THE MAN YOU'RE MEANT TO BE

THE MAN YOU'RE MEANT TO BE

MASTERING YOUR MIND, BODY, AND SOUL

ZAKAREYA AOSSEY

COPYRIGHT © 2025 ZAKAREYA AOSSEY
All rights reserved.

THE MAN YOU'RE MEANT TO BE
Mastering Your Mind, Body, and Soul

FIRST EDITION

ISBN   978-1-5445-4715-2 *Hardcover*
         978-1-5445-4714-5 *Paperback*
         978-1-5445-4716-9 *Ebook*

CONTENTS

1. I HAD EVERYTHING, EXCEPT MYSELF 17
2. THE SPECTRUM OF MAN 21
   THE FOUR STAGES OF A MAN'S LIFE 29
   LIVE WITH IKHLAS 33
3. CHARACTER 37

PART I: BODY

4. REDEFINING STRENGTH 43
5. STRENGTH TRAINING/FITNESS 49
   STRENGTH, SIZE, AND THE LAWS OF NATURE 55
6. WHEN A MAN SHOULD USE FORCE (AND WHEN HE SHOULD NOT) 61
7. NUTRITION 67
8. SUPPLEMENTATION 73
9. SLEEP: THE ULTIMATE PERFORMANCE ENHANCER 79
10. SMILE LIKE A MAN 85
11. THERMAL THERAPY TRAINING 89
12. FASTING IS A PRESCRIPTION 95
    STOP DRINKING ALCOHOL 101
13. D.A.R.E. 107

14. REDEFINING MASCULINITY 111
15. SEX 115
16. STOP MASTURBATION 121
17. LOWERING YOUR GAZE 127
18. GET MARRIED 131
19. CHOOSING THE ONE 137
20. BUILD A BULLETPROOF RELATIONSHIP 143
21. HAIR IS OVERRATED 147
22. GOOD HYGIENE 151
23. DRESS TO IMPRESS 155
    CARE FOR AN ANIMAL 159
24. GET YOUR $ RIGHT 163
25. MONEY WITHOUT MORALS WILL RUIN YOU 167

PART II: MIND

26. THE ENEMY WITHIN 177
27. THE POWER OF OPTIMISM 183
28. MASTERING MINDSET 187
29. NO PORN, IT'S MIND CANCER 191
30. ALWAYS BE LEARNING 195
31. DIG YOUR TRENCH 199
32. DISCIPLINE/SELF CONTROL 203
33. DIVORCE SOCIAL MEDIA 207
34. THE MIRROR GENERATION 213
35. HANDLING DIVORCE AND BREAKUPS 217
36. THE ART OF DOING NOTHING 221
37. REMEMBER YOU WILL DIE 225
38. THE HEALING POWER OF NATURE 229
    LET THE CHILD IN YOU THRIVE 233
39. THE SPIRITUMENTAL CRISIS 237

PART III: SOUL

40. THE HIDDEN THREAT OF SUCCESS 243
41. GIVE MORE THAN YOU TAKE 247
    SELF-REFLECTION (MUHASABA) 251
42. PURIFY THE HEART 255
43. IHSAN 261
44. MASTER YOUR DESIRES 267
45. COURAGE 271
46. BRAVERY 275
47. CHIVALRY 279
48. LOVE 283
49. REFLECTION ON GRATITUDE 287
50. CHARITY 291
51. GUARD THE TONGUE 295
52. TRANSFORMING ANGER INTO STRENGTH 301
53. FORGIVE AND FORGET 305
54. CHECK YOUR EGO AT THE DOOR 311
55. CONFIDENCE 315
56. YOUR "STARTING FIVE" 321
57. HEAVEN IS AT THE FOOT OF YOUR MOTHER 327
58. BUILD STRONG FAMILY 331
59. DIVINE ENERGY 335
60. GOOD MANNERS 339
61. KNOWLEDGE OF SELF 343
62. SUBMIT TO GOD 347
63. LOVE GOD 351
64. PRAYER 355
65. PURIFYING AND STRENGTHENING THE ESSENCE WITHIN 363
66. REFLECTIONS AND REMINDERS 367
67. PATIENCE 369
68. THE ULTIMATE BLUEPRINT FOR MASCULINITY: LESSONS FROM THE
    PROPHET MUHAMMAD (PBUH) 375
    APPENDIX 383

FULLY OPTIMIZE YOUR MIND, BODY, HEART, AND SOUL TO ACHIEVE excellence in character, fierce confidence, eternal peace, and purpose.

In the Name of God, the Most Gracious, the Most Merciful.

All that is good in this book comes from God. Any error is a reflection of my own limitations.

I pray the words within these pages serve as a mirror, a compass, and a fire. May they inspire reflection, ignite conviction, and restore the dignity that has been stripped from far too many men. You were created with brilliance, carved with intention, and designed for greatness.

At some point, every man faces the quiet but deafening question: Am I truly the man I was created to be?

Perhaps you've already felt that weight. Maybe it's what brought you here. A knowing. A restlessness. A signal from within that something more is expected of you—more strength, more clarity, more impact. But how does one reach that higher state of manhood? How do you become a man marked not by noise, but by weight?

It starts by returning to first principles. Before we rebuild, we must strip away the lies.

Ask yourself plainly: What shaped your view of manhood? Was it strength? Image? Approval? Pain?

Society has blurred the definition, feeding men illusions: avatars of dominance, seduction, and material power. The alpha archetype obsessed with conquest. The mogul driven by ego. The influencer masking insecurity with performance. These aren't men to admire. They're symptoms of a deeper sickness. Their influence has infected the culture, and their false strength has contributed to a crisis of character.

Real strength does not need to be loud.

We live in an age where power is worshipped but rarely understood. Too many use influence to indulge themselves and betray others. These are not strong men. They are fractured. Outwardly bold, inwardly broken.

So let's be clear about what this book is here to do.

We're not here to play dress-up with masculinity. We're here to return to what is real. We will break down the false foundations and lay new ones built on timeless truths: discipline, purpose, honor, and obedience to God. You'll learn how to command your life, your habits, your thoughts, and your relationships with the strength of a man who knows who he is and who he serves.

This isn't about performance. This is about becoming the man your Creator intended you to be. For your own growth, for your family's stability, for your community's revival, and for the pleasure of God.

WHAT IT DOESN'T MEAN TO BE A MAN

Being a man is not defined by your income, your résumé, or your following. It is defined by your integrity when no one is watching.

It's not the businessman who conquers the boardroom but loses his marriage and children. That's not a man. That's a boy with money.

It's not the playboy who objectifies women and leaves wreckage behind him. That's not confidence. That's emptiness in disguise.

It's not the elite who uses status to shame others. Arrogance is not leadership. Influence without morality is a virus.

It's not the influencer with millions of fans but no soul left to speak of. A real man values substance over applause.

It's not the man who "has it all" but dies young, stressed, isolated, and bitter. A real man doesn't self-destruct chasing false victories.

WHAT A REAL MAN *IS*

A real man:

- Serves from a place of strength, not ego.
- Makes principled decisions even when they cost him.
- Honors his wife, protects his children, uplifts his community.
- Fights temptation through self-mastery, not suppression.
- Speaks the truth with kindness and holds silence with wisdom.
- Seeks knowledge relentlessly and lives with spiritual depth.
- Stands for what is right even when it is unpopular.
- Loves with power, leads with humility, and submits to God.

This book is your blueprint. Not for imitation, but for transformation. Not for public praise, but for private integrity. We're building men who can be trusted, not just admired.

THE BLUEPRINT: BODY, MIND, SOUL

To become that kind of man, you must be aligned from the inside out. This book is structured around the three domains that shape you:

The Body—your vehicle for action. Strength. Energy. Vitality. You'll learn how to build and maintain the physical discipline required to carry out your mission.

The Mind—your control center. Discipline. Clarity. Mental resilience. You'll learn how to train your thinking and eliminate patterns that weaken you.

The Soul—your anchor. Purpose. Faith. Integrity. Without it, everything else collapses. You'll learn how to stay grounded, sharpen your conscience, and align your life with your Creator.

THE BODY

Your body is your armor. It is the physical manifestation of your discipline and respect for the life you've been given. Strength is not about vanity; it is about function, vitality, and resilience.

A well-maintained body impacts everything: energy, confidence, and your ability to provide and protect. This section will teach you how to:

- Build endurance, power, and longevity.
- Train for strength, discipline, and mental clarity.
- Fuel your body with proper nutrition and recovery.
- Develop the physical discipline required for excellence.

A man in control of his body is in control of his future.

THE MIND

Your mind is your greatest weapon. Every great achievement, every act of strength, every moment of discipline begins in the mind. Yet many men allow fear, doubt, and external pressures to dictate their thoughts.

A strong mind is not inherited; it is built. The ability to remain calm in chaos, make sound decisions under pressure, and push through adversity is cultivated through conscious effort. This section will teach you how to:

- Develop mental toughness and resilience.
- Channel the power of discipline to shape your destiny.
- Rewire negative thought patterns and build an unstoppable mindset.
- Master patience, focus, and emotional control.

A great mind seeks wisdom, knowledge, and the strength to lead with clarity and conviction.

THE SOUL

Without a guiding purpose, even the strongest mind and body will drift. Your soul is the core of who you are and the source of your values, faith, and mission. Without spiritual grounding, a man becomes a slave to his impulses and desires.

A man with a strong soul stands firm in his principles. This section will teach you how to:

- Strengthen your faith and build an unshakable foundation.
- Cultivate inner peace, humility, and gratitude.
- Align daily actions with your higher purpose.
- Lead with integrity, honor, and selfless service.

Throughout history, cultures have marked the transition from boyhood to manhood with rites of passage. These trials were designed to create discipline, resilience, and purpose. Today, these rites are absent, leaving men adrift. But the need for transformation has not disappeared. True transformation happens when all three are optimized in perfect harmony. You don't need perfection; you need alignment. You don't need hype; you need truth. This isn't motivation; this is calibration.

CHAPTER 1

I HAD EVERYTHING, EXCEPT MYSELF

I WAS BORN INTO CHAOS. MY PARENTS HAD DECIDED TO DROP everything and travel the world. My mother carried me through Jerusalem, Morocco, Tunisia, and then in Cairo, Egypt, it happened. A hospital room buzzing in a language my parents couldn't understand. My mother was in pain. My father was helpless. And me? I came into this world silent. Not a cry. Not a sound. Minutes passed. Still nothing.

Some call it a medical delay. I call it my first fight. I believe something tried to grab hold of me that day—something dark. But God held me. Protected me. Even then.

Four weeks later, I was on my first international flight back to America. A baby with a passport and no idea how turbulent life would get.

I was born Zakareya Tarik Aossey and raised in a devout Muslim household. Islam wasn't a part of our life—it *was* our life. Our identity, our rhythm, our anchor. And yet, as we settled into Cedar Rapids, Iowa, that identity became the very thing that made me different. One of the only Muslim kids in school. One of the only kids of color in the entire town.

I was the chubby kid who loved dinosaurs, *Star Wars*, math, reading, and football. I got good grades, played every sport, and lived for validation. When we moved to Texas when I was seven years old, the spotlight on my difference only grew brighter. The "weird Muslim kid" jokes followed me. So did the 9/11 jokes, the side-eyes, the questions, the three-on-one fights, and the rejection.

But I kept smiling.

I poured myself into football. I transformed my body. I trained like I had something to prove—because I did. I became All-State, top of my class, recruited by the biggest schools in the country. Harvard and Stanford both came calling. I chose Harvard.

From the outside, I was a dream come true: a straight-laced, clean-cut, All-American Muslim kid with a full ride to the Ivy League. No drinking. No dating. No partying. I was the golden child. A perfect record.

But what nobody saw was the cost.

I wasn't living for God. I was performing for everyone *but* God.

And performance is exhausting.

I thought I could make a deal with God. If I did everything perfect, stayed away from sin, he would give me superstardom on the field and guide me to the league. But you don't make deals with the Almighty for this Dunya. What you think may be best for you may be a curse, and what you think is terrible for you may be what's best for you.

I got hurt—again and again. ACL. Ankle. Knee. Crutches through the halls, into the weight room, back into surgery. Every time I got close to full strength, it slipped away. I questioned everything. Why would God give me this gift only to take it away?

Then came Harvard.

Loneliness hit me like a freight train. No family. No friends. The only Muslim on the team. The only one fasting while everyone else bulked up. I cried on the phone to my dad, ready to quit. He told me that if I left, I'd regret it for the rest of my life.

He was right.

I stayed. I fought through the isolation. I healed. I studied. I won championships. I made lifelong friends. But life had more tests coming. A heartbreak. A soul-crushing illness. Months in bed, wrecked by mono, trying to hold myself together while the world spun around me.

I made it through. Graduated. Traveled Europe. Laughed again. Then I stepped into the real world and stepped into the darkest chapter of my life.

Six figures. Fancy job. New car. Designer wardrobe. Nights out. Women. Status. The "good Muslim boy" became a master of the double life. On paper, I had it all: Harvard degree, high-rise apartment, respectable image, masjid, upstanding community member, the golden child.

Behind closed doors? I was spiraling.

I chased women like trophies. Drank to forget. Partied to feel something. I was addicted to validation, money, lust, status. I lived for dopamine and clout. I posted highlight reels while quietly bleeding inside.

Eventually, I got fired from my job and I hit rock bottom for the first time.

That's when I met my first wife. We got married quickly—too quickly. We wanted it to work. We tried. But we weren't ready. We were never aligned in values, purpose, or vision. And when it ended in divorce, it shattered me.

I never saw it coming. On Instagram, we looked like the dream couple. High-rise living, exotic trips, luxury everything. But it was all performance. And when she left, the mask cracked.

I didn't heal. I went darker. I reached an even deeper bottom.

I made more money. Traded stocks recklessly. Gambled six figures like a walk in the park. Flew girls out. Flew around the world for girls. Bottle service every night. Bought a lime-green Aston Martin just to flex. I thought I was living the dream.

But the truth? I was living my death sentence.

I was a millionaire in my twenties and spiritually bankrupt. My soul was bleeding and my ego was growing. I lost sight of everything: God, my purpose, myself.

Then one night, I looked in the mirror after a weekend I don't remember. And I didn't recognize the man staring back.

He had everything the world said would bring happiness.

But he had no peace.

That's when I broke. Not publicly. Not dramatically. Quietly. I walked away from the life I had built. Moved back home. Thirty years old, in my parents' basement. No money. No status. No applause. Just me and God.

And that's when I met *her*—my wife now. A woman who had her own wild story. And somehow, God brought us together. But I knew I wasn't ready. I told her: I need time. I need to get right.

So I disappeared for six weeks. No dating. No distractions. Just prayer. Reflection. Discipline. Fasting. And it changed everything.

We got married. She embraced Islam. God gave us a child. And He gave me back my soul.

I'm not writing this book as a man who figured it all out. I'm writing this as a man who's been to the edge, who's lived both lives, and who finally found the path back.

This isn't a book about perfection. It's a manual for realignment.

If you're chasing money, women, status, or applause—I've done it. And I promise you: It doesn't work. It'll never be enough. What you're looking for isn't out there. It's inside you. And above you.

You were not created to be ruled by your urges or applauded for your image. You were created for greatness. For leadership. For legacy. For God.

CHAPTER 2

THE SPECTRUM OF MAN

EVERY MAN WALKS A SPECTRUM.

On one end, he is capable of descending into the lowest depths of beastliness: driven by desire, blinded by arrogance, and enslaved by impulse. On the other end, he can ascend to a level higher than the angels: living with purpose, guided by discipline, and devoted to his Creator.

God has honored mankind above creation with a unique gift: choice. Unlike animals, which operate purely on instinct, and angels, who are incapable of disobedience, man was created with free will. This is both our greatest privilege and our greatest test.

The human soul is constantly pulled in opposing directions. One path is paved with pleasure, ego, and indulgence.

Every man is at war.

Not with the world. Not with his enemies. Not with the economy or his past.

With himself.

There is a battle raging inside you every single day. A battle between your discipline and your desire. Your patience and your pride. Your vision and your vices. One side wants to elevate. The other wants to escape. One side wants to lead. The other wants to indulge.

And here's the truth most men never hear: **If you don't win that war inside, you'll lose everything outside.**

I've lived both lives. The man who prays in the dark and the man who parties in the dark. The man driven by purpose and the man controlled by impulse. And I'm telling you right now, nothing destroys a man faster than being mastered by himself.

THE THREE SELVES EVERY MAN CARRIES

Centuries ago, Imam Al-Ghazali described the three natures that exist within every man:

1. **The Beast (Bahimiyyah):** This is the lower self. The part of you that craves food, pleasure, lust, laziness, and distraction. It wants ease. It wants gratification. It lives for the next hit of dopamine.
2. **The Predator (Sab'iyyah):** This is the ego-driven self. It wants power, control, status, dominance. It's fueled by arrogance and comparison. It's the part of you that would rather be feared than respected.
3. **The Angelic Self (Malakiyyah):** This is your higher self. The part rooted in discipline, wisdom, worship, and service. It's calm, resilient, clear. It seeks God, not gratification. Purpose, not praise.

The question isn't whether you have these natures. You do.
The question is: Who's running the show?

For most men today, the beast is in charge. He wants comfort, pleasure, sex, food, entertainment, escape. So we obey him. We scroll. We swipe. We binge. We chase. We consume. All the while, the soul—our angelic self—shrinks in silence.

Let's examine how each nature manifests in real life.

THE MAN WHO FOLLOWS DESIRE

When the beast rules, the man becomes a slave. He doesn't think; he reacts. He doesn't lead; he chases. Hunger dictates his day. Lust drives his choices. Comfort defines his identity. The discipline required to become a man is sacrificed on the altar of cheap pleasure.

And what does the world do with this man? It celebrates him. Rewards him. Sells his image back to society.

The celebrity drowning in vice. The influencer peddling hedonism. The man who confuses indulgence with success. But behind the filters and the fame, there's a hollow ache. A soul starving for meaning.

The Qur'an warns of this very descent:

> Have you seen the one who takes his desires as his god? God has left him astray knowingly and sealed his hearing and his heart and put a veil over his vision. Who, then, will guide him after God? Will you not take heed? (Qur'an 45:23)

Animals follow instinct. They are not accountable. But man? He has knowledge. He has will. When he surrenders his intellect to lust, he doesn't just fall, he degrades. He becomes less than what he was created to be.

THE MAN WHO CRAVES POWER

The second danger is more deceptive: a man not enslaved by pleasure, but by power.

This is the predator.

He doesn't want to feel good; he wants to dominate. His worth is measured in submission. His success, in fear. He manipulates. He conquers. He destroys…and calls it leadership.

He's the tyrant who bathes in applause while bleeding his people dry. The mogul who crushes others to elevate himself. The politician who sells truth to buy influence.

But God and His Messenger were clear:

> Two hungry wolves let loose among sheep are not more harmful than a man's craving for wealth and status is to his religion. (Tirmidhi 2376)

A man consumed by the predator within may rise high, but he will fall hard. Power without righteousness corrupts. His legacy will not be honored; it will be mourned.

THE MAN WHO WALKS WITH THE ANGELS

And then, there is the rare man. The one who submits to something greater than himself.

He doesn't deny his desires; he disciplines them. He doesn't suppress his strength; he refines it. He is not guided by pleasure or power, but by purpose.

He chooses prayer over ego. Restraint over impulse. Service over self.

This man is not weak; he is principled. He is not passive; he is patient. He stands firm, not out of arrogance but out of alignment with truth, with justice, with God.

The Qur'an describes such a man:

> Indeed, those who say, "Our Lord is Allah," and then remain steadfast, the angels descend upon them, saying, "Do not fear and do not grieve, but receive good tidings of Paradise, which you were promised." (Qur'an 41:30)

To become this man requires more than wishful thinking. It requires sacrifice. It requires prayer, fasting, purification of the heart, and brutal honesty with oneself.

This battle isn't won once. It is fought every day. Every morning, you decide who you will be. Every night, you measure who you were.

Will you choose ease or excellence? Ego or integrity? The world or the One who created it?

Al-Ghazali said, "The key to salvation lies in knowledge and action." You must know your weaknesses. And you must act against them.

- Do you understand what drives you?
- Do you recognize what enslaves you?
- Are you building the angel within or feeding the beast?

The strongest man is not the one who lifts the most weight. It's the one who carries his soul in obedience and refuses to bow to anything less than God.

WHY YOU'RE LOSING—AND DON'T KNOW IT

Modern society is designed to keep men weak. Not physically. Spiritually.

We're told real strength is having money, women, clout, and control. But nobody tells us the truth:

The strongest man is the one who conquers himself.

You can bench four hundred pounds but still be a slave to lust. You can make millions but be spiritually bankrupt. You can be the man everyone admires and still hate yourself in silence.

I know, because I've lived that life.

I had the résumé. The accolades. The money. The penthouse. The exotic trips. The image of a successful man. But inside, I was empty. Every time I fed the beast—another party, another girl, another purchase—I felt emptier. I was dying slowly, and smiling for the camera while I did it.

It doesn't matter how "successful" you look. If the wrong part of you is in charge, you're headed for destruction.

God didn't create you to live for comfort, lust, or applause. He created you for strength. For submission. For significance. Not worldly significance—*eternal* significance.

You weren't created to drift. You were created to lead.

But before you can lead others—your wife, your kids, your team—you have to lead yourself. And that starts by declaring war on the parts of you that are quietly killing your potential.

So what does that look like?

- It looks like silencing the beast when it begs for another hit.
- It looks like humbling the predator when your ego wants to lash out.
- It looks like strengthening the angelic self through discipline, worship, truth, and action.

Most men don't lose their life in one big moment. They lose it inch by inch. Click by click. Compromise by compromise. Until one day, they wake up and don't recognize the man in the mirror.

This isn't just a book. It's a blueprint. A training ground. A modern rite of passage.

Here's yours:

1. **Identify your dominant self.** Which part of you has been in charge? Be honest. Are you led by lust? By ego? Or by clarity and discipline?
2. **Choose who leads from here.** Make a *decision* today: My beast is no longer running this house. My ego doesn't sit in the captain's chair. I submit to a higher path. I live for more.
3. **Say it out loud.** "I am not a slave to my urges. I am not a slave to validation. I was created for more. I choose the man I'm becoming."

Say it. Mean it. Then back it up.

In the chapters ahead, we're going to break this war into winnable battles.

- You'll learn how to master your mind and make it your strongest weapon.
- You'll learn how to build a body that commands respect—and reflects discipline.
- You'll learn how to anchor your soul to something eternal so no storm can shake you.
- And you'll learn how to become the kind of man God trusts with influence, responsibility, and legacy.

This isn't about being perfect. It's about being *ready*.
And readiness begins with war.
Win the battle inside. Or lose everything that matters.
Let's build the man you were meant to be.

BE LIGHT

Staring up at the dark purple sky deep in the Moroccan desert, a thought occurred to me. Despite how densely dark it was, the stars of light in the sky illuminated our surroundings with angelic radiance. At that moment I realized, **even the darkest sky can be lit up by the brightest star**.

God says in Surah Ibrahim, Verse 1:

> (This is) a Book which We have revealed to you (O Muhammad), that you might bring mankind out of darkness into the light by permission of their Lord—to the path of the Exalted in Might, the Praiseworthy.

Since the dawn of creation, the struggle between light and darkness has shaped existence. Light is more than a physical phenomenon; it is a force of profound symbolism and transformation. It embodies hope, guidance, truth, and clarity in the face of uncertainty and illusion. Darkness, by contrast, represents ignorance, fear, and despair. Yet, darkness is powerless on its own, existing only in the absence of light. Its dominance is but an illusion, dispelled by even the faintest flicker of illumination.

The power of light to overcome darkness is a universal metaphor, resonating across cultures, religions, and philosophies. It captures the human journey of our innate desire for enlightenment, both intellectual and spiritual. To bring light into darkness is to reveal truth, confront ignorance, and uncover what was once hidden. This metaphor extends beyond the physical world, advocating for wisdom, transparency, and virtue in a world often shadowed by deception and misunderstanding.

In the physical world, light's transformative power is undeniable. Step into a dark room, and the introduction of even the smallest flame alters everything. Light doesn't merely make the unseen visible. It redefines the environment, shifting perception, changing the atmosphere, and awakening new possibilities. Where darkness once obscured, light brings clarity, hope, and direction.

On a grander scale, the celestial rhythms of light and darkness remind us of light's essential role in life. The sun, the ultimate source of energy, nourishes the earth and dispels the night with its radiant strength each morning. Its presence commands the rhythms of nature, from the turning of seasons to the growth of all living things. The moon, though a reflection of the sun, serves as a guide through the night. Its softer glow brings quiet illumination, shaping tides and symbolizing constancy amid the unknown.

These celestial bodies remind us that light is not merely illumination; it is life itself, a force that shapes and sustains us. Across religious and philosophical traditions, light symbolizes purity, goodness, and the divine. It represents higher truths and transcendent power, guiding humanity out of ignorance and sin. In Islam, the invocation of "SubhanAllah" when reflecting on the sun and moon expresses awe and reverence for the Creator's design. These celestial marvels are not just physical phenomena but signs of divine orchestration, reminders of the eternal battle between light and darkness.

To walk in the light is to seek clarity, integrity, and connection to the divine. Spiritual light transforms the soul, guiding it away from shadowy desires and into alignment with truth and purpose. It is a catalyst for change, not merely existing but acting, transforming, and renewing. The introduction of light into darkness is not just a shift in visibility but in possibility, carrying with it the potential for growth, wisdom, and hope.

The battle between light and darkness serves as a powerful reminder: Just as light transforms physical spaces, it also transforms lives. By embracing light through wisdom, faith, and action we rise above the shadows. The natural cycle of day and night reflects this truth. No matter how long the night may seem, the dawn is inevitable.

Light remains a profound force for good, a guide through life's challenges, and a beacon of hope in even the darkest times. When we choose light we honor its transformative power. The victory of light over darkness is not just symbolic; it is a call to action, urging us to illuminate both our inner selves and the world around us.

THE FOUR STAGES OF A MAN'S LIFE

BEFORE WE LAY DOWN THE STRATEGIES AND DISCIPLINES REQUIRED to rise into a man of excellence, we must first confront a reality that too many ignore: Life does not happen at random. It unfolds in defined phases, each stage carrying its own unique temptations, distractions, and defining tests. These aren't mere seasons; they are sacred battlegrounds for character, clarity, and calling.

In Arabic, the word *Dunya* refers to this world and its glitter, its illusions, its ephemeral pleasures. The Dunya makes promises it can't keep. And unless you understand how its influence shifts across the stages of your life, you risk being mastered by what was meant to be mastered by you.

Your mission as a man is not to coast through these phases but to move through them with conviction. You were not created to drift. You were created to navigate with wisdom, to refine your soul, and to leave behind a legacy that echoes beyond your name.

Here's the truth: Every phase of life is a proving ground. Let's break them down.

1. CHILDHOOD: INNOCENCE, IMAGINATION, AND THE FIRST BLUEPRINT

The world of a child is filled with wonder. No ego, no pressure, no masks. A stick becomes a sword, a cardboard box becomes a spaceship, and the heart is still untouched by the bitterness of comparison or the noise of opinion.

Don't dismiss this phase. This is where the blueprint of your character begins. Seeds of faith, love, trust, and curiosity are planted here. A child who feels safe learns to love. A child who is nurtured learns to believe. The foundation of manhood begins long before muscles and milestones. It begins with purity of heart.

But childhood is not meant to last forever. The danger arises when grown men try to relive it. The pursuit of escape through drugs, endless entertainment, or sexual indulgence is often a disguised longing for the simplicity of youth. But manhood requires leaving behind the sandbox. The joy of innocence must evolve into the strength of responsibility.

You are not a boy anymore. Stop living like one.

2. TEENAGE YEARS: DISTRACTION, ILLUSION, AND THE BATTLE FOR DISCIPLINE

As adolescence hits, a new enemy appears: distraction. You gain access to the tools of adulthood without yet developing the wisdom to wield them. Social media, video games, sports, entertainment, it all pulls you outward when what you need most is inward grounding.

This is the era of false maturity. Teenagers often believe they've outgrown innocence, yet they have no idea what sacrifice means. It's a dangerous illusion: thinking you're grown while your soul remains untested.

This is where your habits begin to form. Lust, ego, rebellion—all these roots either take hold or get uprooted. And this phase determines one thing above all: whether you build discipline or become owned by your desires.

The Dunya enters strong here. You don't beat it with brute force; you beat it by anchoring yourself in purpose, prayer, and presence.

The habits you create here will either carry you or curse you later. Choose wisely.

3. EARLY ADULTHOOD: THE SEARCH FOR IDENTITY AND THE SEDUCTION OF APPLAUSE

You enter adulthood thinking you're building your future, but often you're building a mask.

In this phase, men become hyperaware of perception. The chase for validation intensifies. You curate your life instead of living it. Everything becomes performance: the filtered photos, career moves for clout, and relationships that feed ego over growth.

This is the era of *image worship*. Men begin to confuse confidence with comparison and purpose with popularity. But behind every highlight reel is a man secretly unsure of who he is without the applause.

The unfortunate truth is that the world will always find a way to reward what's shallow. But faith rewards what's unseen.

Masculinity at this level is not measured by how many people clap for you. It's measured by what remains when no one is watching. The question is no longer "Do they like me?" but "Am I still me?"

Real men build their identity on purpose, not popularity.

4. MATURITY AND LEGACY: FROM SUCCESS TO SIGNIFICANCE

Eventually, the noise fades.

You no longer chase likes or trends. You begin to reflect. The mirror becomes less about your face and more about your life. And the question arises: What did I actually build?

This is the phase of reckoning. You realize wealth is not the goal, but impact is. The obsession with being seen fades, and what matters is who you've become in silence.

This is when a man understands that legacy isn't about being remembered. It's about being useful. What will your children say about you? What kind of values did you engrain in your home? What kind of presence did you leave behind in every room?

The Dunya shifts form here. It no longer seduces with vanity; it tempts with comfort and complacency. But men of substance don't retire from responsibility. They refine it.

This phase is your last chance to pour your wisdom into others, to mentor, to serve, and to shape a generation. Don't waste it building a monument to yourself. Use it to build men who will outlive your name.

Understanding these stages is not just about insight; it's about alignment. You must know what stage you're in. More importantly, you must act like it.

Many men are stuck in one phase while pretending they're in another. Some are forty years old, still chasing attention like a nineteen-year-old. Others are teenagers already burnt out by the burdens of adulthood they were never equipped to carry.

Your job is to be honest about where you are, and intentional about where you're going.

This is not about perfection. It's about progression. And the only way forward is to live with vision.

So ask yourself:

- Am I being pulled forward by purpose or dragged backward by distraction?
- Have I built habits that reflect the man I want to become?
- Do I live in response to truth or in reaction to temptation?

Great men don't stumble into excellence. They *design* it.

They don't worship youth, approval, or money. They serve God, protect their families, uplift others, and leave behind legacies that echo into eternity.

Wherever you are today, whether just entering manhood or deep into maturity, own it. Learn the test of your season. Pass it with honor. Because boys react. Men respond. And great men rise.

LIVE WITH IKHLAS

LIFE IS NOT ABOUT HOW LONG WE LIVE BUT HOW DEEPLY WE LIVE. Seneca once said, "It is not that we have a short time to live, but that we waste a lot of it." Time is the one currency we can never earn back. Each passing second is a sealed door. You cannot rewind. But you can decide how to walk forward.

When my grandfather turned eighty-nine, he looked me in the eye and said, "It's not how long you live, it's how you live." That stayed with me. Not as a cliché, but as a confrontation. It made me stop and ask: Am I living with purpose, or just existing? Am I aligned with what matters or am I being distracted by what doesn't?

The difference between a life that matters and a life that fades into obscurity is Ikhlas, or in English, sincerity. Ikhlas is the Arabic word for purity of intention. It is the invisible force behind every action that counts. It is what transforms ordinary acts into timeless deeds. It is the heartbeat of a meaningful life.

The Prophet Muhammad (PBUH) said, "Actions are judged by intentions." (Bukhari & Muslim). Two men can do the same thing. They can give charity, pray, and serve others, but only one walks away with reward: the one who did it for God alone.

A man with Ikhlas is untouchable. He cannot be manipulated by praise or discouraged by criticism. He does not chase applause, nor does he fear being overlooked. He lives above the noise. His purpose isn't people; it's God. His integrity isn't rented; it's rooted.

He doesn't ask, "Will this make me look good?" He asks, "Is this the right thing to do?" He does not act for optics. He acts for impact. His character is his currency, and he spends it wisely.

Ikhlas is not a motivational quote. It's a lifestyle. And if you want your life to leave a mark on the people you love, the community you serve, and the soul you must return, then it has to be built on sincerity.

CULTIVATING IKHLAS IN DAILY LIFE
1. BEGIN EVERYTHING WITH INTENTION

Before you move, ask why. Why are you working, training, posting, giving, speaking? If the answer is ego, status, or attention, then pause. Realign. Recalibrate.

Make intention a pre-action ritual. Say to yourself, "For God." Let that become your internal compass. Live for legacy, not for likes. Seek reward from the One who never forgets, not from the world that barely notices.

2. PRACTICE SILENCE AND SECRECY

Social media has taught us to perform. To broadcast. But sincerity thrives in the shadows. Learn to do good in silence. Give without announcing. Pray without posting. Help someone who will never repay you.

Private deeds train your heart to stop seeking recognition. They teach your soul to find fulfillment in serving and not in being seen.

3. ANCHOR YOUR WORK IN THE ETERNAL

Every worldly pursuit fades. Money comes and goes. Looks vanish. Titles expire. But sincerity turns temporary acts into eternal investments.

Whether you're building a business, raising children, or learning a craft, try to tie it to something higher. Do it for God. Do it with excellence. Do it with the intention of service. Then even the mundane becomes sacred.

4. LIVE WITH DEATH IN MIND

Nothing humbles like death. Nothing clarifies like remembering that your name will one day be etched on stone, your body lowered into silence.

When you internalize that truth, you stop wasting time. You stop caring about petty drama and empty praise. You start asking, What will remain when I'm gone?

The Prophet (PBUH) said, "When a man dies, his deeds end except for three: ongoing charity, beneficial knowledge, or a righteous child who prays for him." (Muslim)

Each of these requires sincerity. And each of them outlives you.

5. REFINE YOUR WORSHIP

Ikhlas starts in the heart, and the heart is shaped most powerfully through worship. Ask yourself:

- Do I pray out of routine or out of love?
- Do I fast to detox or to draw near to God?
- Do I give charity to impress or to purify?

The answers matter. Because it's not just the act, it's the *why* behind the act that is recorded.

The man who lives with Ikhlas leaves behind more than memories. He leaves behind a *legacy of substance*. People remember how he made them feel. How he served without needing to be thanked. How he worshipped with humility. How his presence elevated the space, not because he tried to be seen, but because he carried something sacred within.

He doesn't need to preach with words. His life is the message.

Ask yourself: When my name is spoken after I'm gone, what will follow it, a trail of impact or a trail of noise? A legacy of contribution or one of consumption? Will the people I loved remember me as sincere?

You do not control how long you live. But you decide how you show up in the time you are given. And the best way to live is with Ikhlas. In every move. Every prayer. Every relationship. Every decision.

Sincerity is not weakness. It is strength in its purest form. It is doing the right thing, especially when no one's watching. It is loving God more than applause. It is becoming the kind of man who doesn't just live well, but dies well.

Because in the end, it's not the length of your life that people will remember. It's the weight of it.

CHAPTER 3

CHARACTER

THE ASPECT THAT GOVERNS ALL THE ABOVE IS CHARACTER. YOUR character defines you. It is not a reputation. It is not what people think of you. Character is who you are when no one's looking. Who you are when the cameras are off, the crowd is gone, and the world has nothing to offer you in return. It's the decisions you make in silence, the battles you fight in your mind, and the standards you uphold when there's no applause, no consequence, and no recognition. It is truth lived, not just spoken.

In a culture that thrives on perception, it's easy to fall into the trap of performance. I used to believe that if I looked like a man of integrity, then I *was* one. So I curated my life like a highlight reel of perfection: neat, respectable, and admired. But behind the scenes, I was fractured. I said the right things but didn't always live them. I wanted to be seen as good more than I wanted to *be* good. That's not strength. That's self-deception and hypocrisy.

The harshest realization I ever came to was this: **You cannot outrun yourself.** You can't drown out the voice that knows the truth. The one that speaks in the quiet and won't be silenced by likes, titles, or distractions. You can fool the world, but you can't fool your own soul. And you can't fool God.

A man living out of alignment, projecting virtue while harboring vice, isn't just living a lie; he's waging war against his own soul. That war might be silent, but it's deadly. Hypocrisy eats away at you. Slowly. Quietly. It separates who you are from who you claim to be until there's nothing left but performance. And performance won't save you when life hits.

A man without character is like gold-plated filth; shiny on the outside, rotten underneath. He may impress for a season, but when pressure comes, he collapses. When temptation strikes, he caves. When responsibility calls, he disappears. Why? Because there's no backbone. No weight. No moral anchor. Just polish.

But a man of character, real, tested character, cannot be moved. He's the same in public and in private. He lives by principle, not preference. He speaks the truth, even when it costs him. He walks away from what's wrong, even when no one would know. That's not weakness. That's strength. That's clarity. That's freedom.

True character is not built for public approval. It is built for divine accountability. It is forged in prayer, discipline, and the quiet resistance to temptation. It is the decision to choose right over easy, truth over comfort, obedience over ego. It is knowing that one day, you will stand alone before your Creator, and all facades will fall.

The man of character isn't swayed by trends or applause. He doesn't need the world to approve of him because he answers to something higher. He understands that every thought, every action, and every intention will be weighed. And so he lives like it matters—because it does.

Character is the bridge between who you are and who you are called to become. Without it, you will build a life on sand. With it, you will endure storms that destroy others. But it is not easy. It requires vigilance. You must guard your heart from pride, your eyes from envy, and your actions from hypocrisy. You must be brutally honest with yourself and willing to confront your own darkness.

This is the soul's daily war between your higher self and your base instincts. The reward isn't popularity. It's peace. Alignment. Strength. And ultimately, the pleasure of God.

Look at the life of the Prophet Muhammad (PBUH). He was the embodiment of unwavering character. He was truthful when lies would have protected him. Just when injustice would have favored him. Gentle in a world that honored cruelty. His greatness didn't come from wealth or influence; it came from a soul refined by sincerity, humility, and faith. His example isn't just to be admired. It's to be followed.

This book isn't meant to be a motivational talk. It's a mirror. It's an audit of your inner life. Are you the same man in secret that you are in public? Are your values consistent when tested? Does your private self honor the God you claim to serve?

Each section of this book will walk you through key pillars of character: discipline, honesty, humility, courage, restraint, and resilience. These are not just moral traits; they are weapons. Tools for building a life that lasts. Without them, you will be tossed around by emotions, opinions, and circumstances. With them, you will stand unmoved.

Master your character, and you master your soul. Master your soul, and your destiny will follow.

PART I

BODY

CHAPTER 4

REDEFINING STRENGTH

AS A CHILD, I REMEMBER SITTING WIDE-EYED IN FRONT OF THE television, watching the World's Strongest Man competitions. Giants among men flipped tires, pulled trucks, and hoisted stones taller than most people. I thought to myself, "That is strength."

But over time, I learned that physical might, though impressive, is only a fraction of what true strength entails.

Real strength—the kind that endures, inspires, and transforms—is not just found in muscle or mass. It's measured in character. In how a man rises after defeat, restrains himself in the face of temptation, and leads with clarity, courage, and humility. The strongest man is not just a physical force, but a balanced force of mind, body, and soul.

His strength is not loud. It doesn't need to be. It speaks through consistency. Through silent discipline. Through service.

A strong man is not measured by how much weight he can lift, but by how much weight he can carry: the burdens of responsibility, the discipline to live with integrity, the courage to stand alone in truth, and the selflessness to protect and uplift others. Strength is not about dominating others. It's about being dependable—especially when no one's watching.

THE SEVEN PILLARS OF STRENGTH

Real strength is built on a foundation. For men, that foundation rests on seven enduring pillars:

Faith. Fitness. Family. Education. Love. Community. Brotherhood.

These are not ideals we admire from a distance—they are disciplines we live by. They shape a man into someone who doesn't just survive the world, but someone who changes it. Not by force, but by presence. By example.

You may ask, How do I begin cultivating this kind of strength?

It starts with two honest questions:

- What does strength mean to me?
- How can I serve someone today?

Ask those daily, and you won't just build muscle—you'll build meaning.

All true strength begins with faith. Without a connection to something higher than yourself, your strength has no direction. It's like having power with no purpose.

A man anchored in his Creator does not waver when life tests him. He doesn't crumble under pressure or chase every fleeting desire. He stands rooted, calm in chaos, guided by something eternal. His actions aren't fueled by ego, but by alignment.

Temptation will come. So will adversity. But strength is not about avoiding either—it's about rising above them with conviction.

As God reminds us in the Qur'an:

Verily, with hardship comes ease. (Qur'an 94:6)

The body may be powerful, but the mind is the command center. Strength without wisdom is reckless. Intelligence without humility is fragile.

Socrates once said, "The only true wisdom is in knowing you know nothing." That humility is where growth begins.

A strong man is always learning. He reads. He reflects. He listens. He knows arrogance is a disguise for insecurity, and that real strength is quiet and curious.

Intellectual growth sharpens our ability to lead, to connect, and to build legacy. A wise man never stops becoming wiser.

Emotional mastery is the unseen strength that governs everything.

Too many men suppress their emotions, only to explode later in ways that destroy trust, peace, and purpose. A truly strong man doesn't numb his emotions—he understands them, processes them, and chooses to respond with control and maturity.

Mindfulness. Self-awareness. Emotional discipline.

These are muscles too. And they must be trained just like the body.

A man who can remain calm in the storm, who can love without fear and lead without pride, becomes an anchor for everyone around him.

In a world obsessed with hollow metrics like followers, income, and titles; we need to redefine what it means to win.

Wealth, status, and influence are tools. They're not the end. When used with wisdom, they can serve a higher purpose. But when they become the goal, they rob a man of joy and clarity.

The truly successful man asks, How can I use what I have to elevate others?

Impact is greater than income. Legacy outweighs luxury. When you live for a purpose bigger than yourself, you become immortal—not in years, but in meaning.

Strength thrives in community. A man becomes sharper, wiser, and more disciplined when he is surrounded by others who challenge him and hold him accountable.

Brotherhood is essential.

We were never meant to walk this road alone. The strongest men build each other. Iron sharpens iron. Real strength is not isolation—it's interdependence.

If you want to go far, walk with others. Share wisdom. Admit weaknesses. Grow together.

Modern life has made us soft. Food delivered. Air-conditioned comfort. Entertainment at our fingertips. But comfort, left unchecked, breeds complacency. And complacency is the enemy of strength.

The hard truth is strength is born through struggle.

Recall the age-old adage: "Hard times create strong men. Strong men create good times. Good times create weak men. Weak men create hard times."

So choose hardship.

Wake up early. Train hard. Delay gratification. Say no when it's easy to say yes. These small acts of discipline build the internal armor you need to withstand life's hardest seasons.

Discipline is not about being extreme—it's about being consistent. Every day, you're either reinforcing strength or surrendering it.

Imam Suhaib Webb once told me over a cup of coffee: "How can one dream of saving the world if they can't muster the discipline to lift their blanket for predawn prayer?"

Pain is not punishment; it's preparation. Adversity is not your enemy; it's your assignment.

Every setback carries a seed of strength, if you're willing to extract it.

I've faced moments that nearly broke me—injuries, heartbreak, loss—but they didn't end me. They refined me. My knee injury in college taught me endurance. My divorce taught me surrender. Both brought me back to faith. Both made me a better man.

The strongest men you'll ever meet didn't have it easy. They had it meaningful.

Angela Duckworth, the psychologist behind the concept of *grit*, discovered that it's not talent that determines long-term success—it's perseverance. The refusal to quit. The resolve to keep going, especially when the fire dies out.

Winston Churchill is credited with the phrase: "If you're going through hell, keep going."

Strength isn't a sprint. It's a quiet, stubborn refusal to quit.

Neuroscience backs this up. Every time you overcome a challenge, you rewire your brain. You build resilience. The more you endure, the stronger you become.

Strength is more than a physical feat. It is a way of life.

It's found in faith, forged in hardship, sustained by discipline, and amplified by community.

It's quiet, unshakable, and deeply rooted in purpose.

So build your body, sharpen your mind, and anchor your soul. Face discomfort. Ask better questions. Surround yourself with men who make you better.

And remember this:

The man with the strongest soul will always outlast the man with the strongest body.

Because real strength doesn't fade. It echoes.

CHAPTER 5

STRENGTH TRAINING/FITNESS

IF I TOLD YOU THAT LIFTING WEIGHTS COULD SHAPE YOU INTO the strongest, sharpest, and most resilient version of yourself, would you believe me?

Most people think of strength training and immediately picture chiseled abs, flexed arms, or the cover of a fitness magazine. But the truth is those are just the side effects. The real transformation lies far deeper.

There's a reason why the saying goes, "A strong body is the greatest status symbol." Not because of how it looks—but because of what it takes to build it: discipline, grit, patience, and intention. Strength is not just muscle. It is the framework for mental clarity, emotional stability, and unwavering confidence. When your body is strong, your mind and soul follow suit. Strength training prepares you to carry life's heaviest loads—physically, yes, but also mentally and spiritually.

I still remember the first time I gripped a barbell. I was at the YMCA with my father. I didn't know it then, but that simple act would become a defining rhythm in my life. The clang of the weights, the scent of iron, the pulse of music in my headphones, the burn in my muscles—it was the first place I ever felt free. Free from confusion. Free from frustration. Free to become who I was meant to be.

Twenty years later, I can count on one hand how many days I've missed willingly. The gym isn't a hobby. It's a cornerstone. A sanctuary. My therapy. My reset. It's how I express gratitude to God for the body He's entrusted to me on this temporary journey.

This chapter is not about aesthetics—it's about building internal fortitude. It's about forging a body capable of leading, protecting, and enduring. This isn't a hobby. This is a practice. A discipline. A way of life.

WHY EVERY MAN MUST LIFT

1. PHYSICAL STRENGTH BUILDS MENTAL STRENGTH

Lifting weights doesn't just shape the body. It rewires the mind.

When you train, blood flow to the brain increases, sharpening focus, memory, and stamina. But the deeper benefit lies in the release of brain-derived neurotrophic factor (BDNF)—a compound that strengthens neural connections, boosts learning capacity, and fuels creativity. Lifting becomes a brain workout. With every rep, your mind gets stronger.

2. THE BARBELL BUILDS CONFIDENCE

Every time you push through fatigue, add another plate, or hit a new personal best, you prove to yourself: "I can do hard things." That self-assurance doesn't stay in the gym. It bleeds into your relationships, your career, your leadership, and your goals.

You begin to carry yourself differently—not arrogantly, but intentionally. Your posture improves. Your handshake is firm. Your eyes don't flinch.

3. LIFTING IS STRESS RELIEF IN ITS PUREST FORM

Strength training releases endorphins, the body's natural antidepressants. It balances cortisol, the stress hormone that, when unchecked, damages your mood, your immune system, and your mental clarity.

Former NFL player Brandon Marshall is a powerful example. Diagnosed with borderline personality disorder, he used training, alongside therapy and faith, to regain balance. His story is proof that wellness is not one-dimensional. Mental health must be fought for on all fronts: physically, emotionally, and spiritually.

4. IT PROTECTS AGAINST MODERN LIFE

Muscle isn't just about appearance. It's metabolic armor.

Strength training increases insulin sensitivity, improves glucose metabolism, and activates genes that protect against type 2 diabetes, heart disease, and premature aging. It reduces the inflammation caused by processed food, sedentary living, and chronic stress.

Your body was not designed to sit all day and live on processed fuel. Strength training is the antidote to a lifestyle that weakens men from the inside out.

5. STRENGTH BALANCES YOUR HORMONES

Testosterone. DHEA. Growth hormone. These are the hormones that fuel vitality, masculinity, and recovery. They decline with age, but consistent training reverses that decline.

Weightlifting also combats estrogen dominance, which can lead to mood swings, energy crashes, and unwanted fat gain. A strong body is a balanced body, and hormonal health is the engine.

6. STRONG BONES = LONG-TERM INDEPENDENCE

Resistance training stimulates osteoblasts, the cells responsible for building new bone tissue. This increases bone density, decreases the risk of fractures, and keeps you mobile well into old age.

You're not just training for today. You're building a body that won't abandon you decades from now.

7. LIFTING IMPROVES SLEEP QUALITY

Weight training regulates adenosine, the chemical that prepares your brain for sleep. As your circadian rhythm improves, you fall asleep faster, recover better, and wake up with sharper energy and focus.

Quality training leads to quality rest. And deep rest is where the real growth happens.

Your body is not just flesh and bone. It is a sacred trust. Strength and discipline are not luxuries—they are responsibilities. They reflect how much you value the life you've been given.

Training is a physical act, but for men of faith, it is also spiritual. It is a way to honor the gift of health, to show gratitude through effort, and to prepare yourself for leadership and legacy. Every set. Every rep. Every drop of sweat becomes an offering.

Here's a simple but effective weekly template to develop strength, improve composition, and enhance endurance:

Day 1: Upper Body

- Bench Press: three sets of eight to twelve reps
- Pull-Ups: three sets of eight to twelve reps
- Shoulder Press: three sets of eight to twelve reps
- Bent-Over Rows: three sets of eight to twelve reps
- Bicep Curls: three sets of twelve to fifteen reps
- Tricep Dips: three sets of twelve to fifteen reps

Day 2: Lower Body

- Squats: three sets of eight to twelve reps
- Dead Lifts: three sets of eight to twelve reps
- Leg Press: three sets of twelve to fifteen reps
- Lunges: three sets of twelve to fifteen reps
- Calf Raises: three sets of twelve to fifteen reps

Day 3: Rest or Active Recovery

- Light cardio, walking, yoga, or stretching

Day 4: Upper Body

- Incline Bench Press: three sets of eight to twelve reps
- Lat Pull-Downs: three sets of eight to twelve reps
- Arnold Press: three sets of eight to twelve reps
- T-Bar Rows: three sets of eight to twelve reps
- Hammer Curls: three sets of twelve to fifteen reps
- Skull Crushers: three sets of twelve to fifteen reps

Day 5: Lower Body

- Front Squats: three sets of eight to twelve reps
- Romanian Dead Lifts: three sets of eight to twelve reps
- Leg Extensions: three sets of twelve to fifteen reps
- Leg Curls: three sets of twelve to fifteen reps
- Seated Calf Raises: three sets of twelve to fifteen reps

Day 6: Full Body

- Clean and Press: three sets of eight to twelve reps
- Pull-Ups: three sets of eight to twelve reps
- Dead Lifts: three sets of eight to twelve reps
- Push-Ups: three sets of twelve to fifteen reps
- Plank: three sets of one-minute holds

Day 7: Full Rest

- Optional light walk, meditation, or stretching

Daily Add-On:

Incorporate at least thirty minutes of cardio to improve stamina, burn fat, and support heart health:

- Stairmaster
- Incline treadmill walking
- Jogging
- Fast-paced walking outdoors

Some days, you'll feel unstoppable. Other days, it'll take everything just to show up. But remember: The goal is not perfection—it's consistency.

Every time you lift, you are not just building muscle. You're training your mind to endure. You're proving to yourself that effort still matters. That you are capable of growth. That you are worth the investment.

A strong body creates a sharp mind. A sharp mind leads a clear life. And a clear life builds an unshakable legacy.

So lift—not for applause, not for vanity, but because a man of strength is a man prepared.

And the world needs more of them.

STRENGTH, SIZE, AND THE LAWS OF NATURE

NOTHING COMMANDS ATTENTION LIKE UNDENIABLE PRESENCE. It's why Arnold Schwarzenegger became a global icon. Why stories like David and Goliath echo across generations. And why my friend and brother Tacko Fall, who stands seven foot seven inches, can't walk the streets of Saudi Arabia without being swarmed for photos.

There's something about physical power that captures the eye and stirs something ancient within us. But it's more than visual impact. Strength and size are primal signals—deeply encoded in our biology and psychology. They're not just about admiration. They're about survival, security, and leadership. To understand this is to understand how we're wired as men—and how we're meant to carry ourselves in the world.

I know this personally. I'm six foot two, 260 pounds, built like an NFL linebacker. I played football. I trained like a savage. And whether I walk into a boardroom, a room full of strangers, or a street in a foreign country, my presence is felt before I say a word.

That isn't arrogance. That's reality. Because presence is a currency.

And strength is power, not just in muscle, but in confidence, command, and control.

In the wild, strength and size are not symbolic—they are strategic.

The lion doesn't dominate the savannah because of his roar. He reigns because of his frame—his power to hunt, defend, and protect. Without strength, there is no kingdom.

The silverback gorilla leads through sheer physical presence. He protects his troop, commands order, and holds peace through dominance that's understood without needing explanation.

These animals don't debate their worth. They live it.

This is the law of nature: **Power demands presence.**

It's not just *survival of the fittest*, it's *survival of the strongest*—the most grounded, the most prepared, the most capable.

Strength isn't just visual—it's physiological. Testosterone, the hormone that drives male vitality, is directly linked to strength training. Lifting weights naturally boosts testosterone and other key hormones, such as DHEA and growth hormone, which enhance:

- Muscle development and recovery
- Mental clarity and emotional resilience
- Confidence and assertiveness
- Long-term energy and vitality

This is not bro-science—it's biology. Physical strength isn't merely aesthetic. It's chemical. And it affects how you think, feel, and show up in the world.

Muscle is metabolically active tissue. Unlike fat, it's constantly working for you, even while you rest. Building and maintaining lean mass leads to:

- Better fat-burning at rest
- Improved insulin sensitivity
- Reduced risk of chronic illness
- Greater joint stability and injury prevention

A well-built body is not decoration—it's demonstration. It reflects effort, structure, and personal standards. It's visual proof of your ability to commit, to endure, and to evolve.

Throughout history, strong men were the protectors, the providers, the decision-makers in times of chaos. They didn't just lift spears—they lifted communities. They stood at the gate when the enemy approached. They didn't ask for safety. They *became* the safety.

- They survived brutal winters and brought food back to the tribe.
- They fought enemies face-to-face.
- They earned respect through sacrifice, not just stature.

That instinct—**to trust strength**—still lives in us today.

Even in a modern society that tries to domesticate masculinity, people naturally respect and gravitate toward men who move with quiet power. It's subconscious. It's built into our evolutionary design. When you walk into a room with strength, it signals: This man can lead. This man can protect. This man is built for more.

We no longer need to hunt or fight off wild animals, but the need to train is still urgent. The enemies are different now:

- Stress
- Weak posture
- Sedentary living
- Poor hormone profiles
- Low self-worth
- Emotional fragility

The gym is where you go to build your armor. Every rep is an act of resistance—not just against gravity, but against mediocrity.

Strength training is how you fight back. It's how you reclaim discipline in a world that promotes indulgence. It's how you rewire your mind to choose effort over excuse.

A strong, well-developed body doesn't just improve health. It improves outcomes. Studies show that people perceive strong men as more competent, more trustworthy, and more persuasive. Strength influences:

- How you're treated
- How you lead
- How you negotiate
- How others respond to your authority

You don't have to be a bodybuilder. But you do have to be *intentional*. Because people see your body before they hear your voice.

Your body isn't something to be worshipped. It's something to be sharpened. Strength is not a luxury—it's a duty.

If you were handed a high-performance machine and told to carry precious cargo across dangerous terrain, would you neglect it? Of course not. You'd prepare it. Tune it. Strengthen it for the road ahead.

That's what your body is: the vehicle of your mission.

- When it's strong, you think clearly.
- When it's strong, you lead decisively.
- When it's strong, you don't fear conflict—you're built for it.

Let's be clear: Physical strength alone does not make a man. But it *does* elevate everything that does.

- It reinforces self-discipline.
- It boosts energy and endurance.
- It improves mental health and hormonal balance.
- It gives you an edge—in how you move, lead, and protect.

Strength is not optional. It is **required** for every man who wants to rise above comfort and lead with clarity.

You don't need to be the biggest man in the room. But you should be the most prepared. And preparation begins with honoring your body—not through ego, but through intention.

Because strength isn't about being better than others.
It's about being ready when others need you most.

CHAPTER 6

WHEN A MAN SHOULD USE FORCE (AND WHEN HE SHOULD NOT)

A MAN SHOULD NEVER BE KNOWN FOR HIS VIOLENCE, BUT HE should always be *capable* of it.

There is a time to speak, and a time to act. A time to lead with compassion, and a time to set boundaries with force. The wise man understands both and uses each only when it aligns with his principles, not his emotions. Violence, when driven by ego or unchecked anger, destroys. But when guided by justice, necessity, and self-control, it becomes a last-resort defense that is measured, purposeful, and often unavoidable.

It's easy to confuse power with dominance. To believe that "might makes right." But a man of character doesn't swing first. He assesses. He measures. He leads with his mind, not his fists.

The Prophet Muhammad (PBUH) said:

> The strong is not the one who overcomes the people by his strength, but the one who controls himself while in anger. (Sahih al-Bukhari)

Self-control is strength. Anyone can lose their temper. Anyone can lash out. But the man who pauses, who restrains his wrath even when provoked, displays a higher form of power.

There are situations when physical force is not just acceptable—it is righteous.

1. **To protect the innocent.** When your wife, children, loved ones, or even strangers are in imminent danger and words have failed, a man must not hesitate. In this case, force is not aggression—it is protection.
2. **In legitimate self-defense.** If someone threatens your life or physical safety, you have every right to defend yourself. But there is a difference between defense and retaliation. The goal should always be to neutralize, not annihilate.
3. **To stop harm or injustice.** Whether it's breaking up a violent assault, protecting someone being harassed, or intervening when no one else will—act decisively. But again, with measured intent. Not to inflict pain, but to halt harm.
4. **As a final option, not the first.** Physical action should come only after reason, dialogue, and boundaries have failed. Then, and only then, does force become a righteous tool.

I used to fight—a lot.

Growing up, it felt good to let the anger out. To throw a punch instead of talking. To assert control over chaos in the only language I thought the world respected: violence. I left holes in the walls. I got into wild 6th Street brawls. I threatened physical violence many times. That's one of the reasons I fell in love with football. It was legal aggression. Controlled violence. You could knock someone's lights out, and not only was it allowed, but it was celebrated. That kind of release was addicting.

As I got bigger, stronger, and more imposing, people stopped testing me. They'd think twice before raising their voice or stepping out of line. And to be honest, that power was intoxicating. It felt like I could do whatever I wanted and get away with it. There was no real fear of consequence.

Despite this, even when at my angriest, it never felt *good* to hurt people. Not deep down. There was no peace in it and no real victory. Just a temporary high followed by a spiritual low.

Over time, I began to understand a deeper truth: All beings are God's creation. Whether saint or sinner, friend or foe, every person is sacred. And unless there is true danger or real harm, violence is not just unnecessary, it's destructive. Not just to others, but to your own soul.

That shift in perspective changed everything. I began to find more peace in *defusing* tension rather than escalating it. There was more strength in walking away, more satisfaction in restraint. The real man, I realized, is the one who can destroy but chooses not to.

I'll never forget one moment that tested this.

I was out, up to no good, but minding my business…or so I thought. Someone attacked me. Out of nowhere. It was aggressive, personal, and unprovoked. I had every right to respond with force. I could have snapped his ribs in a second. In the past, I would have. But something stopped me. I remembered a Hadith of the Prophet Muhammad (PBUH), when he was grabbed and choked from behind in the streets. His response? He didn't retaliate. He didn't strike. He had his companions give the man *charity* and let him go.

That story stayed with me.

So I made a choice. I didn't fight back. I didn't escalate. I de-escalated. And in that moment, the situation didn't just end; it transformed. What could've led to serious injury or long-term consequences became a moment of clarity, mercy, and unexpected reward. I walked away with my peace intact, and more importantly, I walked away knowing I had chosen God's approval over my ego's satisfaction.

But don't confuse that restraint with weakness.

There was another very different moment I faced. An active shooter situation unfolded inside our building. My family was inside. Lives were on the line. I didn't hesitate. I had my .45 loaded and in my hand and my body stationed by the door, prepared to do whatever was necessary to protect them. That's not violence driven by pride; that's protection born from responsibility.

And that's the line.

Violence is never for vengeance. Never for ego. Never for showing off or proving who's tougher. That's the behavior of children and cowards. But if someone is threatening your life, your family, or the innocent then you don't ask questions. You act. You protect. And you do so *in accordance with God*, with a clean heart and clear intention.

The truth of it is that **the strongest man is not the one who fights the most, but the one who knows *when* to fight and when to forgive.**

Too many men confuse masculinity with aggression. They think being feared is the same as being respected. That is a lie.

- **When it's fueled by ego.** If your pride is wounded and your instinct is to "prove" yourself physically, you've already lost. A man who fights to save face is not strong; he's insecure and reckless.
- **When it's used to intimidate.** Raising your voice or your hand to assert dominance, especially in your own home, is a betrayal of your duty. The strongest man in the room is the one who makes others feel *safe*, not scared.
- **When it's a reaction, not a decision.** Violence should never be an impulse. If you strike out in a moment of anger or stress, you've surrendered your authority to your emotions.
- **To prove you're a "man."** If you're using force to feel validated as masculine, it means you haven't yet understood what masculinity truly is.

If the moment arises when you must act physically, here's how to carry it with integrity:

- **Pause before you strike.** Breathe. Assess. Your greatest weapon is your calm.
- **Use the minimum necessary.** The goal is to stop the harm, not to punish the person.
- **Stay anchored in your intent.** If your heart is clean and your goal is protection, you'll sleep at night.

- **Lead after the conflict.** Once safe, use your words. Show maturity. Teach if you can.
- **Don't glorify the moment.** Walk away with humility, not celebration. Reflect. Learn. Purify your intention.

Violence is a last resort, not a personality trait. The world doesn't need more violent men. It needs more *capable* men. More *principled* men. Men who are not afraid to act but are wise enough to know when *not* to.

If you must be dangerous, let it be to those who prey on the weak. If you must be feared, let it be by those who seek to harm the innocent. But to your loved ones, to the righteous, and to your community be the man they turn to when trouble comes. Not the cause of it.

CHAPTER 7

NUTRITION

MY COLLEGE STRENGTH COACH AT HARVARD, JAMES FRAZIER, USED to say, "You can't outwork a bad diet." Simple. Brutal. True.

You can train like a beast. Grind for hours in the gym. Push every limit. But if your nutrition is garbage, your results will be too.

This isn't about abs or aesthetics. It's about discipline. Clarity. Longevity. Because what you eat isn't just fuel—it's a direct reflection of how much you value yourself, your mission, and the vessel God entrusted you with.

Imam Al-Ghazali once said that man's two greatest desires are those of the stomach and the loins.[1] Of the two, the stomach comes first. And controlling it is one of the hardest, most defining tests a man will ever face.

Food is culture. It's nostalgia. It's celebration, comfort, and connection. But let's not ignore the other side of it.

It's also one of the leading causes of chronic disease, low energy, poor mental health, and early death.

The rise of ultra-processed, high-sugar, high-sodium foods—and

---

[1] Abu Hamid Muhammad al-Ghazali, *Disciplining the Soul and Breaking the Two Desires: Books XXII and XXIII of the Revival of the Religious Sciences*, trans. T. J. Winter (Islamic Texts Society, 1997).

a culture that glorifies excess—has created a health crisis. Super-sized portions, drive-throughs on every corner, and chemical-laden "foods" have turned our plates into weapons against us.

Make no mistake: This isn't just about taste. It's business. The food industry profits while your body pays the price.

But you don't have to play victim. You can opt out. You can treat your diet as your **competitive edge**.

Because once you take control of what goes on your plate, you take control of everything else.

Let's be honest. Most of us have had those long days: stacked meetings, stress, no time to cook—and fast food calling your name. The convenience is seductive, but the price is steep.

Poor nutrition wrecks more than your waistline. It fuels:

- Chronic inflammation
- Brain fog and decision fatigue
- Anxiety and emotional volatility
- Low testosterone and poor recovery
- Weakened immunity

On the other hand, smart nutrition builds a fortress around your mind and body. Ancient wisdom has always emphasized balance and moderation. Now, science confirms it: What you eat determines how well you **think, perform, recover,** and **lead**.

Here's how you reclaim control and fuel your life with precision:

1. **Prioritize whole foods.** Lean proteins, vegetables, fruits, whole grains, and healthy fats should dominate your plate.
2. **Eliminate processed junk.** Cut out the packaged, sugary, chemical-laced stuff designed to hijack your brain.
3. **Plan and prepare.** Meal prep isn't trendy—it's tactical. It eliminates excuses and guarantees you're always fueled with intention.
4. **Stay consistent.** Consistency beats perfection. Over time, the simple habits stack up and compound into massive results.

If your goals include fat loss, muscle growth, or peak performance, here's how to dial it in:

- **Caloric balance:** Slight deficit (three hundred to five hundred calories) for fat loss. Slight surplus for muscle gain.
- **Protein intake:** Aim for at least one gram per pound of body weight daily. This repairs, rebuilds, and protects muscle.
- **Smart carbs and fats:** Use complex carbs (quinoa, sweet potatoes, rice) to fuel your sessions. Include essential fats (avocados, fatty fish, nuts) for hormone health.
- **Hydration:** Water is nonnegotiable. Half your body weight in ounces—minimum.

Your body is a high-performance machine. You wouldn't fill a McLaren with low-grade fuel. So why feed your body like a junkyard when you expect it to operate like a war machine?

Islamic teachings echo what modern science confirms: Nutrition is sacred.

The Qur'an calls us to eat that which is Tayyib—pure, wholesome. Not processed. Not excessive.

The Prophet (PBUH) ﷺ said:

> The son of Adam does not fill any vessel worse than his stomach. It is sufficient for the son of Adam to eat a few mouthfuls to keep him going. If he must do that, then one-third for food, one-third for drink, and one-third for air. (Sunan Ibn Majah 3349)

That wisdom counters everything modern culture promotes: indulgence, excess, and emotional eating.

Fasting, particularly during Ramadan, re-centers us. It resets blood sugar, regulates hormones, enhances self-control, and sharpens mental clarity. It's more than spiritual—it's biochemical refinement.

Ask yourself:

- Do I eat to live, or live to eat?
- Do I use food to numb stress, anxiety, or boredom?
- Do I celebrate wins with junk and call it "reward"?

I used to celebrate with fast food. After a win, I'd go for burgers, pizza, or sugar bombs. But eventually, I realized I wasn't rewarding myself—I was numbing myself. What I craved wasn't the food. It was the dopamine spike. The comfort.

Now, I celebrate with things that serve me: a quiet walk, a hard lift, a sauna, a writing session.

Redefine what reward means. Choose habits that reinforce the man you want to become.

THE 80/20 RULE: DISCIPLINE WITH ROOM TO LIVE

Let's be real: This isn't about perfection. It's about control.

I love a good burger. I've had my fair share of ice cream and cheat days. But I don't live there. I visit, then return to discipline.

The 80/20 Rule works like this:

- 80 percent of the time: clean, whole, intentional eating
- 20 percent of the time: flexibility, enjoyment, no guilt

This is how you stay sharp without burning out. This is how you build lifelong habits.

A SAMPLE MEAL BLUEPRINT

MONDAY

Breakfast: Spinach-and-mushroom omelet + whole-grain toast
Snack: Greek yogurt + berries + almonds
Lunch: Grilled chicken + quinoa + roasted vegetables
Snack: Apple slices + almond butter
Dinner: Baked salmon + sweet potato + asparagus

TUESDAY

Breakfast: Protein smoothie (spinach, berries, protein powder, almond milk)

Snack: Baby carrots + hummus

Lunch: Turkey-and-avocado wrap on a whole-grain tortilla

Snack: Hard-boiled eggs + celery

Dinner: Grilled steak + roasted brussels sprouts + brown rice

Repeat variations throughout the week with seasonal produce and lean proteins. Simplicity is strength. Focus on lean meat and proteins, fruits, complex carbs; minimize sugar and highly processed foods; and minimize high-sodium seasoning.

The Pareto Principle says that 80 percent of your results come from 20 percent of your actions. In nutrition, that 20 percent is your food choices.

You are not a victim of your cravings. You are not a slave to convenience.

You are a man with a mission. And that mission demands a clear mind, an energetic body, and unwavering discipline.

Your transformation starts at the table. What you eat today becomes who you are tomorrow.

CHAPTER 8

SUPPLEMENTATION

WE'VE COVERED TRAINING. WE'VE COVERED NUTRITION. BUT THE often-overlooked edge—the **X-factor** in performance—is smart supplementation.

The right supplements, taken with intention and consistency, don't replace discipline. They *amplify it*. When layered on top of solid training, recovery, and nutrition, they serve as force multipliers: sharpening focus, accelerating recovery, boosting hormonal function, and extending your capacity.

This isn't about shortcuts. It's about optimization.

I remember the exact moment it all started. I had just gotten my hands on the original Jack3d preworkout—one of the most powerful formulas ever created (and eventually banned).

One scoop. Tingling skin. Heart racing. I felt like a caged animal finally released.

That workout lasted nearly three hours.

Growing up, my parents didn't allow caffeine, supplements, or anything artificial. But as my senior football season approached, I started experimenting cautiously. What followed was years of research, trial, and refinement as I trained alongside NFL athletes and bodybuilders, aiming to feel and perform my best—without compromising integrity or health.

What follows is the product of that journey.

THE MEN'S OPTIMIZATION SUPPLEMENT PROTOCOL

This blueprint is designed for peak performance: mentally, physically, and hormonally. It's not about hype—it's about results.

UPON WAKING: PRIMING THE SYSTEM

Your first hour shapes your physiology for the entire day. Start clean.

- **Greens blend (AG1, BPN Super Greens):** Gut health, immune support, nutrient insurance.
- **Manuka honey (1 tbsp):** Antibacterial, prebiotic, clean energy.
- **Bovine colostrum (2–3g, e.g. Armra):** Gut lining repair, immune resilience, recovery support.
- **Delay caffeine 60–90 minutes:** Allow cortisol to peak naturally before adding stimulation.

MORNING ENERGY AND FOCUS STACK

Build sustainable mental clarity without caffeine dependency.

- **L-theanine:** Smooths focus, prevents overstimulation.
- **L-carnitine:** Enhances fat metabolism and cognitive energy.
- **Maca root:** Boosts endurance, libido, and hormonal stability.
- **Ashwagandha:** Lowers cortisol, supports testosterone.
- **Vitamin B12 (methylated):** Key for energy, cognition, and nervous system health.
- **Ginseng extract:** Enhances mood and physical endurance.
- **Rhodiola rosea:** Improves stress resilience and mental clarity.

This stack offers clean, focused energy without the post-caffeine crash.

PREWORKOUT (TWENTY TO THIRTY MINUTES BEFORE TRAINING)

Your body needs raw material for intensity and output.

- **Preworkout formula (1 scoop):** Choose one that enhances blood flow, focus, and stamina without trash ingredients.
- **Creatine HCl (5g):** Increases power, strength, and cell hydration.
- **Citrulline and arginine:** Boost nitric oxide for performance and muscle pump.

Training fasted? Add electrolytes for hydration and endurance.

INTRAWORKOUT SUPPORT

Fuel the engine while you train.

- **BCAAs (1 scoop):** Protects muscle during long or fasted sessions.
- **Creatine HCL (optional):** Split dose with preworkout stack if preferred.
- **HMB (3g):** Reduces muscle breakdown and speeds recovery.

POSTWORKOUT RECOVERY

Anabolic windows are real. Don't miss yours.

- **Whey protein (25–50g):** Rapid absorption for muscle repair. Go grass-fed when possible.
- **Fast-digesting carbs (optional):** Banana, honey, or dextrose to replenish glycogen.

Struggle with digestion? Opt for plant-based protein with enzymes.

EVENING: SLEEP AND HORMONAL RESET

Growth happens in deep sleep. Guard it.

- **Magnesium glycinate (300–500mg):** Promotes relaxation, recovery, and sleep depth.
- **Zinc (30mg):** Supports testosterone and immune defense.
- **ZMA formulas:** Highly effective for sleep quality and recovery.

ADVANCED OPTIMIZATION STACK

For those serious about hormonal health and elite performance.

- **CoQ10 (100mg):** Supports mitochondrial function and cardiovascular health.
- **Boron (3–6mg):** Aids testosterone metabolism and bone density.
- **DHEA (25–100mg):** Balances hormone levels and supports energy.
- **Tongkat ali (400–500mg):** Boosts testosterone and sexual health.
- **Fadogia agrestis (500mg):** Synergistic testosterone support.
- **Tribulus terrestris (1,000mg):** Strength and libido enhancer.

Cycle these herbs periodically to prevent tolerance.

Supplements aren't magic. They're magnifiers. They don't create results—they **enhance** results you're already earning through discipline, sleep, movement, and nutrition.

Think of them as the final 1 percent. The polish. The edge that separates the dedicated from the elite.

The right stack:

- Enhances focus and brain performance
- Increases strength and muscular output
- Speeds up recovery and sleep quality
- Optimizes hormone balance and vitality
- Helps push past physical and mental plateaus

But none of it matters without consistency.

The secret isn't in a capsule or powder.

It's in the decisions you make every day—the food you eat, the workouts you show up for, the hours you sleep, the temptations you resist, and the effort you repeat.

Supplements are tools. They're not saviors.

Use them with wisdom, not dependence.

Use them to refine, not replace.

Because the strongest, sharpest, most dominant version of you isn't built by shortcuts.

He's built by habits.

CHAPTER 9

SLEEP: THE ULTIMATE PERFORMANCE ENHANCER

WHAT IF THERE WERE A MAGIC POTION THAT SHARPENED YOUR mind, enhanced your physical performance, stabilized your emotions, and elevated your mood? The kind of fuel that takes you from foggy and fatigued to focused and unstoppable?

It exists. And it's not a supplement, stimulant, or secret hack.

It's sleep.

If you're serious about building strength, clarity, and spiritual discipline, then there's one nonnegotiable law you must live by:

Get at least seven hours of high-quality sleep every night.

In my early twenties, I wore the grind like armor. "I'll sleep when I'm dead" was my mantra. I thought I was built different. Late nights. Early mornings. Double scoops of caffeine and back-to-back sessions. I thought I was optimizing. But in reality, I was burning out from the inside.

The symptoms crept in:

- Fat gain despite training harder than ever

- Elevated resting heart rate
- Brain fog that made me feel like a shell of myself

I wasn't just tired. I was breaking down. And instead of slowing down, I doubled down—more caffeine, more supplements, more denial. Until my body finally gave out.

The turning point came when I joined WHOOP as director of sales. Surrounded by elite recovery science and top-tier data, I started tracking my own sleep, HRV, and recovery metrics. What I discovered changed everything.

SLEEP IS NOT REST. IT'S RESTORATION.

Once I made sleep a true priority, everything changed.

- My mind cleared.
- My body leaned out.
- My energy stabilized.
- My discipline returned.

Sleep wasn't just fixing fatigue. It was rebuilding me from the inside out.

Here's what happens when you get real, restorative sleep:

1. ELEVATED TESTOSTERONE AND GROWTH HORMONE

The majority of your testosterone and growth hormone is released during deep sleep. These two hormones drive:

- Muscle repair
- Fat burning
- Libido
- Vitality

You can train hard, but without sleep, you'll stay stuck.

2. MUSCLE GROWTH AND RECOVERY

Your muscles don't grow in the gym—they grow at night.

Deep sleep is when your body repairs damaged muscle fibers and rebuilds stronger tissue. Poor sleep = reduced gains and stalled progress.

3. SHARPER BRAIN FUNCTION

Sleep strengthens memory, learning, creativity, and decision-making.

Lack of sleep leads to:

- Poor judgment
- Slower reaction time
- Impulsivity
- Mental fog

For high-performance living, mental sharpness is nonnegotiable.

4. NERVOUS SYSTEM RESET AND HEART RATE VARIABILITY

Your HRV—a powerful indicator of recovery and stress—is directly impacted by sleep quality. The lower your recovery, the more stress your body holds.

Chronic sleep deprivation increases risk of:

- Burnout
- Anxiety
- Cardiovascular disease
- Premature aging

Think you're tough for skipping sleep? Real strength is measured in longevity, not sacrifice.

Elite sleep isn't random—it's built with precision. Here's how to dominate your nights so you can dominate your days:

1. **Cut caffeine by 2:00 p.m.** Caffeine has a long half-life. What you drink at 4:00 p.m. might still be disrupting your sleep at midnight.
2. **Black out your room.** Light = enemy of melatonin. Use blackout curtains or an eye mask to protect your deep sleep.
3. **Keep it cool.** Optimal sleep temp? 65–68°F. A cool room signals your body it's time to wind down.
4. **Eliminate blue light.** Phones, laptops, TVs—they all emit blue light that tricks your brain into thinking it's still daytime. Go screen-free for thirty to sixty minutes before bed. Read. Pray. Reflect.
5. **No late-night eating.** Finish your last meal two to three hours before bed. Let your body rest—not digest.
6. **Track your patterns.** Use tools like WHOOP or the Oura Ring to monitor sleep quality, HRV, and recovery metrics. Data reveals the truth.
7. **Use white noise or sound machines.** A consistent audio backdrop can block out distractions and improve deep sleep.
8. **Aim for at least seven hours of real sleep.** Not time in bed—actual sleep. Factor in time to fall asleep and wake-ups. Shoot for seven to eight hours consistently.

SLEEP IS SPIRITUAL

This isn't just about hormones and muscles. It's about your soul.

I used to suffer from sleep paralysis. I'd feel a dark presence. I couldn't move. Couldn't breathe. A shadow would press on my chest, choking me. Science calls it a REM glitch. But I knew better. After speaking with scholars, I understood this wasn't just neurological—it was spiritual.

Sleep is the "little death." During sleep, our souls temporarily leave our bodies. It's a vulnerable state, one that requires purification and protection.

To sleep in peace, you need more than a cool room and blackout shades. You need spiritual shielding.

Here's what I do nightly:

- Recite Ayat al-Kursi (three times) before bed: "Whoever recites it before sleeping, no harm shall come to him until morning."
- Make Dua (supplication), asking for protection, forgiveness, and peace.
- Keep the room clean of negative energy: no dark symbols, toxic content, or distractions from remembrance

The Prophet (PBUH) said:

When you go to bed, Satan ties three knots at the back of your head. He whispers, "You have a long night ahead, so sleep." If you remember Allah, one knot is undone. If you make wudu, another is undone. If you pray, all three are untied—and you wake up energized and in good spirits. If not, you wake up lazy and moody. (Sahih al-Bukhari 1142)

This is real.

Spiritual discipline directly impacts physical and emotional strength. Stop treating sleep like a luxury. It's the foundation.

Every high performer—whether an elite athlete, entrepreneur, or leader—protects their sleep like a fortress. They know that focus, resilience, emotional stability, and hormonal balance all begin in the bedroom.

When you sleep better, you:

- Train harder
- Think sharper
- Lead stronger
- Recover faster
- Live longer

Sleep isn't weakness. It's strategy.

Sleep isn't escape. It's equipping.

Sleep isn't soft. It's sacred.

Starting tonight, make sleep part of your discipline. Optimize your environment. Build a spiritual routine. Cut the noise, clean your space, and prepare your body and soul for renewal.

This one shift will transform how you train, think, lead, and worship.

Because the strongest version of yourself?

He's not sleep-deprived.

He's not overcaffeinated.

He's clear. Centered. Recharged and ready.

CHAPTER 10

SMILE LIKE A MAN

A SMILE IS MORE THAN A FACIAL EXPRESSION; IT'S A STATEMENT. A nonverbal declaration of confidence. A signal of strength that doesn't need to be loud to be felt. It cuts through tension, disarms pride, and connects people before a word is even spoken. In a world hardened by competition and ego, it's often the softest expression that holds the most power.

The world tells men to look serious, stay guarded, and withhold emotion. We're conditioned to believe that stoicism is strength and that a smile is a crack in the armor. But this mindset has it backward. A man who smiles isn't weak; he's secure. He doesn't need to prove himself through intimidation or detachment. His presence says, "I'm grounded. I'm in control. I'm not here to impress; I'm here to uplift."

A genuine smile carries weight. It shifts atmospheres. It softens hardened hearts. It builds bridges without needing to speak.

Try this: Spend one day intentionally smiling at everyone you pass. Not a forced grin, but a sincere, grounded smile. Watch what happens. Strangers nod. Eyes soften. Even the most guarded expressions begin to crack. That's not coincidence; that is human design.

Smiling is not just about positivity alone. In the right hands, it's a tool that enhances presence, builds connection, and commands respect without aggression.

1. IT SHAPES FIRST IMPRESSIONS

Before you speak, people feel you. A smile communicates confidence and composure. According to studies published in *Neuropsychologia*, smiling activates the brain's reward circuitry in those around you, making you more likable, trustworthy, and competent. That's influence before you've said a single word.

2. IT UPLIFTS AND DISARMS

Smiling triggers mirror neurons in the brain, making it biologically contagious. You smile, they smile—it's automatic. This is how you interrupt someone's stress without even talking. This is how you change a room's temperature without raising your voice.

3. IT BUILDS BROTHERHOOD

Every strong bond is built on trust, and trust grows fastest in the presence of warmth. The Prophet Muhammad (PBUH) said, "Your smile in the face of your brother is charity." (Tirmidhi 1956) Something as effortless as a smile can be the spark that ignites brotherhood, forgiveness, or unity.

4. IT DE-ESCALATES CONFLICT

In tense environments, people expect confrontation. A man who maintains his smile in heated situations isn't soft; he's composed. Smiling doesn't eliminate boundaries; it reinforces that you're in control, not reactive. That's real power.

Masculinity doesn't mean emotionless. It means responsible emotional leadership. And that begins with mastering your energy, including your face.

- **Confidence without ego:** A smile says you're not performing. You're present. You're at ease in your skin. That type of energy can't be faked, and it can't be ignored.
- **Influence without intimidation:** A Princeton University study found that leaders who smile are seen as more competent, trustworthy, approachable, and inspirational.[2] Power is less about pressure, more about presence. And presence begins with warmth.
- **Strength with kindness:** Society still clings to the outdated idea that kindness is weakness. That's noise. True masculinity balances compassion with clarity. Smiling doesn't erase strength; it refines it.

THE SCIENCE BEHIND THE SMILE

Smiling doesn't just change how others see you. It actually changes your biology.

- **Mood booster:** Smiling releases dopamine, serotonin, and endorphins, which are your brain's natural mood enhancers.
- **Stress reducer:** It lowers cortisol, reducing physical and emotional tension.
- **Blood pressure and immune support:** It relaxes your body, improving circulation and immunity.
- **Productivity and creativity:** Positive emotional states improve memory, focus, and innovation.
- **Longevity:** Studies in *Psychological Science* found those with genuine smiles live longer lives.[3]

The Prophet (PBUH) was a man of unparalleled gentleness. His smile was constant. Welcoming. Disarming. Comforting.

---

[2] Scott Mautz, "Want to Make Great First Impression? A Princeton Psychologist Says Be Aware of 3 Snap Judgments People Make," Inc.com, March 27, 2019, https://www.inc.com/scott-mautz/a-princeton-psychologist-says-people-make-these-3-snap-judgments-within-milliseconds-of-meeting-you.html?utm_source=chatgpt.com.

[3] E. L. Abel and M.L. Kruger, "Smile Intensity in Photographs Predicts Longevity," *Psychological Science* 21(4) (2010), 542–544.

I never saw anyone who smiled more than the Messenger of God. (Tirmidhi 3641)

Smiling in the face of your brother is charity. (Tirmidhi 1956)

His smile wasn't just social; it was spiritual. It reflected inner peace and God-consciousness. It told people: "You are seen. You are safe. You matter."

Smiling, then, isn't just a habit; it's a Sunnah. A practice that fuses character with faith, kindness with purpose.

Strength doesn't always look like clenched fists and hardened stares. Sometimes, it's in the man who walks into the room with calm eyes and an open face. The one who knows who he is, doesn't need to flex, and still commands attention without saying a word.

That man doesn't seek approval; he gives it. Doesn't need to dominate because he connects. And when he smiles, it's not for show. It's a reflection of what's already anchored within: certainty, peace, and presence.

So smile like a man. Not because you're trying to be liked. But because you know who you are.

CHAPTER 11

THERMAL THERAPY TRAINING

FOR CENTURIES, CIVILIZATIONS ACROSS THE GLOBE HAVE TURNED to thermal therapy—not as a trend, but as a foundational tool for recovery, clarity, and renewal. From the Roman bathhouses where emperors and generals recharged their bodies, to the ice-cold streams of Japanese misogi, to the smoke-filled Finnish saunas tucked into the woods, this practice has always been more than relaxation.

It's been training.

In my travels through Scandinavia and Eastern Europe, I saw it firsthand. Saunas, steam rooms, cold plunges, all woven into the rhythm of daily life. Not luxury. Lifestyle. Just as routine as brushing your teeth. And it shows. These cultures rank among the healthiest and most resilient on earth—not just physically, but emotionally and spiritually.

In the United States, we treat thermal therapy like a spa day. An indulgence. A bonus.

But the truth is, it's a necessity.

A discipline.

A form of stress rehearsal.

When I began incorporating thermal work consistently—morning and night—cycling through sauna, cold plunge, hot tub, and steam, the results were undeniable.

- My recovery improved.
- My mood stabilized.
- My energy sharpened.
- My mind calmed.

This wasn't subtle. It was a shift. A reset. A recalibration of both body and nervous system.

At WHOOP, we studied the effects of contrast therapy on high performers: athletes, executives, and operators. The results were clear: No recovery protocol offered greater benefit to **resilience, recovery,** and **regulation** than heat and cold exposure.

Thermal therapy works because it does what every effective training system does: It introduces **stress** in a controlled environment—and forces you to adapt.

HEAT EXPOSURE (SAUNA + STEAM)

The heat simulates stress. Your heart rate increases. Your body works to cool itself. You sweat, release toxins, and stimulate endorphins.

Benefits include:

- Improved circulation
- Enhanced cardiovascular function
- Boosted growth hormone
- Better sleep and sharper cognition

This is cardiovascular conditioning without movement. It's passive endurance.

Stillness under strain.

COLD EXPOSURE (PLUNGE + ICE BATHS)

The cold activates your fight-or-flight response instantly. Your breathing spikes. Your brain tells you to flee. But you don't. You slow it down. You stay present.

Benefits include:

- Reduced inflammation
- Stronger immune response
- Elevated dopamine and mood regulation
- Increased mental resilience

This is where you train your ability to override panic and sit inside pain—without running.

CONTRAST THERAPY (HOT + COLD ROTATION)

Moving between extremes demands full-system adaptation.

Benefits include:

- Enhanced HRV and blood flow
- Faster recovery
- Hormonal balance
- Sharpened mental edge

Each switch—hot to cold, cold to hot—is a rehearsal for change. For life's rapid transitions. For staying grounded when nothing else is.

THE PROTOCOL: THREE TO FOUR TIMES A WEEK

You don't need a fancy spa. You need consistency and commitment. Here's a sample protocol built around performance, recovery, and mental conditioning:

- **Sauna (fifteen to twenty minutes):** Enter with intention. No phone.

No noise. Hydrate beforehand. Breathe slowly. Use this time to reflect, visualize, or simply endure.
- **Cold plunge (three to five minutes):** Step in slowly. Breathe through your nose. Let the shock hit—but stay calm. The pain is your teacher. Stay until your breath slows and your mind clears.
- **Hot tub (ten to fifteen minutes):** Let your body recalibrate. Focus on full relaxation. Let stillness challenge your attention.
- **Steam room (ten to fifteen minutes):** End with restoration. Inhale deeply. Let the heat cleanse your lungs and quiet your nervous system.
- Rinse with cool water to seal the session.

This isn't just recovery. It's resilience training.
Strength training builds muscle. Fasting refines your soul.
Thermal therapy? It teaches **composure** under pressure.
Each round is a controlled confrontation with discomfort. You're not just healing from stress—you're preparing for it.
Because when life hits, you don't get to pause. You respond with whatever nervous system you've trained. Thermal therapy trains you to respond from **centered stillness**, not panic. From calm, not chaos.

THIS IS NOT A SHORTCUT. IT'S A STRATEGY.

A man who chases ease becomes soft.
A man who embraces discomfort becomes unbreakable.
Thermal therapy builds that kind of man.

- The man who holds his breath steady when everything's shaking.
- The man who leads calmly in high-stakes situations.
- The man who doesn't fold when life gets cold.

This isn't wellness. This is warfare—against passivity, anxiety, and reactivity.
You won't just recover better. You'll live better.
Because the man who trains his nervous system…

Trains his leadership.
Trains his fatherhood.
Trains his faith.
Trains his presence.
So sweat. Freeze. Breathe.
And step out sharper than you were when you stepped in.

CHAPTER 12

FASTING IS A PRESCRIPTION

MASTERING YOUR MIND IS NONNEGOTIABLE IF YOU WANT TO LIVE with excellence. But self-mastery doesn't begin in the mind alone—it begins with the body. And nothing trains the body, mind, and soul more effectively than fasting.

In a culture ruled by instant gratification, fasting is a radical act. It cuts against the grain of a society addicted to consumption and distraction. It's not a trend. It's an ancient tool—time-tested, God-ordained, and biologically validated.

Fasting isn't about deprivation. It's about **dominion**.

It's about taking back control over your impulses, cravings, and base desires—and directing that energy toward purpose, presence, and discipline.

More than two billion people around the world engage in fasting every year during the sacred month of Ramadan. From dawn until sunset for thirty days, Muslims abstain from food, drink, sexual activity, gossip, and mindless distractions—not just to reset the body, but to elevate the soul.

It's not just a ritual. It's a full-body transformation—physical, emotional, and spiritual.

> O you who have believed, fasting has been prescribed upon you as it was prescribed upon those before you so that you may attain *taqwa* (God-consciousness). (Qur'an 2:183)

That verse captures the essence: **Fasting is a path to higher awareness.**

I remember fasting during brutal Texas summers—two-a-day football practices in 100-plus-degree heat, while juggling classwork and training. You'd expect performance to dip. But by God's will, I was thriving.

One game stands out: I broke a school record with **twenty-five tackles**, all while fasting. That season ended with All-State honors. Not despite fasting—but because of it.

Fasting taught me that energy doesn't just come from calories—it comes from conviction. It comes from aligning with something higher than hunger.

I was inspired by the likes of Hakeem Olajuwon and Muhammad Ali, who trained and competed at the highest levels while fasting. That's when it clicked: **Fasting isn't a limitation—it's a lens.** It reveals who you are when comfort is stripped away.

While fasting is primarily spiritual, modern science confirms its physical and mental power. Whether through intermittent fasting or prolonged fasts during Ramadan, fasting activates several powerful biological processes:

1. AUTOPHAGY

Your body's natural detox system. It breaks down and recycles damaged cells, supporting long-term health and slowing aging.

2. HORMONAL OPTIMIZATION

- Boosts growth hormone
- Improves insulin sensitivity
- Enhances fat burning and energy levels

3. IMMUNE AND INFLAMMATORY RESPONSE

- Reduces chronic inflammation
- Strengthens immune defenses
- Supports gut health and brain function

4. COGNITIVE SHARPNESS

- Improves focus and memory
- Reduces brain fog
- Enhances emotional regulation and discipline

Fasting is the **reset button** your body and mind are starving for.

FASTING FLIPS THE SCRIPT ON MODERN LIFE

Modern society is engineered for overindulgence. We scroll, consume, click, snack, repeat. Every moment is designed to seduce you into comfort.

Fasting is your protest.

It's how you reclaim stillness in a noisy world. It breaks the cycle of mindless consumption. It realigns your soul with purpose, restraint, and remembrance.

Fasting trains you to say *no*—not out of fear, but out of **freedom**. You're not being controlled. You're choosing what—and who—you serve.

Ramadan is sacred. But fasting can also be integrated throughout the year for physical, mental, and spiritual growth.

Intermittent fasting (IF) has gained global traction for good reason: It works. When paired with resistance training, clean nutrition, and deep sleep, it becomes a powerful system for renewal and performance.

BENEFITS OF INTERMITTENT FASTING (IF):

- Greater insulin sensitivity and fat metabolism
- Sustained energy and reduced inflammation

- Sharper focus and better memory
- Increased willpower and emotional resilience
- Activation of autophagy for cellular health

If you're ready to experience the power of fasting, start with intention and discipline.

1. **Set your intention.** Fasting is more than skipping meals. Define your *why*: spiritual clarity, mental toughness, physical reset.
2. **Ease into it.** Start with a twelve- to fourteen-hour fasting window. Gradually build to sixteen hours or more as your body adapts.
3. **Reflect and realign.** Use fasting windows to pray, meditate, or journal. Let hunger remind you of purpose, not lack.
4. **Hydrate strategically.** During nonfasting hours, prioritize water and electrolyte balance. Dehydration kills performance.
5. **Break your fast with intention.** Fuel your body with nutrient-dense foods—lean protein, healthy fats, slow carbs, and micronutrients.
6. **Be consistent.** Like any discipline, fasting compounds with time. Your body adapts. Your mind sharpens. Your spirit strengthens.

Fasting is not about what you're giving up. It's about what you're gaining.

- Focus instead of distraction
- Clarity instead of chaos
- Discipline instead of indulgence
- Spiritual elevation instead of emotional numbness

In a world obsessed with feeding every craving, fasting teaches restraint. And in that restraint, you find power.

This is how you build the strongest version of yourself—not just physically, but mentally, emotionally, and spiritually.

Trade comfort for clarity. Trade excess for excellence. Trade distraction for devotion.

Fasting is not a punishment.

It's preparation.

And when used with purpose, it unlocks the version of you that God always intended.

STOP DRINKING ALCOHOL

LOOK AROUND. ALCOHOL IS EVERYWHERE.

It's on your screens, in your social feeds, and at the center of almost every gathering. Commercials sell it as confidence in a bottle. A celebration. A lifestyle.

But let's strip away the marketing.

Alcohol isn't your ally.

It's a slow-moving thief—stealing clarity, discipline, vitality, and spiritual alignment. Quietly. Persistently. Strategically.

If you're committed to becoming the man you're destined to be, cutting alcohol might be the single most powerful move you'll ever make.

From the moment alcohol enters your bloodstream, it begins its quiet destruction. No matter how "harmless" it feels at the moment, the physiological effects are real—and they stack up fast.

YOUR LIVER

Alcohol is a toxin. Your liver works overtime to filter it out. Chronic drinking leads to inflammation, fat buildup, scarring, and eventual liver failure.

Why sabotage the engine room of your body's strength?

YOUR IMMUNE SYSTEM

Alcohol weakens your defenses, making you more susceptible to illness and slowing recovery from training, injury, or stress.

YOUR METABOLISM

It disrupts fat-burning, impairs nutrient absorption, and raises cortisol—all of which undermine your efforts in the gym and your goals in the mirror.

YOUR SLEEP

Alcohol knocks you out but robs you of deep, restorative sleep. It interrupts the very cycles your body depends on to rebuild and perform.

You wake up foggy, unmotivated, and reactive—not because you slept poorly, but because alcohol hijacked your rest.

IT'S NOT JUST YOUR BODY. IT'S YOUR MIND.

A few drinks in, and your discipline starts to slip.

You say things you shouldn't.

You make choices you'd never make sober.

You lower your standards and blur the edges of your values.

The issue isn't the drink—it's the ripple effect. Alcohol lingers long after the buzz fades. It numbs your emotional clarity. Dulls your spiritual awareness. Weakens your connection to purpose.

It tricks you into thinking you're in control when, in reality, you're being pulled away from everything you're building.

For most of my life, I stayed away from alcohol. But at one point, I let my guard down. A few drinks turned into bottle service. Parties turned into lifestyle. That lifestyle became chaos.

I lost relationships. I lost control. I almost lost myself.

It led to fights, moments of violence, and situations in foreign countries I could've never returned from. I was surrounded by the wrong people, making the wrong choices, with the wrong mindset—all influenced by alcohol. And worst of all, I was drifting from my relationship with God.

The turning point?

Realizing that the man I wanted to become could not coexist with the man I was becoming under the influence.

My true transformation began the moment I made a vow—for God, for my future, and for my soul—to eliminate alcohol from my life entirely.

THE LIES WE TELL OURSELVES

"It's just one drink."

"I only drink socially."

"I can handle it."

Let's be honest. Alcohol alters your brain. Whether it's one drink or ten, the effect is real. Every time you drink, you weaken your edge.

And if you're building a life of clarity, purpose, and high performance, you don't have room to hand over the steering wheel.

Picture yourself at a gathering. Drinks are flowing. Everyone's on autopilot.

But you?

You make a different move.

You order sparkling water, nod respectfully, and stay locked in. You choose presence over pressure. And with that one decision, you gain:

- **Clear thinking.** You stay sharp, alert, and in control.
- **Deep sleep.** You wake up truly rested and recharged.
- **Faster recovery.** Your body thanks you. So does your brain.
- **Iron discipline.** Every "no" strengthens your self-respect.
- **Better nutrition.** No late-night junk. No next-day cravings. Just consistency.

You're not missing out.
You're moving ahead.

THE HIDDEN COST OF "ONE NIGHT OUT"

Think about this:

You train hard. Eat clean. Live with intention.

Then one night out wipes out days—sometimes weeks—of progress. Why?

Because alcohol doesn't just wreck your sleep. It torches your hormones, spikes inflammation, and sabotages your food choices. That greasy burger at 2:00 a.m.? That's alcohol pulling the strings.

This is how high-performing men lose momentum: one compromise at a time.

Beyond the science, beyond the physical, alcohol disconnects you from your moral compass. It silences the internal voice God placed inside of you—the one that warns you, checks you, guides you.

You feel it. We all do.

And when alcohol enters the picture, that voice gets quieter. Until, eventually, you don't hear it at all.

But the man of discipline—of purpose—he listens. And he protects that connection at all costs.

Try this: Cut alcohol for thirty days. Just thirty.

- Train harder.
- Sleep better.
- Think clearer.
- Reconnect with your goals.
- Rebuild your connection to God.

Then ask yourself: Do I really want to go back?

Chances are, you won't.

You're not giving something up.

You're getting something back:

- Your discipline
- Your mental edge
- Your health
- Your purpose
- Your connection to the Creator

This is about more than sobriety.

It's about sovereignty.

It's about ruling over your impulses instead of letting them rule over you.

Alcohol doesn't deserve a seat at your table.

Not in your habits.

Not in your relationships.

Not in your vision for the man you're becoming.

So tonight, when the drinks are being poured and the pressure creeps in, remember this:

- You don't need the buzz.
- You've got clarity.
- You've got vision.
- You've got purpose.

And that's stronger than anything you'll find at the bottom of a glass.

CHAPTER 13

D.A.R.E.

DRUGS, ALCOHOL, AND SMOKING ARE SOME OF THE MOST DANgerous obstacles on the road to greatness. They promise excitement, escape, and even enlightenment—but behind the high is a harsh reality: These substances are not shortcuts. They're sabotage, designed to lure you in with false promises and strip away the very clarity, discipline, and control required to live with purpose.

They don't just numb your pain; they rob you of your identity.

Growing up, I was taught that saying no to drugs was a mark of strength. I still remember the D.A.R.E. programs, the school assemblies, and the pride of resisting peer pressure. Back then, drugs were painted clearly as something to avoid.

But somewhere along the way, the script changed.

What was once taboo has now been glorified. Drug use isn't just normalized—it's branded as sophisticated, edgy, or even spiritual. From music and movies to influencer culture, we're constantly being fed the idea that substances unlock creativity, expand consciousness, and help us "relax" or "cope." But take a step back and ask yourself: Who's selling this illusion? More often than not, it's people who are already drowning—

promoting habits they barely survive themselves, backed by industries that profit off your spiral.

I wish I could say I never fell for it. But I did.

In high school, I avoided drugs altogether. But one day after practice, a few teammates offered me weed, and I gave in. Instead of feeling calm or carefree, I was flooded with anxiety and paranoia. That should've been enough to stop me for good. But like many things in life, it wasn't a sudden fall—it was a slow erosion.

As I got older, I found myself in circles where substances weren't just available—they were expected. What started as something I dabbled with on weekends became embedded in my lifestyle. Smoking became a daily routine. Party drugs became part of the fun. I began to believe I was living the life of the artists I listened to and the public figures I admired, as if their self-destruction somehow validated mine.

It felt exhilarating—until it didn't.

My performance at work declined. I spent money that should've been building my future on substances that were tearing me apart. I ruined relationships with people who genuinely cared about me. I lost my sense of purpose and let my desires drag me into places and situations that I only escaped by the mercy of God.

One night after a business trip in California, I took a pill to unwind. Within hours, I found myself in a garage surrounded by ex-cons, sensing I had walked straight into something dark. My instincts screamed at me to get out. I sprinted for miles through the city to reach my Uber, then caught a flight home.

On that flight, my body started shutting down. My chest was tight. My breathing shallow. My heart rate dropping. I begged the flight attendant for water, trying to hold back the panic that was flooding my system. I thought that was it—that I wasn't going to make it.

And still…I didn't stop.

That's the cruel grip of addiction. It convinces you that you're fine. That you're just blowing off steam. That you can quit anytime. But deep down, I knew I was lying to myself. I was being manipulated by a force that knew exactly where I was vulnerable. I thought I was the exception—that I could dance in destruction and still come out clean. But with every decision, I was losing more of myself.

What started as casual cocaine use became a weekly habit. Alcohol and women replaced prayer and discipline. My entire value system began to blur. I wasn't living. I was numbing myself. I was surviving—but barely.

Then came the night that changed everything.

After mixing energy drinks, cocaine, alcohol, and Adderall, I pushed my body to its absolute limit. What followed was an entire year of anxiety, panic attacks, and mental fog. My mind became a prison—one I had built with my own hands.

That's when I knew something had to change.

Substance abuse doesn't just affect you in the moment—it lingers. It rewires your brain, distorts your thinking, and steals your ability to make sound decisions. The short-term buzz comes at the cost of long-term clarity.

It weakens your cognition, reduces your emotional resilience, and hijacks your dopamine system—tricking your mind into chasing highs that always leave you lower than where you started. That's the formula: fake pleasure, real destruction.

And it's not just about hard drugs. Nicotine, vapes, and hookah follow the same playbook. They compromise your lungs, accelerate aging, and shave years off your life. Yet we justify it because it seems common, even cultural. But just because something is normal doesn't make it right.

One Ramadan, I witnessed something that put everything into perspective.

It was just before sunset, and we were all gathered, ready to break our fast after a long day of no food or water. But one man stood alone, shaky and pale. I invited him to eat first, but he shook his head and said something I'll never forget:

"I don't need food, man. I need a cigarette."

That was his priority. Not water. Not food. Just a hit of nicotine.

That's what addiction does. It reverses your instincts. It turns survival into slavery.

And this is why, for the man serious about his mission, abstaining from drugs, alcohol, and smoking isn't optional—it's foundational.

At some point, every man must decide.

Will you be the guy who stays up all night chasing a high, nursing hangovers, wasting time, money, and potential?

Or will you become the man who chooses clarity, strength, and spiritual alignment—who trains his mind to lead, his body to endure, and his heart to remain grounded?

True strength isn't found in numbing your pain. It's found in facing discomfort without reaching for a crutch. It's choosing discipline over indulgence, and building a life so fulfilling you don't feel the need to escape it.

SAY NO TO THE HIGH. SAY YES TO THE HIGHER YOU.

This isn't just about saying no to substances. It's about saying yes to who you really are.

- ☐ Yes to long-term health
- ☐ Yes to mental clarity and confidence
- ☐ Yes to meaningful relationships
- ☐ Yes to self-respect and divine alignment
- ☐ Yes to a life of depth, peace, and impact

Greatness isn't built in moments of escape. It's forged in intentional choices, through steady discipline, and by showing up with full presence.

You weren't created to escape. You were created to lead.

Substances only offer the illusion of control. They dull your edge, drain your energy, and blind you to purpose.

So draw your line. Make your vow. Reclaim your clarity, your strength, and your mission.

CHAPTER 14

REDEFINING MASCULINITY

The cry of "be a man!" or "man up!" echoes across generations. It's a call that demands strength but often silences pain. For many, this phrase isn't just advice—it's a verdict. It has shaped how boys become men, not through guidance or wisdom, but through pressure, expectation, and confusion.

Manhood, for most, was never clearly taught. It was absorbed—through media, culture, and the unspoken rules of masculinity passed down in locker rooms, barbershops, and homes. And while masculinity has always been contextual, defined by society's shifting winds, one thing has remained constant: the quiet expectation that manhood must be earned. Not by truth or integrity—but through performance.

The problem? We've inherited a framework of manhood that's deeply flawed. Many of us were raised between two extremes: one that glorified emotional suppression, and another that criticized every expression of traditional masculinity as inherently toxic. Stuck in the middle, we were left with questions few dared to answer: What does it really mean to be a man? What does strength look like when it isn't masking fear?

For too long, men have been conditioned to wear a mask—one that hides fear behind bravado, buries sadness under sarcasm, and replaces connection with conquest. This is what people now call *toxic masculinity*, but it's more than a buzzword. It's a generational illness that leaves millions of men suffering in silence.

The consequences are devastating:

- A silent epidemic of depression, addiction, and suicide.
- The normalization of emotional numbness as strength.
- Shallow relationships, broken homes, and unresolved trauma.

This isn't manhood. It's imprisonment.

The mask may win you applause, but it will cost you your peace. It may shield your ego, but it will starve your soul. True strength isn't found in suppression—it's revealed in authenticity.

The world doesn't need more hardened men. It needs men who are whole.

Redefining masculinity does not mean abandoning strength or leadership. It means clarifying what they actually require.

A real man doesn't fear his emotions; he understands them. He doesn't chase dominance; he builds respect.

Masculinity, in its highest form, lives at the intersection of:

- **Self-awareness:** The ability to acknowledge weakness without shame.
- **Emotional courage:** The willingness to be honest, even when it's uncomfortable.
- **Relational strength:** The capacity to create connection rather than control.

Real strength is not reactive. It's rooted. It doesn't seek validation. It operates from conviction. It is not built through domination—it is built through discipline, truth, and purpose.

The redefined man embodies three essential traits:

- **Integrity:** Choosing principle over popularity, even when no one is watching.

- **Compassion:** Leading with empathy, not ego.
- **Authenticity:** Living without performance. Being the same man in public as he is in private.

He balances power with presence. Confidence with humility. Resilience with vulnerability. He's not afraid to admit his flaws because he knows his identity is not defined by them.

To become this kind of man, we first need to recognize what shaped us.

- **Social conditioning** taught us boys don't cry.
- **Media narratives** glorified stoic, emotionless, hyperaggressive men.
- **Peer pressure** rewarded conformity and punished honesty.
- **Fatherlessness or poor role models** left a vacuum where wisdom should have lived.

These are the forces that created the mask. And the only way to become free is to unlearn what was never true to begin with.

This isn't about rejecting masculinity. It's about reframing it in alignment with growth, truth, and divine purpose.

SMALL SHIFTS. LIFELONG CHANGE.

Transformation is not instant. It's built in the quiet, intentional moments:

- **Physically:** Choose discipline over comfort. Lift when you don't feel like it. Move with purpose.
- **Emotionally:** Replace self-judgment with self-honesty. Speak what's real.
- **Spiritually:** Spend time in reflection. Reconnect with the higher purpose for which you were made.

Progress isn't about perfection. It's about movement in the right direction.

One of the greatest battles modern men face is the onslaught of hypersexualized media and pornography. These aren't harmless indulgences. They are corrosive forces that distort desire, fracture intimacy, and enslave the soul to false ideals.

Porn teaches men that women are objects. It creates addiction to fantasy and weakens the discipline needed for real connection. It replaces meaning with momentary pleasure, leaving behind shame and isolation.

True masculinity requires *self-mastery*, not self-indulgence.

To reclaim your masculinity:

- Refuse to participate in systems that degrade others.
- Rebuild your mind through faith, discipline, and accountability.
- Choose relationships that are real, rooted, and sacred.

The strongest men are not those who take what they want. They are those who govern what they crave.

A NEW MASCULINITY. A HIGHER CALLING.

Masculinity is not obsolete. It is misunderstood. We don't need less masculinity. We need more *noble masculinity*.

Men who:

- Stand in truth, even when it's unpopular.
- Love their wives and raise their children with presence.
- Sacrifice for others and live for something greater than themselves.

The world doesn't need more men in masks. It needs men of depth, vision, and courage. Men of God. Men of purpose. Men of legacy.

This is your call.

You can continue pretending. Or you can rise—free from the false ideals—and step into manhood that brings peace to your soul and strength to your home.

The choice is yours.

CHAPTER 15

SEX

SEX IS A FUNDAMENTAL PART OF HUMAN LIFE. AT ITS BEST, IT deepens the emotional, physical, and spiritual bond within a committed marriage. Yet for many men, sex remains a topic wrapped in confusion, shame, and misinformation. With pornography, hookup culture, and distorted portrayals in media, many of us grew up learning about sex from all the wrong sources.

The result? A generation caught in extremes. Some repress their desires entirely. Others indulge them recklessly. Both approaches are destructive. What we're missing is a balanced understanding—one that doesn't view sexual energy as something to suppress or exploit, but as a force to harness, refine, and transform.

Because sexual energy, when left unchecked, leads to chaos.

But when understood and mastered, it becomes fuel for greatness.

Our culture promotes a hollow version of manhood. From Hollywood movies to viral TikToks, the message is loud and clear: "The more women you sleep with, the more of a man you are."

I fell into that trap. Maybe it was the sting of early rejection. Maybe it was the ego boost I thought I needed. Or maybe it was the impact of porn rewiring my brain before I even understood what intimacy really was.

Whatever the reasons, I lost myself in the pursuit of pleasure. Sex became an escape. My mind was consumed. My actions were dictated by desire.

It wasn't just about lust—sexual conquest became my identity. It led to drinking, drugs, superficial relationships, and a growing distance from my Creator. I tied my self-worth to how many women validated me. I mistook attention for confidence and conquest for connection.

At first, I felt guilt. But eventually, I felt nothing.

The thrill became the goal.

My professional focus waned. My relationships became shallow.

And my spiritual life was hanging by a thread.

Lust had me in a chokehold, and I didn't even see it. Not until I hit rock bottom.

It was only after intense self-reflection—and by the grace of God—that I recognized the truth: I was trying to fill a spiritual void with physical encounters. I didn't need more pleasure. I needed purpose.

WHAT ARE YOU REALLY CHASING?

If you're caught in this cycle, you're not alone. Many men feel the weight of lust but don't know how to escape it. Let's confront it head-on—because freedom starts with truth.

Think about the hours, energy, and focus you've spent chasing temporary pleasure. Now imagine redirecting that same energy into your goals: building your career, strengthening your body, deepening your faith, or leading your family. That's power.

The endless chase may feel exciting, but ask yourself: Is it truly fulfilling? Or is it keeping you distracted, disoriented, and distant from your potential?

True masculinity is not defined by how many women you've been with. It's defined by your ability to lead yourself with discipline, restraint, and integrity. The man who can control his desires—who can redirect them toward purpose—is a man who becomes unstoppable.

Sex before marriage is a polarizing topic. But whatever your stance, the emotional, physical, and spiritual consequences are real.

1. **Emotional weight:** Premarital sex creates deep emotional bonds without the foundation of commitment. When those connections break, they often leave behind guilt, confusion, and emotional detachment. Studies have found lower relationship satisfaction and trust in couples who engage in sex before establishing long-term commitment.
2. **Physical risk:** The physical consequences are often overlooked. STIs are still widespread, and many come with lifelong effects. No moment of pleasure is worth your health.
3. **Spiritual drift:** Over time, casual sex leads to spiritual numbness. The act, designed to bond two souls, becomes reduced to a momentary thrill. When sex is stripped of meaning, your connection to God, purpose, and self weakens.

Lust doesn't just tempt you. It robs you—of time, of clarity, of peace.

FROM CHAOS TO CONTROL: MASTERING SEXUAL ENERGY

Sexual desire is not the enemy. It's part of you. But it's not meant to control you. It's meant to be governed, refined, and redirected. Here's how you begin that process:

1. **Acknowledge the urge.** Suppressing or denying your sexual desires doesn't work. Recognize them. Respect them. But don't let them rule you. Acknowledgment is the first step to self-mastery.
2. **Redirect the energy.** Channel the energy you once used chasing validation into something greater: your fitness, your mission, your craft. Sexual discipline fuels productivity, confidence, and creativity.
3. **Guard what you consume.** Pornography and hypersexualized media distort your perception of intimacy. Limit your exposure. Clean up your digital diet. What you feed your mind becomes your reality.
4. **Practice mindfulness.** Mindfulness teaches you to observe your desires without acting impulsively. Meditation, prayer, and reflection give you space to respond rather than react.

5. **Pursue meaningful relationships.** Build connections based on respect, faith, and shared purpose. A relationship rooted in trust and commitment will give you more lasting joy than a hundred empty flings.
6. **Get help if needed.** Whether it's mentorship, spiritual counseling, or professional support, there is no shame in seeking guidance. Real men ask for help when they need it.

The benefits of sexual discipline extend beyond the spiritual:

- **Sharper focus:** Your mental bandwidth increases when your energy isn't being hijacked by lust.
- **Greater motivation:** With fewer distractions, your drive and ambition intensify.
- **Stronger relationships:** Intimacy becomes sacred, not transactional.
- **Emotional stability:** You're no longer pulled by every impulse or consumed by regret.

Mastery isn't about repression—it's about alignment. You take the most powerful force within you and transform it into strength, clarity, and conviction.

You don't need a woman's approval to feel like a man.

You don't need porn to feel satisfied.

And you don't need casual sex to feel confident.

You need purpose. You need truth. You need alignment with your Creator.

True fulfillment won't come from one more night. It comes from waking up clear, centered, and committed to your calling. That kind of peace doesn't come from indulgence—it comes from mastery.

Every man must answer the same question:

Will I master my desires, or will they master me?

Because this is not just about sex.

It's about who you're becoming.

Are you building a life of lasting meaning, or are you chasing fleeting pleasure?

Are you living with discipline, or drifting into distraction?

The choice is yours. And when you choose mastery, everything begins to change.

Your mind clears. Your goals sharpen. Your soul breathes.

You step into the man God created you to be.

Not bound by impulse. But led by intention.

Not chasing validation. But rooted in vision.

This is your invitation:

Walk away from the noise.

Walk toward the truth.

And become the man you were always meant to be.

CHAPTER 16

STOP MASTURBATION

MASTURBATION IS ONE OF THE MOST MISUNDERSTOOD AND OVER-looked weapons used to keep men bound in silence and weakness. It's often dismissed as harmless, laughed off in pop culture, or even promoted as a form of self-care. But beneath the surface lies a habit that, when left unchecked, can quietly erode a man's strength, confidence, and sense of purpose.

For centuries, faith traditions have warned against it—not out of repression, but from a deep understanding of its spiritual, emotional, and physiological consequences. Meanwhile, modern culture has gone the other direction, celebrating it as normal, healthy, and even empowering. Scientific essays praise its so-called benefits, while endless internet articles compare us to animals, justifying indulgence through biology.

What no one talks about nearly enough is the other side of the equation: the long-term cost.

We live in a world wired for instant gratification. With a few clicks or taps, anything you want is available. For many men, the addictive loop of pornography and masturbation starts subtly—but escalates quickly. What begins as a "stress release" or curiosity soon turns into a compulsive pattern.

The impact? It's deeper than most realize.

Over time, this habit conditions your brain to seek pleasure without connection, intimacy without vulnerability, and stimulation without purpose. It diminishes your ability to bond with real partners, weakens your attraction to real intimacy, and trains you to retreat inward instead of stepping forward as a man of responsibility.

That dopamine hit rewires your brain, making it harder to focus, stay motivated, and pursue long-term goals. The more you indulge, the more you feel scattered, unfulfilled, and ashamed—and the cycle repeats.

Unchecked, compulsive masturbation opens the door to a host of deeper issues:

- Emotional detachment
- Social withdrawal
- Sex addiction
- Infidelity
- A growing disconnect from purpose, faith, and identity

This isn't just about lust—it's about self-control.

If you can't say no to yourself in private, how will you stay disciplined when life tests you in public?

Nearly every monotheistic religion affirms this truth: Sexual energy is sacred. It was never meant to be wasted on screens, fantasies, or impulsive gratification. It was designed to bond two souls in a committed, loving relationship. When we strip sex of its spiritual and emotional weight, we don't just cheapen the act—we cheapen ourselves.

True masculinity isn't about chasing pleasure. It's about directing desire with intention and accountability.

Like many young men, I stumbled into masturbation early. At first, it felt like a secret discovery—some kind of forbidden superpower. But over time, the habit grew stronger. What started with imagination became magazines. Magazines became pornography. Soon, it didn't matter where I was—whether writing a paper, studying for a test, or on the way to the gym—I had become a slave to the habit.

I told myself it was harmless. I justified it with excuses: high testosterone, stress, being single. But deep down, I knew it was controlling me. It fed into a bigger web of lust, ego, and detachment that nearly ruined my life.

It dragged me toward porn addiction, sex addiction, and a complete loss of peace. I became emotionally numb, chasing validation and pleasure while my soul withered in the background.

The turning point came when I chose to stop—for good.

And the clarity that followed was undeniable.

Suddenly, my mind was sharper. My relationships became more meaningful. My confidence returned. For the first time in years, I felt like I was standing in my full power—not hiding, not ashamed, but free.

THE REAL COST OF "JUST ONE MORE TIME"

We're told this habit is harmless. But if it were, why does it leave so many men feeling anxious, drained, and guilty?

Here's the truth most won't say out loud:

Masturbation drains your energy.

It dulls your motivation.

It erodes your confidence.

It weakens your spirit.

In contrast, men who reclaim control over their sexual energy report higher focus, stronger relationships, and a greater sense of purpose. Many high-performers, athletes, and entrepreneurs know this—and practice semen retention to increase drive, boost testosterone, and maintain peak performance.

This isn't pseudoscience or hype. It's discipline. And discipline builds kingship.

THE PATH TO FREEDOM

Breaking free from this habit isn't easy—especially in a world designed to pull you back into it. But with faith, strategy, and support, it is absolutely possible.

Here's how to start:

1. **Anchor yourself in a higher power.** Whether you're deeply religious or still exploring faith, connect with something beyond yourself. Submission to a greater truth brings clarity to your mission and the strength to overcome temptation.
2. **Respect your future relationship.** If you're married—or plan to be—recognize that your discipline today protects your connection tomorrow. Self-control preserves attraction, emotional presence, and intimacy.
3. **Control your environment.** Clean up your digital space. Eliminate pornography. Set app limits. Avoid visual triggers. Your surroundings either feed your strength or fuel your struggle.
4. **Redirect your energy.** Don't suppress the urge—transform it. Channel it into training, creative work, business goals, or spiritual practices. Your sexual energy can build something far greater than a few seconds of pleasure.
5. **Create a brotherhood of accountability.** Isolation fuels addiction. But community builds strength. Surround yourself with men pursuing similar discipline. Share your wins. Speak your struggles. Build each other up.
6. **Be patient with the process.** Slipping doesn't mean starting over. Don't confuse failure with finality. Keep showing up. Every victory compounds.

When you reclaim this part of your life, the impact is felt everywhere.

- **Sharper focus:** You stop zoning out and start locking in.
- **Stronger relationships:** You connect from a place of presence, not need.
- **Higher confidence:** No more shame. You walk with conviction.
- **Spiritual strength:** You rebuild the connection to God and purpose that lust once clouded.
- **Unshakable willpower:** If you can master this, you can master anything.

This isn't about demonizing desire.

It's about disciplining it.

You weren't created to be ruled by impulse. You were created to lead—with integrity, focus, and divine alignment.

So ask yourself: Will I master my desires, or will they master me?

Because this decision defines everything else.

When you choose self-control over self-indulgence, you begin to unlock a version of yourself the world rarely sees: a man fully present, deeply grounded, and undeniably powerful.

You become the man who doesn't just survive temptation—but rises above it.

And from that place, you lead. You love. You build.

Not as a slave to lust, but as a man of unwavering strength.

CHAPTER 17

LOWERING YOUR GAZE

IN TODAY'S HYPERSTIMULATED WORLD, DISTRACTIONS ARE AGGRESsively marketed and temptation is only a click away. The discipline of lowering your gaze is no longer just a recommendation—it's a necessity. It's not simply about avoiding sin; it's about reclaiming your focus, protecting your heart, and perfecting your character in a world determined to pull you in every direction but up.

While this concept is often framed around avoiding inappropriate glances at the opposite sex, its true significance runs far deeper. Lowering your gaze means filtering out anything that pulls your soul away from God—anything that sparks dissatisfaction, stirs unnecessary desire, or diverts your energy from what truly matters. Because the truth is this: What you allow into your eyes enters your mind, and what enters your mind eventually settles in your heart. And what sits in your heart shapes your direction—sometimes your entire destiny.

The Prophet Muhammad (PBUH) taught, "The glance is a poisoned arrow of Satan. Whoever lowers his gaze for the sake of God, He will grant him a sweetness of faith that he will find in his heart."

It may seem like nothing—just a glance. But in that single moment, your heart can be pierced by a desire that festers and grows. And just as easily, that same moment can be transformed into a spiritual victory if you resist. The sweetness of faith that God promises in return for your restraint is not metaphorical. It's real. It's peace. It's strength. It's clarity.

This is why Islam places such powerful emphasis on the eyes. Your eyes are not passive; they are portals. What you feed them, you feed your soul. Letting them wander toward what is impermissible may feel harmless in the moment, but it opens a door that's often hard to close. It begins with a look…then a thought…then a craving. And over time, it builds a fire that burns through your discipline, your values, and your sense of self.

Lowering your gaze isn't just about guarding against lust—it's about reclaiming sovereignty over your senses. In a culture that mocks modesty and glorifies indulgence, choosing restraint is countercultural. But it's not repression. It's **respect**. Respect for your soul. Respect for others. Respect for the mission God gave you.

When you lower your gaze, you're making a statement:

- I will not reduce people to objects.
- I will not allow external noise to dominate my internal world.
- I will not compromise my focus, my dignity, or my connection with God.

This practice trains you to view women not as conquests or entertainment, but as sisters in faith—human beings with honor, value, and depth beyond appearance. It reprograms your instinct from consumption to compassion, from fixation to focus. And in that process, your heart begins to heal.

The Prophet (PBUH) said, "From the perfection of one's Islam is leaving that which does not concern him."

Your attention is sacred. And in an age where social media, gossip, and mindless content compete for it constantly, learning to guard it is one of the highest forms of discipline.

Every time you give your eyes to something unworthy, you give your energy to something empty. You allow your thoughts to be shaped by shallow stories, your desires to be stoked by illusions, and your purpose to be clouded by noise. Whether it's lust, envy, greed, or comparison, your eyes are often the entry point to the chaos that clutters your soul.

Even the so-called harmless habits—endless scrolling, window shopping, comparing lifestyles—chip away at your peace. That "just looking" at luxury, wealth, or status can breed dissatisfaction. You start thinking you're missing something. But the Qur'an reminds us:

> Know that the life of this world is but amusement and diversion and adornment and boasting to one another, and competition in increase of wealth and children… (Qur'an 57:20)

Lowering your gaze from what you don't have is how you protect contentment. And contentment is the real wealth.

Pornography and explicit media are more than just sins. They are soul-deforming poisons. They warp your perception of intimacy, distort your expectations of love, and program your mind to crave what will never satisfy. Over time, they lead to addiction, isolation, and shame. What starts as curiosity can quickly spiral into a lifestyle that kills confidence, numbs emotions, and destroys real relationships.

The Prophet (PBUH) said, "There is a piece of flesh in the body, and if it is sound, the whole body is sound; and if it is corrupt, the whole body is corrupt. Verily, it is the heart."

Protecting your eyes is protecting your heart. And protecting your heart is preserving your ability to love, to lead, to grow, and to connect with God.

PRACTICAL WAYS TO LOWER YOUR GAZE

It's not easy. But it's worth it. Because every time you lower your gaze, you raise your standard. Every time you guard your attention, you strengthen your soul.

Here's how to build this practice:

1. **Be aware of your environment.** Online or offline, be intentional. Curate your surroundings. Install blockers. Mute or unfollow triggers. Limit your exposure and set boundaries.
2. **Make Dua for strength.** Ask God for protection. Turn to Him in moments of weakness. This isn't just a battle of will—it's a spiritual struggle, and you don't fight it alone.
3. **Replace, don't just resist.** Fill your time and mind with what benefits you. Read. Train. Create. Learn. Serve. Lust thrives in emptiness. Fill the void with purpose.
4. **Find accountability.** Build a circle of brothers who want the same discipline. Talk openly. Check in regularly. Strength comes in numbers.
5. **Keep Jannah in sight.** Remind yourself of the reward. Every act of restraint is a step toward Heaven. Every temptation resisted is a deposit in your spiritual legacy.

Lowering your gaze is not a weakness—it's a weapon. A weapon that protects your heart from corruption, your mind from distraction, and your life from destruction.

The man who masters his gaze doesn't just avoid temptation. He masters his focus. He becomes clear, grounded, and unshakable. He doesn't follow his impulses—he leads them.

So lower your gaze—not only from lustful images, but from anything that steals your peace.

Lower your gaze from envy, comparison, and distraction.

Lower your gaze from everything that pulls you away from God.

Because in a world that celebrates indulgence, restraint is revolutionary.

And the man who guards his eyes...becomes the man who sees clearly.

CHAPTER 18

GET MARRIED

MEN AND WOMEN WERE CREATED IN PAIRS—DESIGNED NOT TO compete, but to complete one another. In its purest form, marriage is not simply a legal agreement or social expectation. It is a sacred covenant. A divinely inspired union that nurtures the emotional, physical, and spiritual dimensions of both partners. At its best, marriage becomes the foundation upon which legacies are built, strong children are raised, and thriving communities emerge.

But let's be clear: This chapter isn't about prescribing a single path to fulfillment. It's about honoring the profound purpose marriage can bring while recognizing that joy, growth, and alignment can be found in many life choices—whether single, dating, or married. The true question is not, "Are you married?" but, "Are you living in alignment with your values, your mission, and your faith?"

Choosing marriage means stepping into something greater than yourself. It's no longer just about your ambitions, your plans, or your comfort. It's about merging your individual purpose with someone else's, creating a shared life built on intentionality, commitment, and love.

When nurtured with sincerity and vision, a strong marriage offers:

- **Emotional strength:** In life's trials, a righteous spouse becomes your anchor—offering support, perspective, and comfort. Research consistently shows that men in healthy, loving marriages experience lower stress, greater happiness, and longer life expectancy.
- **Shared triumphs:** Wins feel sweeter when celebrated together. The milestones you reach as a couple become the building blocks of lasting joy and lifelong memories.
- **Spiritual elevation:** Marriage refines the soul. When both partners are aligned in faith and character, the relationship becomes a vehicle for drawing closer to God—teaching patience, humility, forgiveness, and gratitude.

Marriage, in many ways, is a mirror. It reflects your strengths and exposes your weaknesses. It holds up a light to your character and invites you to grow.

MARRIAGE DOESN'T FIX YOU. IT FORMS YOU.

A fulfilling marriage is never built on perfection. It's built on shared values, mutual respect, and a deep love that matures through time and effort. It requires:

- **Shared principles:** A common foundation of faith, character, and long-term vision.
- **Mutual respect:** Honoring one another with patience, dignity, and understanding.
- **Effective communication:** Listening to understand, not just to respond.
- **Lasting love:** A love that moves beyond feelings into action, sacrifice, and service.

Marriage doesn't magically make you whole. But it does refine you. It teaches you to give when it's hard, to listen when it's uncomfortable, and to serve even when it goes unnoticed. It forces you to grow—not because you have to, but because love demands it.

Before marriage, I was constantly on the move—driven by impulse, chasing fleeting desires, untethered, and spiritually restless. My life had motion, but not direction. Then God placed the right woman in my path, and everything began to shift.

She didn't just love me—she challenged me. She helped me see what I was capable of. She taught me how to lead with humility, how to love with purpose, and how to ground myself in something deeper than ambition. Through her presence, I became a better man, a more intentional provider, and a servant to something greater than myself. Without her, I am half the man I am today.

And still, I don't glorify marriage blindly. I've experienced failure. I've walked through heartbreak. I've learned hard lessons. But I also learned that failure doesn't mean the journey ends. You heal. You grow. You realign. And if it's written, God brings you someone who reminds you why it's all worth it.

Life was never meant to be walked alone.

THE DEEPER PURPOSE OF MARRIAGE

A righteous marriage speaks to the core of what it means to be human: the need for connection, legacy, and shared meaning. At its best, it offers:

- **Social bonding:** A deep emotional connection with someone who sees you, knows you, and chooses you daily.
- **Legacy building:** Raising children who carry not just your name, but your values and vision.
- **Shared responsibility:** Building a home, supporting dreams, and weathering storms—together.

The Qur'an describes this beautifully:

> And among His signs is that He created for you spouses from among yourselves, that you may find tranquility in them; and He placed between you affection and mercy. (Qur'an 30:21)

Tranquility. Affection. Mercy. These are not fleeting emotions. They are the pillars of a marriage built to last.

MARRIAGE ISN'T THE ONLY PATH—BUT IT IS A SACRED ONE

Not everyone will choose marriage, and that's okay. Fulfillment is not confined to one lifestyle. What matters is alignment: with your purpose, your values, and your Creator.

If you do choose marriage, do so with both eyes open. Enter it not for validation or image, but for growth, service, and spiritual elevation. And know that a strong marriage doesn't happen by accident. It requires:

- **Effort:** Daily actions, not just grand gestures.
- **Compromise:** Meeting in the middle, even when it's uncomfortable.
- **Commitment:** Choosing your partner again and again, even on the hard days.

At its heart, marriage is not just a partnership—it's a mission. A journey of shared sacrifice, vision, and transformation. It is one of the most sacred responsibilities a man can accept, and one of the most profound ways to serve God through service to another human being.

But whether your life includes marriage or not, the goal remains the same:

Live with clarity.

Walk with conviction.

Build your life in alignment with what matters most.

If you choose marriage, embrace it fully. Honor it. Nurture it. Let it mold you into the man you were born to become.

And if your path takes a different route, walk it with just as much intention, faith, and devotion. Because no matter the role you play, you were made to lead a life of meaning.

TEN QUESTIONS TO ASK YOURSELF BEFORE MARRIAGE

1. **Why do I want to get married?** Is it for connection, purpose, growth—or is it pressure, loneliness, or image?
2. **Have I done the personal work to become a good partner?** Am I emotionally mature, financially stable, and spiritually grounded?
3. **What values are nonnegotiable for me?** Faith, character, ambition, family dynamics—what truly matters?
4. **Can I lead with love and humility?** Leadership in marriage requires strength and gentleness. Do I embody both?
5. **How do I handle conflict and correction?** Do I shut down, lash out, or seek understanding?
6. **Am I ready to serve—not just be served?** Do I see marriage as a mutual mission or a personal reward?
7. **What does a successful marriage look like to me?** Have I defined success by love, service, growth, faith—or by image and status?
8. **Am I sexually disciplined and emotionally available?** Can I offer my partner integrity, presence, and trust?
9. **Do I have mentors, role models, or support systems in place?** Marriage isn't meant to be navigated in isolation. Who am I learning from?
10. **Have I prayed about this decision—and am I willing to walk away if God says no?** Am I choosing from alignment with God or from fear, fantasy, or impatience?

MARRIAGE READINESS CHECKLIST

☐ I understand my purpose and values.
☐ I've worked on my emotional health and healing.
☐ I'm financially aware and planning with responsibility.
☐ I seek growth, not just comfort.

- ☐ I'm ready to lead with faith and serve with love.
- ☐ I respect women and reject objectification.
- ☐ I've forgiven past relationships and let go of resentment.
- ☐ I can communicate with clarity and empathy.
- ☐ I'm committed to sexual integrity and spiritual growth.
- ☐ I've sought counsel, prayed intentionally, and feel peaceful—not pressured—about this step.

CHAPTER 19

CHOOSING THE ONE

CHOOSING A LIFE PARTNER IS ONE OF THE MOST PIVOTAL DECIsions a man will ever make. It shapes not only his home, but his future, his character, and his legacy. A wise man does not choose a wife based solely on impulse or physical desire. He chooses with discipline, with foresight, and with God-consciousness. Because the woman you commit to will either help you rise—or slowly pull you away from everything you're striving to build.

She will either be a source of strength or a weight of distraction. An anchor or an oar. This is not a choice to make in haste, nor in the haze of lust. It is a covenant that will affect every corner of your life: emotionally, spiritually, generationally.

Marriage isn't just about romance. It's about alignment. It's about partnering with someone whose presence inspires purpose, whose character earns trust, and whose vision walks beside your own.

1. BEAUTY: BEYOND THE SURFACE

Physical attraction matters. It's part of human nature. But the man who makes this his foundation builds a house on sand. Over time, beauty changes, but the radiance of a woman's character endures.

Ask yourself:

- Does her presence bring peace or provoke unrest?
- Is her beauty more than what meets the eye—reflected in her speech, her conduct, her character?
- Do her inner qualities make her more beautiful as time passes?

A mature man isn't mesmerized by superficial charm. He is drawn to dignity, grace, warmth, and integrity—beauty that time cannot touch.

2. LINEAGE: VALUES OVER STATUS

Her family background can offer insight, but it should never be the final measure. Nobility is not inherited—it's lived. A woman's true worth is reflected in her resilience, humility, and character, not in the name she carries.

Consider:

- Does her upbringing reflect values you want to pass to your future children?
- Is she respectful, grounded, and principled regardless of her background?
- Will she stand beside you through trials, not just ease?

A woman of character will elevate your home—not because of her bloodline, but because of the standards she upholds.

3. WEALTH: CHARACTER OVER CURRENCY

Financial comfort is important—but wealth, on its own, is a poor foundation for a lifelong bond. A woman's relationship with money reveals far more than her bank balance.

Ask yourself:

- Is she financially responsible and content, or driven by materialism?
- Can she handle hardship without resentment?
- Does she view money as a means to serve—or as a source of status?

The right woman is rich in loyalty, in faith, in strength—not just in possessions. She will build with you, not expect to be handed ease without effort.

4. CHARACTER: THE TRUE GEM

Character is what sustains a marriage when attraction fades and circumstances shift. Look for a woman whose actions reflect sincerity, whose values reflect depth, and whose presence brings stability.

Evaluate:

- How does she treat those who can do nothing for her?
- Is she consistent, trustworthy, and rooted in principle?
- Does she uplift others, or does she belittle, compete, and compare?

Kindness, loyalty, humility, and faith—these are the marks of a woman who will become the backbone of your home.

5. COMMUNICATION: THE ART OF PEACE AND PARTNERSHIP

No marriage survives without healthy communication. It's not just about talking—it's about understanding. A strong woman knows how to listen with presence and speak with wisdom.

Reflect on:

- Can we discuss hard things without defensiveness or manipulation?
- Is she emotionally open and honest, or avoidant and reactive?
- Do we resolve tension through patience and respect?

Words can heal or destroy. Choose a partner who uses them to build, not to wound.

6. SHARED VALUES: ALIGNMENT OVER ATTRACTION

Compatibility matters—but alignment matters more. Two people can love each other and still be walking in opposite directions. A woman's beauty cannot compensate for conflicting beliefs.

Ask yourself:

- Do we share the same values when it comes to faith, family, and the future?
- Are our life goals in harmony, or are we living parallel but divided lives?
- Will she support your mission—and will you support hers?

When your values align, even life's fiercest storms won't shake your foundation.

7. RED FLAGS: WHAT TO AVOID

No one is perfect, but some traits point to deep-rooted instability. Pay attention to:

- **Materialism:** Obsession with wealth, fame, or status
- **Financial irresponsibility:** Reckless spending or hiding debt
- **Emotional immaturity:** Inability to handle discomfort, anger, or conflict

- **Lack of emotional depth:** Avoidance of real connection or vulnerability
- **Controlling behavior:** Jealousy disguised as love or possessiveness masked as protection
- **Inconsistency:** Repeated promises broken without accountability

Trust your gut. A wise man sees the signs others ignore—and walks away before it's too late.

MARRIAGE IS NOT ABOUT PERFECTION— IT'S ABOUT PARTNERSHIP

The goal isn't to find the perfect woman. She doesn't exist. The goal is to find a woman who is **willing to grow with you, not just shine for you**. A woman who builds, not one who waits to be handed a kingdom. A woman who makes you better—and whom you make better in return.

TO BUILD A RELATIONSHIP THAT LASTS

- **Invest in each other.** Show appreciation. Celebrate growth. Encourage peace.
- **Prioritize growth.** Individually and as a team. Challenge each other respectfully.
- **Be patient.** Love matures slowly. Let trust and connection deepen over time.
- **Stay committed.** Love is not just a spark. It's a daily decision. A sacred vow.

A wise man does not chase beauty, titles, or ease. He seeks character, alignment, and spiritual depth. He understands that his wife will influence his thoughts, his habits, his children, and ultimately, his standing before God.

So choose slowly. Choose intentionally. Choose with the long view in mind.

The right woman won't just complement your lifestyle—
She will multiply your growth.
She will reflect your discipline.
She will strengthen your faith.
And she will help you become the man you were always meant to be.

Choose wisely. Because who you marry is not just a personal choice—it's a generational one.

CHAPTER 20

BUILD A BULLETPROOF RELATIONSHIP

ONCE YOU'VE FOUND THE RIGHT WOMAN AND COMMITTED TO marriage, never forget: the real work begins there. Marriage is not a destination—it's a lifelong covenant. A living, breathing commitment that requires presence, patience, and purpose. Love may spark the connection, but it's shared values, daily effort, and unwavering discipline that sustain it.

After walking through two marriages, I can tell you this truth firsthand: Success in marriage is not about perfection. It's about partnership. It's about progress. It's about building something bigger than yourself, and doing so with love, responsibility, and faith at the center.

My first marriage didn't fail because of one major event—it unraveled slowly because I failed to show up in the ways that mattered most. I did many things right. But I also let my vices, impulses, and unchecked habits weaken the foundation. I wasn't grounded enough to lead. And if you're not leading yourself, you have no business trying to lead a household.

Your relationship will only rise as high as your personal discipline allows. Every weakness you ignore—whether it's pride, anger, lust, or distraction—will find its way into your marriage. If you want to build something strong, you must first become someone strong.

As the man, you set the emotional tone. Your attitude, consistency, and leadership style determine whether your home is filled with peace or tension. And it starts not with grand gestures, but with small, daily choices.

A five-second kiss before bed. Holding her hand on a walk. Saying "I love you" when she least expects it. Washing the dishes. Choosing silence instead of escalation during an argument. These moments are not trivial—they're the invisible bricks that build trust, intimacy, and emotional safety.

I used to believe love was self-sustaining. That if the connection was real, it would carry itself. I was wrong. Love needs maintenance. It needs attention. It needs intention. Time apart cannot be compensated with expensive gifts or forced apologies. Connection must be cultivated. Through presence. Through humility. Through effort.

My wife and I now make it a priority to check in with each other. If one of us feels distant or distracted, we say so. We adjust. We reconnect. A relationship only thrives when both people remain aware and invested.

This is the person you've chosen to walk through life with. The one who will witness your best and your worst, your failures and your victories. She is your most important relationship outside of your connection with God. That doesn't mean losing your individuality—but it does mean your marriage gets your best, not your leftovers.

I still prioritize time alone: my workouts, my walks, my worship, my brotherhood. But never at the expense of the relationship that God entrusted to me. That balance is not optional—it's essential.

Be present. Be intentional. Serve your wife. Lead your family. That is the key.

Emotions are seasonal. Love will ebb and flow. But commitment is the current that keeps the marriage alive. A healthy relationship requires action. It requires both partners to keep showing up, even on the hard days. Growth, both personal and shared, is the oxygen that keeps love from suffocating under life's demands.

Without effort, even the strongest love can fade. But when both partners make the daily decision to nurture the relationship—to choose patience, to choose service, to choose forgiveness—marriage becomes a source of unshakable strength.

Strong communication is not about talking more—it's about listening better. It's about presence. It's about putting down your phone, turning off distractions, and giving your partner the respect of your full attention.

Speak honestly, but with kindness. Listen without the urge to fix or dominate. Conflict is inevitable, but it's not the enemy. The way you handle disagreement will either build trust or quietly chip away at it.

The goal is not to "win." It's to understand. It's to preserve the bond.

A man who disrespects his wife disrespects himself. Period. Respect isn't conditional on agreement. It's expressed through patience, consistency, and kindness. It's how you speak to her. How you listen. How you show up even when it's inconvenient.

Respect means valuing her dreams, honoring her thoughts, and never dismissing her struggles. When a woman feels truly seen and heard, she doesn't just stay—she thrives.

Intimacy is more than physical closeness. It's trust. It's shared laughter. It's knowing and being known. It's the safety to be vulnerable without judgment. A thriving marriage nurtures both emotional and physical intimacy—open communication, rituals of affection, and the quiet bond formed in daily life.

Sexual connection is important, but it cannot compensate for emotional distance. Build both, and you'll create a love that feels alive, not just functional.

A real man doesn't lead through control. He leads through example. His strength is steady, not forceful. His leadership is rooted in service, not entitlement. He creates an environment where his wife and children feel secure, valued, and empowered.

Great marriages are not built through dominance, but through mutual leadership—two people committed to helping each other grow.

Marriage without alignment is chaos. You don't need to be identical, but your foundations must match. Faith. Family. Finances. Life vision. When both partners share these pillars, decisions become easier. Direction becomes clearer. And the relationship feels like movement—not conflict.

A couple that moves in sync, anchored by shared values, will not be easily shaken.

In Islam, marriage is described as a bond built on love, tranquility, and mercy. It is not just a worldly agreement, but a divine trust. When approached with sincerity, it becomes a source of spiritual elevation.

> And among His signs is that He created for you spouses from among yourselves that you may find tranquility in them; and He placed between you affection and mercy... (Qur'an 30:21)

When marriage is rooted in faith, it transcends the struggle. It becomes a shelter. A sanctuary. A legacy.

Marriage will test you. It will stretch your character. But the goal is never perfection—it's progress. It's being a little better each year. More patient. More present. More humble.

A man of strength doesn't abandon his responsibilities. He protects them. He leads not with ego, but with wisdom. He serves with love, not pride. And when marriage is approached with faith, discipline, and purpose, it becomes more than a partnership—it becomes legacy.

Let your marriage be your masterpiece. One forged in love, refined through effort, and anchored in faith.

CHAPTER 21

HAIR IS OVERRATED

I'LL NEVER FORGET THE MOMENT. THERE I STOOD—DIVORCED, disoriented, and cracked open by the weight of failure. My first marriage had ended, and with it came a tidal wave of loss, confusion, and identity crisis. Everything felt fragmented. I didn't just need healing—I needed a declaration. A symbolic act to reclaim control, to mark the beginning of my rebuilding.

So I shaved my head.

For centuries, masculinity has been tied to appearance—especially to hair. Thick, flowing hair has long been seen as a symbol of youth, virility, and strength. But what happens when it starts to fade? For many men, hair loss feels like watching a piece of their identity slip away. I've seen brothers spend thousands on procedures, potions, and powders. I've watched friends return from Istanbul, heads bandaged, clinging to a hope that their hairline might give them back their confidence.

But here's the truth most won't say out loud: Holding onto what's already leaving you is a slow form of self-sabotage.

Masculinity isn't rooted in appearance. It's built on confidence, self-command, and the ability to adapt and rise when life shifts beneath your feet.

My own battle with hair loss began in my twenties. Sharp fades became strategic comb-overs. Thickening shampoos, late-night Google searches, and mental gymnastics just to make it all look "normal." Each receding inch felt like a quiet hit to my self-image. Then, life threw me an even greater curveball: divorce.

In the midst of grief and redefinition, I found myself looking for renewal. Not just emotionally, but symbolically. That's when the idea hit me—not as vanity, but as ritual.

Across faith traditions and cultures, shaving the head has long signified transformation. In Islam, men shave their heads during Hajj as a symbol of submission and spiritual rebirth. Buddhist monks do so to embrace detachment and humility. In both contexts, the act is not just external—it's an inner shift made visible.

I walked into the barbershop, stared into the mirror, and told the barber, "Take it all off."

What little I had left—along with the weight of ego and insecurity—fell to the floor.

At first, I wasn't sure what to feel. I looked…different. Exposed. Raw. But with each passing day, I began to feel more like myself—like I had finally stopped pretending. The confidence didn't come from the look. It came from reclaiming my agency.

Shaving my head wasn't just cosmetic—it was cathartic.

Beyond symbolism, the decision came with some unexpected practical benefits:

- **Time and money saved.** No more costly haircuts, no clutter of styling products.
- **Better hygiene.** Simpler grooming, cleaner scalp.
- **Elimination of the illusion.** No more denial, no more stress about how it looks in photos or under bright lights.
- **Confidence boost.** Ownership beats insecurity every time.
- **Low maintenance.** Less fuss, more freedom.
- **Symbol of strength.** A visible sign of transformation and resilience.

And the data backs it up. Research by Dr. Albert Mannes at the Wharton School found that bald men—when fully shaved—were consistently rated as more dominant, confident, and authoritative than even men with full heads of hair.[4] Ironically, men clinging to thinning hair were perceived as the least confident of all.

Think about the icons: Michael Jordan, the Rock, Jeff Bezos, Jason Statham. Nobody questions their power. Not because of their hair, but because of their presence. Their confidence. Their clarity.

Most men aren't afraid of being bald. They're afraid of what it represents: aging, decline, a loss of desirability. But that fear only has power if you feed it. When you take control—when you make the bold move before life forces your hand—you change the narrative. You're no longer the man hiding behind baseball caps or hat filters. You're the man who chose freedom.

Shaving your head isn't just about aesthetics—it's about mindset. It's about transformation. It's about letting go.

WHAT I LEARNED FROM LETTING GO

1. **Confidence comes from clarity.** I didn't find confidence in the mirror—I found it in the act of ownership. The decision to stop hiding. To start owning.
2. **Control is a choice.** Life will take things from you—youth, comfort, plans. But you always get to choose how you respond. Shaving my head reminded me: I still get to decide who I am.
3. **Letting go creates space.** When you release what no longer serves you—hair, ego, fear—you create space for growth. For strength. For peace.

---

4 Albert E. Mannes, "Shorn Scalps and Perceptions of Male Dominance," *Social Psychological and Personality Science* 4(2) (March 2013): 198–205, DOI:10.1177/1948550612449490.

IF YOU'RE ON THE EDGE—JUMP

If you're staring at your reflection, unsure if it's time, let me save you the mental load. Let it go. Not just the hair—but the weight of shame, denial, and distraction.

Because here's the truth: It's not the hair that's holding you back—it's the fear.

So pick up the clippers. Take a deep breath. And watch what falls away.

What you'll gain is far more valuable than what you lose: confidence, clarity, and the freedom to walk through the world exactly as you are—undistracted, unburdened, and unapologetically yourself.

CHAPTER 22

GOOD HYGIENE

FIRST IMPRESSIONS ARE POWERFUL—AND OFTEN PERMANENT. Before you speak a word, people are already reading your presence. And nothing shapes that presence more immediately than personal hygiene. Science confirms what instinct already tells us: People form opinions within seconds, and hygiene often outweighs even style, physique, or posture—especially in social, professional, and romantic environments.

But hygiene isn't just about appearance or smell. It's a window into your self-discipline, your respect for others, and your spiritual and emotional state.

I know this from experience. As an athlete, hygiene wasn't always my strong suit. I can still remember collapsing into bed after brutal workouts, drenched in sweat, skipping showers and instead drowning myself in clouds of Axe body spray like it was a ritual of toughness. It wasn't about neglect. It was about blind spots—places in my personal discipline I hadn't yet matured.

It was my wife who gave me the honest truth: Hygiene isn't about vanity. It's about self-respect. It's about honoring your body as a gift and presenting yourself to the world with care and intention.

Most of us don't notice when our standards start slipping. The nails we forget to trim. The stale breath we grow accustomed to. The cologne masking what should have been a shower. What feels "normal" to us can be jarring to those around us.

True excellence demands detail. You wouldn't tolerate a dirty uniform on game day. Why tolerate it in life?

There's a proverb that says, "Cleanliness is next to Godliness." Islam teaches that "Allah is beautiful and loves beauty," and Prophet Muhammad (PBUH) emphasized cleanliness as half of faith. When we care for our hygiene, we're not just respecting ourselves—we're honoring the body God entrusted us with. A clean body reflects a clean heart. A clean presentation reflects an intentional life.

WHY HYGIENE IS NONNEGOTIABLE

- **It builds confidence.** A man who smells fresh, dresses clean, and moves with intention carries himself differently. You don't need to say a word—your presence communicates self-respect.
- **It protects your health.** Good hygiene reduces the risk of infections, illness, and skin issues. Oral care, handwashing, and grooming aren't luxuries. They're acts of prevention.
- **It commands respect.** People take notice when you show up well groomed. Hygiene sends a message: "I take myself seriously, and I respect you enough to show up at my best."
- **It fuels mental discipline.** The ritual of hygiene promotes mental clarity. When life feels chaotic, the simple act of caring for your body creates structure, control, and a sense of renewal.
- **It aligns with faith and spiritual discipline.** In many faiths, cleanliness is an act of devotion. In Islam, ablution before prayer is more than ritual—it's a physical and spiritual reset, five times a day.

DAILY HABITS THAT SET THE STANDARD

- **Shower daily:** A nonnegotiable. Especially if you train, sweat, or work in close environments. Use antibacterial soap if needed and always apply deodorant after drying off.
- **Oral hygiene:** Brush twice a day, floss regularly, and use mouthwash. Invest in a good tongue scraper and visit the dentist every six months. Bad breath is not a quirk—it's a signal.
- **Dress clean:** Even the most expensive outfit looks sloppy if it's stained or unwashed. Fresh clothes signal care and preparation. Avoid rewearing anything that's absorbed sweat or odor.
- **Trim and maintain:** Keep nails short and clean. Maintain your beard, hairline, and any facial hair with precision. These are small things, but they speak volumes.
- **Hand hygiene:** Wash often. Carry sanitizer if needed. Dirty hands carry germs, smell, and give a terrible first impression during handshakes.
- **Skin care matters:** Use a gentle cleanser, moisturize daily, and apply sunscreen if you're outdoors. Healthy skin reflects self-care, not vanity.

HYGIENE IS A STATEMENT

A declaration: *I respect this body. I value my presence. I'm becoming a man of discipline.*

Just as a warrior sharpens his blade, a man sharpens his image—not for attention, but for excellence. You're not doing it for likes, compliments, or approval. You're doing it because your appearance reflects your values. When you raise the standard for yourself, others rise to meet it.

The right hygiene habits will improve your relationships, open doors professionally, enhance your mental clarity, and even help you attract a quality spouse. More importantly, they will build your self-image and daily confidence brick by brick.

This body is a gift—a trust from the Creator. It's not about worshiping it, but it is about honoring it. You wouldn't neglect a priceless tool if you knew your mission depended on it. Your physical form is that tool.

So clean it. Care for it. Present it with excellence.

It may start with brushing your teeth or changing your shirt—but in time, it becomes the rhythm of a man who takes himself seriously. And that kind of man? He's noticed. He's respected. And most of all, he's trusted—with leadership, with love, and with legacy.

CHAPTER 23

DRESS TO IMPRESS

YOU'VE HEARD THE PHRASE, "LOOKS LIKE A MILLION BUCKS." IT'S more than just a catchy saying, but it's a powerful reminder of how much our appearance influences both our self-perception and how others see us.

Your clothing choices are an extension of your identity. Studies consistently show a strong connection between attire and perception. A recent study titled *The Power of Professional Dress: Competence, Confidence, and Generational Shifts* highlights that well-dressed individuals are seen as more competent, confident, and dependable.[5] But it goes deeper than external impressions. The effort you put into your appearance signals to your brain that you value yourself, boosting self-esteem and equipping you with the confidence to take on challenges. When you look good, you feel good, and when you feel good, you perform better.

People form opinions within seconds of meeting you, and your clothing plays a significant role in that assessment. Whether it's a job interview, a first date, or a networking event, your attire sets the tone

---

[5] Emma Dillon, The Power of Professional Dress: Competence, Confidence, and Generational Shifts (East Carolina University, 2024).

for how others perceive and interact with you. Dressing professionally signals competence and attention to detail. Studies in *Social Psychological and Personality Science* reveal that men who wear formal attire perform better in negotiations and are perceived as more serious and capable.[6] The right outfit can open doors, acting as a silent ambassador for your skills and potential.

Beyond the workplace, dressing well enhances your social presence. It makes people more likely to approach you, engage with you, and view you in a positive light. A sharp appearance communicates respect for yourself and for the people you interact with. Dressing well isn't just about external validation alone; it's more importantly about how you see yourself. Wearing clothes that fit well and reflect your personality can elevate your mood, improve posture, and help you approach challenges with a sense of empowerment.

I have seen this so many times. The guy who has it all. The great mindset, the looks, the career, good character, strong connection to God, and then it's like, did you get dressed in the dark!? It's like the finishing touch on the masterpiece. You don't have to be draped in designer head to toe, but color coordination and the right tailored fit go a long way. I struggled heavily with this in my early twenties. I thought I had it all, and I even thought I had my style down…I was delusional. Oversized, mismatched, and tacky outfits. When I played football, I always lived by the "look good, feel good, play good" mantra, and I swagged out on the field, which translated to All-American performance. Yet, outside the field, I could not put a fit together if my life depended on it. Understanding the right fit and coordination, asking for feedback from those I trusted, and studying the right outfits and appearances allowed me to put my own spin on my unique style and add that finishing touch to my body.

Contrary to popular belief, dressing well doesn't require a fortune spent on designer brands. It's about making smart, intentional choices.

---

6 Michael W. Kraus and Wendy Berry Mendes, "Sartorial Symbols of Social Class Elicit Class-Consistent Behavioral and Physiological Responses: A Dyadic Approach," *Journal of Experimental Psychology: General* 143(6) (2014): 2330–2340.

A well-fitted suit or shirt instantly upgrades your appearance. Tailored clothing flatters your body shape and communicates attention to detail. Start with timeless, versatile pieces: a crisp white dress shirt, a tailored navy or charcoal suit, dark denim jeans, and a classic leather belt and shoes. These essentials transition seamlessly between professional and casual settings.

Choose clothing that works across different contexts. A blazer paired with chinos can take you from a business meeting to a dinner party with ease. Clothing should always be clean, well ironed, and free of damage. Details like polished shoes and neat accessories complete your look. Your wardrobe should reflect your personality. Whether you prefer classic, bold, or modern aesthetics, ensure your clothing choices align with who you are.

Dressing well transcends fashion trends. Across cultures and religions, presenting oneself with dignity and respect is a shared value. In Islam, for example, men are encouraged to wear clean, modest, and well-kept clothing. The emphasis isn't on extravagance but on self-respect and community respect. The Prophet Muhammad (PBUH) highlighted the importance of cleanliness and presentation, reminding us that outward appearance should reflect inner values.

It builds confidence, earns respect, and signals that you take yourself and your goals seriously. By curating a wardrobe that fits well, reflects your personality, and suits your lifestyle, you transform not just your appearance but your mindset and opportunities.

So next time you get dressed, think beyond the clothes. See it as an opportunity to present the best version of yourself to the world and most importantly to yourself. When you master the art of dressing well, you'll realize it's not about vanity; it's about self-respect, intention, and the image of excellence.

CARE FOR AN ANIMAL

FOR MOST OF MY LIFE, I AVOIDED HAVING PETS AT ALL COSTS. NOT because I didn't love animals, but because I feared the responsibility. I equated pet ownership with a loss of freedom, an end to spontaneity, and the onset of daily obligations I wasn't ready to embrace. But that all changed when we welcomed JJ, our dog, and later Jagger, our Maine coon cat, into our home. These two companions reshaped not just my routine, but my perspective on life, responsibility, and even faith.

Owning pets, I learned, isn't a burden, but a gift. It's a path to becoming more patient, more compassionate, and more mindful of the world around us. In caring for JJ and Jagger, I've grown as a servant of God, a husband, and a family member. These lessons weren't just personal—they were spiritual, emotional, and even physical. The journey of caring for animals has been as much about their well-being as it has been about my own growth.

Throughout history, great leaders and prophets have cared for animals, emphasizing the wisdom and growth that come from this act. The Prophet Muhammad (PBUH), for example, was known for his compassion toward animals, urging kindness and care for all creatures. This wasn't just a moral directive; it was a way of cultivating patience, humility, and empathy. By caring for animals, we learn to prioritize something beyond ourselves, furthering discipline and a sense of stewardship that extends to every area of life.

Before JJ and Jagger entered my life, I underestimated the depth of the bond between humans and animals. Now, I realize that this relationship is transformative. It teaches us to slow down, to be more present, and to nurture life in a way that strengthens our own character. I swear my cat Jagger wakes me up for my morning prayer when the alarm doesn't go off. Looking at these creatures just shows the beauty of God and how loving, compassionate, intricate, and beautiful His creations are. It makes me think: If they are this reliant on us, then how reliant are we on God? He facilitates, He provides for us, and the beauty of animals and pets brings us closer to Him.

Seeing our dog, JJ, finally come out of his shell and interact with other animals and humans is mind-blowing. He could barely leave the apartment and walk on a sidewalk due to his past abuse and trauma before we rescued him, and now this guy runs around the dog park like he owns the place. Watching his transformation reminded me that healing takes time, trust is earned, and consistent love has the power to reshape a soul. The same is true for us as men. We often carry trauma, fears, and limitations from our past, but with the right discipline, environment, and faith, we can break free and thrive.

Scientific research confirms what pet owners have always known. Animals have an uncanny ability to calm our minds. A study by Washington State University found that spending just ten minutes with a therapy dog significantly reduces levels of cortisol, the stress hormone.[7] Whether it's the rhythmic motion of petting a dog or the soothing purr of a cat, these interactions lower blood pressure, slow heart rates, and create a sense of peace. JJ's wagging tail and Jagger's quiet companionship have turned countless stressful moments into opportunities for calm and clarity.

But pets provide more than companionship as they also offer a

---

7   Patricia Pendry and Jaymie L. Vandagriff, "Animal Visitation Program (AVP) Reduces Cortisol Levels of University Students: A Randomized Controlled Trial," *AERA* Open 5(2) (2019), https://doi.org/10.1177/2332858419852592.

sense of purpose. Knowing that JJ and Jagger rely on me for their well-being has brought stability and joy to my life. For those struggling with loneliness, pets can bridge the emotional gap, providing support and connection. Studies show that pet owners are less likely to suffer from depression, as the act of caring for an animal promotes engagement and lifts the spirit.

Owning pets inherently promotes physical activity. From taking JJ for walks to chasing Jagger around the house, these small acts of movement contribute to better health. According to the CDC, regular interaction with pets can lower cholesterol, improve cardiovascular health, and encourage more exercise. For me, these moments of activity have become joyful rituals, blending physical wellness with emotional connection.

On a deeper level, caring for animals nurtures the soul. Many faith traditions, including Islam, view animals as sacred gifts. The Qur'an reminds us that animals, like humans, are part of God's intricate design, teaching us humility and interconnectedness. By caring for them, we fulfill our role as stewards of the Earth.

Caring for JJ and Jagger has become a spiritual practice for me. Their innocence and dependence remind me of my duty to serve my family, my community, and my Creator. Through them, I've learned to value patience, empathy, and the quiet beauty of stewardship.

Owning pets is about much more than feeding, walking, or cleaning. It's about cultivating virtues that ripple outward into every aspect of life. JJ's unwavering loyalty has taught me about unconditional love, while Jagger's calm demeanor has shown me the importance of stillness and presence. Together, they've made me a better person who is more attentive, more disciplined, and more grateful.

Caring for animals is a journey of growth, one that enriches every facet of your life.

It's a path that transforms the lives of the animals we care for as well as our own. In embracing the responsibility of pet ownership, we open ourselves to lessons in love, patience, and purpose, which are all lessons that bring us closer to our true selves and our Creator.

So, if you've ever hesitated to bring a pet into your life, pull the trigger. JJ and Jagger have shown me that in caring for others, we find ourselves. They've enriched my life in ways I couldn't have imagined, and for that, I am forever grateful.

CHAPTER 24

GET YOUR $ RIGHT

MY IPHONE SHATTERED AGAINST THE WALL, THE CLOSET DOOR slammed shut, and my fist connected with the drywall with a force that would impress Mike Tyson. The chaos in that moment mirrored the storm within me, triggered by two seismic events: a catastrophic $50,000 commodities trade loss due to an Iraqi base attack and a disheartening news report on CNN. But it wasn't just about the money; it was the realization that I had lost control.

This wasn't the culmination of one bad trade. It was the breaking point in a years-long cycle of addiction to wealth, fueled by a relentless desire to prove myself and combat the stereotypes that shadowed me as a Muslim in a post-9/11 world. Financial success had become more than just a goal; it had become my identity, my validation, and my everything. The stock market had me under its spell. I was hooked into the constant highs and lows and could not leave the roulette table if my life depended on it.

Chasing after wealth had consumed me long before that fateful night. I was intoxicated by the promises of capitalism and the illusion of control the stock market offered. My Harvard degree became both my advantage and my Achilles' heel. In those early years, I experienced exhilarating highs. Predicting an oil price crash due to political moves by Trump made me feel invincible, while a $250,000 gain in a single week pushed me past the millionaire milestone. But those wins only deepened my addiction. Each gain made me hungrier for the next, and each loss sent me spiraling into despair. I had become a slave to the market, my self-worth rising and falling with every fluctuation.

Special acquisition companies, margin trading, and speculative bets fueled my downfall. Instead of cutting losses, I doubled down, throwing borrowed money at sinking investments. When the inevitable crash came, it wasn't just my portfolio that crumbled. It was my confidence, my identity, and my sense of purpose.

The lowest point wasn't the financial losses. It was sitting alone in my closet, drowning in the realization that I had lost myself. My lavish lifestyle of Aston Martins, Rolexes, and Michelin-star dinners all felt like a hollow facade. The more I spent, the emptier I became. The market's volatility wasn't just financial; it seeped into my mental and emotional state, leaving me unstable and directionless.

But from that wreckage came clarity. Quick wealth was a lie, a mirage that offered no real satisfaction. If I was going to rebuild, it had to be on a foundation of patience, discipline, and sustainable growth.

1. REDEFINING SUCCESS THROUGH A STABLE CAREER

I shifted my focus from trading to a performance-based role in software sales. Here, I found purpose in the process. Every closed deal brought tangible rewards, and I thrived on the structure and challenge of my work. This career allowed me to stabilize my income while also giving me a sense of accomplishment that wasn't tied to market volatility. Eventually, I out-earned the CEO of my team, proving to myself that sustainable effort beats speculative gambling every time.

2. ADOPTING A DISCIPLINED INVESTMENT STRATEGY

I automated my investments, dedicating a consistent portion of my income to low-cost index funds. Dollar-cost averaging became my ally, smoothing out the highs and lows of the market. This strategy required no emotional decision-making and it was simple, steady, and effective.

3. LIVING INTENTIONALLY, NOT EXCESSIVELY

Having nice things isn't the problem; overextending yourself to get them is. I still own luxury items and enjoy the finer things in life, like sports cars and high-quality timepieces. But the difference now is that I don't live beyond my means to acquire them. These indulgences don't come at the expense of my financial security or peace of mind.

Living paycheck to paycheck or racking up credit card debt to maintain a lifestyle you can't afford is a ticking time bomb. Instead, I focus on building wealth first, then using my financial successes to reward myself responsibly. I've learned that true wealth isn't about flaunting what you have, but about appreciating what you have and the freedom to live without financial strain.

4. DIVERSIFYING FOR LONG-TERM SECURITY

To safeguard against future crashes, I diversified my investments. Real estate and startup ventures became key components of my strategy. Allocating 10 percent of my income to these assets spread my risk and opened new opportunities for growth.

5. CREATING A SAFETY NET FOR PEACE OF MIND

One of the most liberating decisions I made was building an emergency fund of six months' worth of living expenses set aside in cash. This safety net became a shield against fear, allowing me to navigate market downturns with confidence.

The road to financial independence taught me that wealth isn't about the zeros in your bank account; it's about freedom, security, and peace of mind. It's about living free from the stress of paycheck-to-paycheck survival and making intentional, long-term decisions that align with your values.

You don't have to abandon the idea of owning nice things or indulging in life's luxuries. But those things should come as rewards for sound financial planning, not as crutches for self-worth or status symbols to impress others. True wealth is about living life on your terms. Where your possessions serve you, not the other way around.

Today, thanks to God alone, I stand on a foundation of sustainable wealth, peace of mind, and a renewed sense of purpose. The G Wagon in my driveway isn't a symbol of excess or show; it's a reminder of the blessings and gifts God bestows on us. I no longer chase wealth for validation; I embrace the freedom and security it provides.

You are not a man simply because you provide. You are a man because you provide *righteously*. Every dollar you earn either brings you closer to divine mercy or further from it. The pursuit of wealth is not inherently evil—but how you earn, spend, and view that wealth determines whether it's a blessing or a burden.

CHAPTER 25

MONEY WITHOUT MORALS WILL RUIN YOU

"Every soul will taste death, and you will only be given your [full] compensation on the Day of Resurrection. So whoever is spared from the Fire and admitted into Paradise—he indeed is successful."

—QUR'AN 3:185

THE LIE YOU'VE BEEN SOLD

Modern society has created a false definition of success: high income, multiple revenue streams, a packed calendar, and a lifestyle you can flex on social media. You're taught to believe that if you're not grinding 24/7, you're falling behind. That if your money isn't working for you, you're losing. That if you don't have passive income, stocks, crypto, or interest-bearing investments, you're doing it wrong.

But here's the truth no one wants to say: Most of the financial world today is built on sin.

And worse than that—it's been normalized. It's been marketed to you as wisdom.

But God doesn't reward hustle if it's hollow. He doesn't bless wealth earned in rebellion to Him.

You've been conditioned to think financial shortcuts are just strategy. But shortcuts that violate divine principles aren't strategies—they're spiritual sabotage.

Let's be blunt: Riba (usury or interest) is a disease. It doesn't just pollute economies—it poisons hearts. It feeds on desperation. It capitalizes on need. It profits from pain.

In the Qur'an, God doesn't just warn against Riba—He declares war on it:

> O you who believe! Fear Allah and give up what remains of your demand for usury, if you are indeed believers. If you do not, then be warned of war from Allah and His Messenger… (Qur'an 2:278–279)

This is not a metaphor. This is war.

Interest isn't wealth—it's inflation of the ego. It creates an illusion of gain while stripping away Barakah (blessing). It may look profitable on paper, but it leaves your soul bankrupt.

So ask yourself: Why chase wealth that puts you at odds with the One who provides it?

I know this isn't just theory—because I lived it.

There was a time I made $250,000 in one month. On paper, it looked like I had cracked the code. I used high-interest margin loans to trade highly leveraged bubble stocks. Every day, the numbers went higher. The balance sheet looked incredible. But in my heart, I knew I was earning in an unethical way.

It didn't feel like a win. It felt like a slow moral collapse dressed up as financial success.

That night, I sat alone in my sports car in the parking garage. The engine off. Silence. You'd think I'd be on top of the world, right? I just pulled in a quarter million in a few weeks. But I remember crying.

Not tears of joy. Tears of guilt. Tears of emptiness. Because no amount of gain feels good when it comes from disobedience.

And to make matters worse—I lost it all in the months that followed. The greed took over. I pushed harder. Took on more margin. Tried to double down.

God didn't just let me fall. He checked me.

He stripped it away before that Haram wealth could poison my future. Before it became the foundation for my home, my giving, my investments. And for that—I'm grateful. That money was never mine to begin with. It would've only cursed everything it touched. What felt like a loss turned out to be mercy.

It's not just about interest. It's about everything we justify in the name of survival. Selling Haram products. Cheating taxes. Lying on résumés. Pushing deceptive marketing. Joining unethical businesses just to "make ends meet."

There is no blessing in money that comes at the cost of your morality.

Prophet Muhammad (PBUH) said:

A time will come when one will not care how one gains one's money, lawfully or unlawfully. (Bukhari)

We are living in that time.

But your standard is higher. Your income is not just a paycheck—it's a form of worship. Every transaction is either a seed for reward or a path to regret. When you earn clean, your wealth becomes a force of good. When you earn dirty, your wealth becomes a curse in disguise.

God does not just look at what you earned. He looks at how you earned it.

Let's flip the narrative. Earning Halal may not bring overnight wealth, but it brings unmatched peace. You sleep deeper. You walk lighter. You speak clearer. Because when your income is clean, your conscience is too.

Halal income is not just lawful. It is liberating.

It reminds you that provision comes from God—not people, not platforms, not algorithms. You hustle, yes, but you know that blessings and wealth are divinely allocated. You don't beg. You don't sell your soul. You do your part and trust the rest to your Creator.

This mindset transforms your career from a trap to a tool.

DON'T LET WHAT YOU DO DEFINE WHO YOU ARE

One of the biggest lies of modern masculinity is that your job is your identity. Your title, your income, your industry—that's who you are, right?

Wrong.

You are not your résumé. You are not your tax return. You are not your business card.

A man of God is defined by his character, not his career.

If your job disappeared tomorrow, who would you be? Would your values still stand? Would your faith remain intact?

When your self-worth is tied to your position, your soul becomes enslaved to performance. You begin to value yourself by how others see you, not by how your Creator sees you.

Let your work serve your purpose. But never let it replace your purpose.

STRIVE FOR BARAKAH

In contrast to the Western model of material success, Islamic wisdom introduces a more powerful concept: Barakah. Barakah is a divine blessing that brings expansion, harmony, and fulfillment to what you already have. It's not about having more. It's about making more out of less. A man with Barakah might not earn the highest salary, but his time stretches, his money sustains, and his work nourishes others.

Barakah isn't logical. It's spiritual. It defies economic formulas. It's the difference between a home filled with peace and a mansion filled with tension. Between wealth that destroys and wealth that uplifts.

Barakah enters a man's life when he aligns his earning, spending, and intentions with God. Consider two men earning the same income: One lives in scarcity and discontent, while the other supports his family with ease, gives to others, and feels anchored in purpose. The second is not luckier. He is blessed.

To invite Barakah into your life:

- **Earn righteously.** Money gained through honesty carries spiritual weight. Wealth accumulated through deceit often becomes a burden.
- **Work with integrity.** Let your income reflect sincerity. Let your business reflect values. What is built on truth will outlast what is built on greed.
- **Purify your intentions.** When your money serves a higher purpose—providing for your family, uplifting your community, seeking the pleasure of God—it multiplies in meaning.
- **Avoid interest-based transactions.** Islam prohibits Riba not just as a religious formality, but because it corrupts balance and justice. Ethical finance preserves dignity.
- **Give generously.** "Charity does not decrease wealth," said the Prophet (PBUH). Giving invites divine favor.
- **Practice gratitude.** Gratefulness draws more blessing. Studies confirm what faith has long taught: The more you appreciate, the more you experience fulfillment.
- **Trust in God.** True peace comes not from the number in your account, but from knowing that provision comes from the Creator. A man of Tawakkul walks with calm even when income is tight.

Barakah enriches from within. It magnifies the essence of what's already there.

Across the world, ancient Eastern thought echoes a similar call—not to possess more, but to live wisely. Taoist philosophy, particularly the Tao Te Ching, teaches the art of alignment: with nature, with time, and with oneself.

The Tao emphasizes simplicity, patience, and surrender. Where Barakah blesses what you have, the Tao teaches you how to live with less and still be whole.

Key teachings of the Tao include:

- **Simplicity over excess.** A man at peace with little is freer than a man with much who constantly wants more.
- **Patience with life's rhythms.** Just as winter gives way to spring, hardship gives way to relief. Forced control breaks things. Wisdom flows with timing.
- **Wu wei—effortless action.** This isn't passivity; it's strategic restraint. A wise leader does not micromanage but trusts the process. Real power is calm.
- **Let go of control.** The tighter you grip, the more life resists. Letting go doesn't mean apathy. It means understanding what is—and isn't—yours to manage.
- **Honor duality.** The Tao recognizes yin and yang: strength and softness, action and stillness, ambition and contentment. These are not contradictions. They are balance.

Western culture tells men to dominate, accumulate, and chase endlessly. But both Barakah and the Tao call you to a different success—one where peace is not the result of arrival, but the presence of alignment.

CHASE BARAKAH, NOT JUST BREAD

The goal isn't just to make money. The goal is to make money that matters.

Barakah is when little goes far. When God puts blessing into your time, your money, your energy. When a modest income sustains your entire household. When your savings stretch. When your heart feels full—even when your account doesn't.

You can have a six-figure salary and still feel broke. You can live in luxury and still live in anxiety. That's the difference between raw cash and real contentment.

Barakah isn't found in greed. It's found in gratitude.

It's not found in manipulating others. It's found in trusting God.

And it's not found in doing "whatever it takes." It's found in doing what is right, even when it costs you something.

ACTION STEPS TO LIVE WITH BARAKAH AND BALANCE:

1. **Audit your intentions.** Ask yourself: Why am I chasing this? Is it validation, or is it purpose?
2. **Simplify your life.** Eliminate distractions. Cut back on things that steal your energy but don't feed your soul.
3. **Trust the process.** Put in the work, but don't obsess over the result. Sincere effort with surrendered outcomes is the formula for peace.
4. **Give without fear.** Generosity is spiritual investment. It returns in forms you cannot predict.
5. **Balance hustle with stillness.** Ambition without pause is burnout. Stillness without purpose is stagnation. A powerful man does both with wisdom.

A man of depth understands: Success is not about wealth, but impact. Not about power, but peace. Not about status, but sincerity.

In a culture where money shouts and values whisper, let your integrity be the loudest thing about you. Let your income reflect morality. Let your spending reflect humility. Let your life reflect God.

Barakah will take care of the rest.

You are not a product of capitalism. You are a servant of the Most Generous.

Do not sell your soul to buy temporary success.

Remember: What you earn dies with you. What you did with it lives on forever. Earn clean. Live clean. Die ready.

PART II

MIND

CHAPTER 26

THE ENEMY WITHIN

THE ENEMY WITHIN IS YOUR GREATEST ADVERSARY. HE KNOWS YOU better than you know yourself. He knows your vices, your weaknesses, your strengths, and your insecurities. He studies your every move, always waiting, always plotting. He has a counter for every defense, a strategy for every attack, and a fortified resolve that seems impenetrable. This is the Nafs, better known as the base desires, the untamed ego, the inner voice that tempts you toward darkness and away from the light. Conquering the Enemy Within is not just a challenge; it's THE challenge.

Shaykh Muhammad Al Jilani, may God bless and preserve him, imparted a profound truth: The true battle lies within. Once you conquer the self, the adversary in front of you is no match. It is like debt. The more you accumulate, the greater the hole you dig. The same principle applies to the Nafs. Its power grows when it is indulged, but it can be diminished with deliberate action and control.

To defeat the Enemy Within, you must approach it as you would any formidable opponent. You study him. You learn his tendencies. You uncover his weaknesses. And then you cut him off: his food supply, his air, and his access to power. What are these sources of strength for the Nafs? They are the toxic variables we allow into our lives: the sinful acts, the indulgences, and the distractions that corrupt the heart and cloud the soul. Each act of darkness strengthens the Nafs and weakens you, furthering the gap between you and your Creator.

When you consume these toxins, whether it be arrogance, greed, lust, envy, foul speech, anger, or any number of destructive habits, you are not just feeding the Nafs; you are arming him. You are equipping your greatest adversary with the tools he needs to defeat you. The odds are not in your favor.

But this battle can be won. To defeat the Nafs, you must weaken him while simultaneously strengthening yourself. You must starve him of the fuel that gives him power. This means cutting out arrogance, greed, stinginess, foul speech, negative thoughts, envy, rage, fornication, pornography, masturbation, drugs, alcohol, gluttony, bad company, disrespect, judgment, and other toxic behaviors. These actions strengthen the Nafs and also darken your heart, making it harder for the Nur, the divine light, to take root.

Just as you weaken your adversary, you must build your own strength. This comes from fortifying the Nur within you. Think of the Nur as the Force wielded by the Jedi, a light that grows stronger with purity of intent and action. You cultivate this light through daily prayer, Dhikr, acts of charity, seeking knowledge, spreading love, smiling, forgiving, clean speech, gratitude, and cutting out the darkness that poisons your soul. The purer your heart, the stronger your connection to God, and the more indomitable your spirit becomes.

The journey to conquer the Nafs is not an easy one, but the rewards are infinite. With every step toward self-mastery, you gain clarity, discipline, and resilience. You become more aligned with your Creator and more equipped to face the challenges of life.

This battle isn't just about resisting temptation; it's about reshaping yourself into the man you were meant to be. By purging the toxins and nurturing the Nur, you become a man of purpose, of integrity, and of unwavering strength. The Nafs loses its grip, and the Enemy Within, once so formidable, becomes powerless against your discipline and devotion.

An old proverb reminds us, "Do not decrease your own character at the expense of another's lack of character." This wisdom extends inward. Do not allow the Nafs to diminish your light. Do not let it rob you of your potential, your strength, your faith.

When the Enemy Within is conquered, every external battle becomes manageable. It is the same as cutting off the head of the snake or taking out the general of an opposing army. The true war is fought within. Once the Nafs is subdued, every enemy, every obstacle, and every challenge in life becomes surmountable.

This is the essence of self-mastery. The battle is not about perfection, but progression. It is about choosing light over darkness, discipline over indulgence, and purpose over distraction. It is about becoming the man God intended you to be. A man of faith, strength, and unwavering resolve. Once the Nafs is conquered, you are no longer a slave to your desires. You become free. You become unstoppable. You become a true man of excellence.

It's critical for you to face the sobering reality: One in five adults in the US faces mental health challenges, and men are at an even higher risk. Suicide is the seventh-leading cause of death for men in America. This fact alone underscores the importance of making mental health a priority. Many men are taught to suppress emotions or see vulnerability as weakness, but breaking this cycle is critical.

To combat this crisis, we need to dismantle the stigma surrounding men's mental health. Open conversations about mental struggles, seeking help without fear, and practicing self-care are critical steps toward progress. Men need to feel empowered to prioritize their mental well-being without shame.

DEFEATING THE DEVIL

In the war for your mind, body, and soul, there's an invisible force working relentlessly to pull you off course. The devil doesn't need to break you—he only needs to distract you. He doesn't have to destroy you in a moment; he just has to keep you busy long enough for you to forget why you were created.

And today, distraction has never been more accessible.

Satan is a master strategist. He rarely approaches with open evil. He disguises destruction as pleasure. He wraps failure in convenience. Every mindless scroll, every dopamine hit from a video, every hour lost in a game—that's time stolen from your mission. The world is engineered to hijack your attention and rewire your focus toward consumption instead of contribution.

Every time you reach for your phone, ask yourself: Is this helping me grow, or is it keeping me numb?

Materialism plays the same trick. Shopping sprees, brand obsessions, chasing what's next—they promise fulfillment but deliver emptiness. Culture tells you that your worth is measured by what you wear, drive, or own. But the soul starves when its value is tied to things that fade.

The same is true of indulgence. Clubs, parties, meaningless relationships—they offer short-term highs and long-term hollowness. With each indulgence, your self-control weakens. The devil doesn't just want you entertained. He wants you desensitized. He wants your senses dull so you can't hear the voice calling you back to discipline.

Look at your conversations. How much time is lost on gossip, pointless arguments, and small talk that does nothing for your mind or soul? Men of purpose seek depth. They sharpen each other. They speak life, truth, and wisdom. The rest is noise.

The greatest threat to your potential isn't failure—it's comfort. Comfort kills drive. It makes you believe you have time. That there's always tomorrow to change. But the man on a mission knows: Tomorrow is never promised.

The antidote to distraction is intentional living. Delete the apps that waste your time. Replace scrolling with studying. Replace entertainment with elevation. Replace distraction with devotion. Prioritize prayer, Qur'an, reflection, and routines that anchor your day in purpose.

The devil doesn't fear your dreams. He fears your discipline.

Master the basics: Wake up early. Train your body. Eat clean. Do meaningful work. Guard your time. Surround yourself with men who call you higher—not into distraction, but into greatness. Fast often. It renews your mind, sharpens your will, and brings your heart closer to God.

If something isn't making you stronger, wiser, or closer to your Creator, it's a distraction. Cut it out.

The devil doesn't attack like a warrior. He slithers in like a serpent. A glance. A comment. A delay. "It's just one time." "I can handle this." What starts as a moment becomes a habit. Then shame takes over. "I'm too far gone." "God won't forgive me." He'll tempt you with sin and destroy you with guilt. And if sin doesn't work, he'll come for your righteousness through pride.

To win, you must become a fortress.

Train yourself to recognize his voice. When you hear the whisper, reject it. Pray harder. Reflect deeper. Stay in community. Keep your body strong. The devil thrives in isolation. He feeds on idleness. He waits for weakness.

Recite: "I seek refuge in God from the accursed Satan."

There will be days when you slip. When you fall. When you feel like you're losing the war. But hear this:

He only wins if you stop fighting.

God never asked you to be perfect. He asked you to resist. To get back up. To fight for your soul. If you keep standing. If you keep striving. If you refuse to give in—there will come a moment when you realize:

You are no longer afraid of him.

Because now, he's afraid of you.

The war never ends. But neither does the victory of the man who refuses to surrender.

CHAPTER 27

THE POWER OF OPTIMISM

IN A WORLD THAT CONSTANTLY TESTS YOUR FOCUS, RESOLVE, AND faith, optimism isn't just a nice-to-have—it's mission-critical. Life will punch you in the gut. You'll face delays, disappointments, and moments where the path ahead seems foggy, maybe even impossible. But it's not the struggle that defines you. It's how you choose to meet it.

Optimism is more than a mindset. It's a weapon. A filter. A discipline. It's how a man trains his mind to turn adversity into strength, chaos into clarity, and pain into progress.

The man who thinks positively isn't delusional. He isn't blind to suffering. He's simply anchored in the belief that no matter how dark it gets, he has the strength, discipline, and faith to rise.

So let's get practical:

Why does optimism matter?

How does it shape the man you're becoming?

And how do you build it—especially when life feels heavy?

OPTIMISM IS NOT NAIVETY. IT'S RESILIENCE.

There's a misconception that optimism means pretending everything's okay. It doesn't. Real optimism means you see the storm, you feel the wind, and still, you believe in a breakthrough. It's not fake positivity—it's trained perseverance.

Think of the gym. The rep that burns, the set that feels impossible, the moment your body wants to quit. What keeps you pushing? The belief that the pain serves a purpose. That's optimism. It's the mental muscle that keeps you moving when everything in you wants to stop.

SCIENCE CONFIRMS IT. SCRIPTURE COMMANDS IT.

Optimism isn't just feel-good fluff. It's biological. It's spiritual. It's essential.

- **Less cortisol, more clarity.** Optimists produce lower levels of cortisol, the hormone responsible for stress, brain fog, and emotional volatility.
- **Stronger immunity and longer life.** Positive thinkers recover faster, resist illness more effectively, and live longer.
- **Sharper thinking under pressure.** Optimism boosts creativity and problem-solving. When you believe solutions exist, your brain actually finds them.

Spiritually, optimism is an act of faith. It's the quiet confidence that God's plan is unfolding—even when you can't see it.

That's not just comfort. It's a divine promise. The struggle will end. The dawn will break. And the man who holds the line—who stays patient, faithful, and focused—will see it through.

Optimism isn't just for you. It's for everyone watching you.

You're in a crisis. Others are panicking. You stay grounded. You look for answers. That steady, forward-looking energy is leadership. Optimism becomes the anchor your circle clings to when everything else is shaking.

Great men inspire by how they carry their storms. They don't run. They rise—and they lift others with them.

OPTIMISM CAN BE BUILT. LIKE STRENGTH.

This isn't something you're born with. It's something you practice.

1. **Control your inputs.** What you feed your mind shapes your outlook. Cut down on negative media, toxic people, and mindless scrolling. Fill your space with wisdom, inspiration, and truth.
2. **Reframe the struggle.** Stop asking, "Why is this happening to me?" Start asking, "What is this building in me?" Pain is feedback. Learn from it.
3. **Practice daily gratitude.** Every morning or evening, write down three things you're grateful for. This rewires your brain to notice what's right—even when things feel wrong.
4. **Visualize success.** See the win before it happens. Picture yourself overcoming. Prepare your mind to rise before your body even moves.
5. **Speak life.** Words matter. Stop saying, "I can't do this." Start saying, "I've survived worse. I've got more in me."

OPTIMISM IN ACTION: REAL EXAMPLES

- **Nelson Mandela** endured twenty-seven years in prison. He came out not bitter, but full of hope—forgiveness in his heart and a vision for unity.
- **Thomas Edison** failed over a thousand times. He didn't see failure. He saw progress.
- **The Prophet Muhammad (PBUH)** faced betrayal, exile, and war—but he never lost faith in God's promise, and his optimism lit the world.

They weren't handed greatness. They chose it. They built it—on the back of resilience and unwavering belief.

There will be days when it feels impossible to stay positive. Days when loss hits, when dreams collapse, when you feel like you're drowning. In those moments, optimism isn't about pretending. It's about choosing.

Choosing to believe that your pain isn't pointless.

Choosing to believe that you're being shaped—not broken.

Choosing to believe that God still has more for you.

Winston Churchill once said, "The pessimist sees difficulty in every opportunity. The optimist sees opportunity in every difficulty."

BE THE FIRE. NOT THE ASHES.

Optimism isn't a mood. It's a decision.

The man you're meant to be doesn't shrink in adversity. He stands. He lifts. He believes. Not because life is easy—but because he knows who he is, and Who he belongs to.

So ask yourself:

- When life hits hard, will you fold—or rise?
- When failure comes, will you curse it—or learn from it?
- When darkness surrounds you, will you wait for light—or become it?

A man of faith, discipline, and optimism cannot be broken. Only sharpened.

CHAPTER 28

MASTERING MINDSET

YOUR MINDSET IS THE LENS THROUGH WHICH YOU EXPERIENCE everything. It shapes how you interpret hardship, how you respond to loss, and how you build the future you claim to want. A disciplined mind doesn't just react—it leads. It turns chaos into clarity and adversity into strength.

A positive mindset isn't wishful thinking. It's a skill. A habit. A force multiplier. It reduces stress, boosts creativity, enhances problem-solving, and raises the quality of your entire life. The man who commands his thoughts commands his reality. His mindset becomes the architect of his resilience, the engine of his progress, and the compass of his destiny.

YOUR MINDSET SETS THE TONE OF YOUR LIFE

The Stoics were clear: Life isn't about what happens to you—it's about how you respond. What happens outside you matters far less than what you allow inside. A man who has mastered his mind is unshaken by circumstance. He interprets pain through a lens of purpose.

When setbacks hit, train yourself to ask, "What's the blessing I can't see yet?"

An injury? Maybe it saved you from a worse fate.

A breakup? Perhaps it made room for someone better.

A disappointing meal? There are millions without food at all.

This mindset doesn't ignore reality—it honors it by placing it in divine perspective.

The most powerful shift you can make is to place full trust in God. Whatever happens—good or bad—is written by His will and rooted in your benefit, even if you can't yet understand how. How many times has something you once dreaded turned out to be one of the best things that ever happened to you?

Faith reframes everything.

…Perhaps you dislike something and it is good for you… (Surah Al-Baqarah, 2:216)

True optimism isn't blind—it's built on certainty that God's plan is always better than your own.

Mindset isn't just psychological—it's physiological. Positive thinking triggers dopamine, the neurotransmitter tied to motivation, focus, and joy. Negativity, on the other hand, activates cortisol, the stress hormone linked to anxiety, depression, and disease.

The choice is biological: flood your system with momentum or poison it with fear. Train your brain, and your body will follow.

A disciplined man does not allow his mind to become a playground for doubt, resentment, or self-pity. He protects it like sacred territory. He installs practices that make positivity second nature, not just a passing mood.

Here's how to cultivate a bulletproof mindset:

1. PRACTICE DAILY GRATITUDE

Each morning, list three things you're thankful for. This trains your brain to focus on abundance instead of lack.

If you are grateful, I will surely increase you [in favor]. (Qur'an 14:7)

Gratitude multiplies everything.

2. BUILD A CIRCLE THAT SHARPENS YOU

Your environment shapes your mindset. Choose people who challenge you, elevate your thinking, and reinforce your standards.

A person is upon the religion of his close friend… (Sunan Abu Dawood 4833)

Energy is contagious. Surround yourself with people whose presence is a reminder of your potential.

3. REFRAME THE STORY

When adversity strikes, ask better questions:

- "What is this teaching me?"
- "What strength is this building?"
- "What would the man I want to be do right now?"

That's how you turn trials into training.

4. EMBRACE MINDFULNESS

Even five minutes of stillness—through prayer, breathing, or reflection—restores clarity. Mindfulness creates space between stimulus and response. That space is where your power lives.

5. VISUALIZE VICTORY

Close your eyes. See yourself executing at the highest level. Success is built twice: first in the mind, then in the world. Champions don't focus on what stands in the way. They lock in on the outcome.

Optimism isn't just emotional—it's physical. Science shows:

- Lower stress
- Reduced risk of chronic illness
- Stronger immunity
- Longer life

When you think better, you live better. Period.

A strong mind reinforces a strong body. And a strong body sustains a focused, disciplined life. It all works together.

Every man wrestles with self-doubt. The difference between the defeated and the disciplined is what they do with it. You can let it shrink you—or let it sharpen you.

Replace weak self-talk with truth:

- "I've handled worse."
- "I am capable."
- "This is building me."

Speak strength into your life. Celebrate your progress. Keep moving forward.

Stress is a test of your preparation. You don't rise to the level of your potential—you fall to the level of your training. Breathe. Reflect. Move your body. Sharpen your tools. A strong man doesn't ignore pressure—he's built to carry it.

The goal isn't perfection—it's progress. Stay in motion. Keep learning. Keep growing. Take the course. Read the book. Ask better questions. Humility and hunger are the hallmarks of greatness.

The man with a positive mindset doesn't just survive—he builds. He heals. He leads.

CHAPTER 29

NO PORN, IT'S MIND CANCER

FROM A YOUNG AGE, MANY OF US WERE TAUGHT TO SUPPRESS ANY conversation around sexuality. Desire was taboo. Silence replaced guidance. And shame replaced understanding.

I remember being twelve years old, completely naive, thinking that restarting the family computer would erase what I had just watched. I didn't know anything about browser history. The fallout was swift and brutal. My parents found out, and I was punished like I'd committed treason. My father didn't speak to me for weeks.

But instead of that moment ending the behavior, it planted the seed of secrecy. I didn't walk away from it—I walked deeper in. What could have been addressed with compassion was buried in shame, and that shame became a breeding ground for addiction.

What started as curiosity turned into routine. Then into compulsion. At first, guilt screamed like an alarm in my soul. I knew I was playing with fire. But over time, the alarm dulled. Eventually, I stopped hearing it altogether.

Society makes it easy to justify:

- "Everyone watches it."

- "It's normal."
- "It's just a phase."

But normalization doesn't mean harmless. Pornography is everywhere—woven into films, memes, music, and social feeds. It disguises itself as freedom, but it's enslavement in disguise.

At my worst, I was watching it three to four times a day. It didn't matter if I was tired, busy, or in public. Porn had control over me. It dictated my energy, my mood, my thoughts. It stole my time, my focus, and my sense of self.

And it didn't stop there.

Addiction doesn't stay in one lane. It leaks. It expands.

Pornography warped how I viewed love and connection. It fed into casual sex. That opened the door to alcohol. Then to substances. One crack in the fortress became a collapse of the foundation.

The deeper I went, the more detached I became. One partner wasn't enough. Intimacy was replaced by novelty. I wasn't chasing connection—I was chasing a chemical high. And every time, I felt emptier afterward.

That's what addiction does. It promises satisfaction and delivers shame.

Pornography is a Mind Cancer. It rewires your brain. It corrupts your relationships. It kills your potential.

Here's what science tells us about what happens when we watch porn:

- **Mental health decline:** Regular use is linked to anxiety, depression, and lower life satisfaction.
- **Relationship dysfunction:** It breeds unrealistic expectations, dissatisfaction, and emotional disconnection.
- **Isolation and shame:** The secrecy intensifies loneliness and fuels deeper addiction.

Pornography isn't harmless. It's a silent predator—distorting what sex was created to be: sacred, powerful, unifying.

THE INDUSTRY PROFITS FROM YOUR PAIN

This is a billion-dollar machine built on brokenness. On silence. On guilt. And while society tries to brand it as empowerment, what it's really doing is dehumanizing intimacy and glorifying dysfunction.

But here's what you need to know:

- **You are not powerless.**
- **You are not too far gone.**
- **You are not defined by your addiction.**

Even public figures like Terry Crews have spoken about their battles with pornography. Through honesty, therapy, brotherhood, and faith—he overcame. And so can you.

THE PATH TO FREEDOM

Breaking free isn't easy. But it is absolutely possible. Here's the strategy:

1. **Acknowledge the enemy.** Stop justifying it. Call it what it is: an addiction. Own the damage it's doing to your mind, your heart, and your future.
2. **Build a brotherhood.** You cannot win this war alone. Isolation fuels addiction. Open up to someone you trust. Join a support group like NoFap or Sex Addicts Anonymous. Confession isn't weakness—it's power.
3. **Know your triggers.** Understand the emotional states that drive you: stress, loneliness, boredom. Get ahead of them. Build a plan for those moments.
4. **Remove the ammunition.** Use content blockers. Set boundaries. Create barriers between you and temptation. Make it hard to fall.
5. **Redirect the energy.** Channel your time and energy into purpose: lift weights, build a business, serve your community. Idle hands are the devil's playground. Keep your hands busy with something that builds you.

6. **Prioritize your foundation.** Sleep. Nutrition. Mental health. These aren't luxuries. They are weapons in your fight. The stronger your body and mind, the harder you are to shake.
7. **Anchor yourself in faith.** Fasting. Prayer. Qur'an. These spiritual practices rewire your brain and reorient your heart. They don't just cleanse the body—they realign your soul.

> Indeed, the soul is prone to evil, except those upon whom my Lord has mercy. (Qur'an 12:53)

Freedom starts with faith. Victory begins with submission to God.

Make no mistake—this isn't a one-day fix. There will be relapses. Moments of weakness. Days where you fall.

But each time you rise, you reclaim another piece of yourself.

Every small win is a step toward clarity, strength, and peace.

You're not just quitting porn—you're choosing purpose. You're taking back your time, your energy, your masculinity, your future.

You're choosing to become a man who isn't mastered by his desires, but who has mastered himself.

You can remain chained to a fantasy that poisons your mind.

Or you can choose reality, where strength is built, intimacy is sacred, and discipline is your shield.

You are not broken beyond repair.

You are simply a man mid-battle.

And the man you're meant to be is waiting on the other side.

Choose freedom.

CHAPTER 30

ALWAYS BE LEARNING

KNOWLEDGE IS A TREASURE—BUT ITS VALUE IS ONLY REALIZED when it's pursued, applied, and shared. Many men stop chasing it the moment they leave the structure of school, as if a diploma marks the end of growth instead of the beginning. But real success—real fulfillment—belongs to the man who keeps asking questions, seeking wisdom, and evolving through life's lessons.

A man who stops learning is a man who stops growing. Every unanswered question is a locked door. Every ignored curiosity is a path not taken. Today, we live in an age where knowledge is more accessible than ever—yet many of us settle for summaries, sound bites, and surface-level understanding.

We scroll. We consume. But we rarely *study*.

We must shift from passive consumption to intentional learning. Great men develop the habit of questioning assumptions, challenging their own beliefs, and stretching beyond what's comfortable. Growth begins the moment curiosity becomes a discipline.

One of the most overlooked forms of knowledge is found in the art of listening.

Too many men hear only to respond. They prepare arguments instead of absorbing wisdom. But real learning happens when we listen to understand, not to compete.

Conversations are not battlegrounds. They are training grounds for growth.

Listening sharpens the mind, deepens empathy, and expands perspective. Whether you're sitting with a scholar, a mentor, or a brother who's walked a different path—listen. There is wisdom everywhere, but it only reveals itself to the attentive.

In a world dominated by technology, superficial content, and distraction, a man who learns with intention stands out. He becomes adaptable, emotionally intelligent, and unshakable. That's not just intellect—that's leadership.

But knowledge alone is never enough.

You can fill a library with facts and still remain unchanged. True growth happens when knowledge transforms into wisdom through action.

A man who hoards knowledge but doesn't use it is like a warrior who collects weapons but never trains for war. Knowledge must be lived to become real.

THE CYCLE OF MASTERY: LEARN. APPLY. TEACH.

The fastest way to grow is to share what you know. When you teach, you reinforce your understanding. You create ripple effects that stretch beyond your life—into your family, your friendships, your community.

Ask anyone who knows me—they'll tell you I always have a book in my hand.

Much of this book was born through years of reading, researching, reflecting, and applying. At times, it felt like I was building my own PhD in character, faith, and psychology. And I'm still learning—every single day.

I urge you: Find teachers. Find mentors. Sit in the circle. Listen to the wisdom of men who have lived what you're trying to learn. Devour books. Watch lectures. Absorb podcasts. But don't stop there—*live* the knowledge.

Today, "knowledge" often comes dressed in virality—clickbait, reels, sixty-second sermons. But real learning is not about hype. It's about depth.

Social media influencers can entertain. But they are not always your best teachers.

A man of depth seeks wisdom from those who have walked through fire—those who've suffered, succeeded, and stood the test of time. Whether in faith, fitness, finance, or family, find the people who have lived it—and learn from them.

Be cautious about who and what you learn from. Not all wells offer clean water. Misinformation and half-truths can corrupt even the most sincere seeker.

Like a man lost in the desert, you must discern what is pure and what is poison.

Vet your sources. Is the person you're learning from wise—or just popular? Are their words rooted in truth—or ego? Real knowledge is often quiet, humble, and hard-earned. Seek it relentlessly and guard your mind carefully.

KNOWLEDGE WITHOUT ACTION IS NOTHING

Reading is not enough. Listening is not enough. Knowing is not enough.

You must *do* something with what you've learned. Apply it. Reflect on it. Share it.

Wisdom is tested in real life—in your relationships, in your routines, in how you respond under pressure.

A man who learns but never acts will stay stuck. But a man who learns, applies, and teaches becomes a source of change—both for himself and for the world around him.

NEVER STOP ASKING

Growth begins with a single question. And it never ends.

Every answer opens a new door. Every insight reveals a new challenge. That's the beauty of the learning journey—it's infinite.

So keep reading. Keep seeking. Keep showing up for the lessons life is trying to teach you.

But don't learn for yourself alone. Mentor others. Share your insights. Help someone else avoid the pitfalls you've already seen.

When you teach, you grow. When you uplift, you rise. When you share knowledge, you multiply its power.

A man who's committed to learning is a man committed to mastery—of his mind, his character, and his future. Knowledge is not about impressing others. It's about improving yourself.

So stay hungry.

Keep asking.

Keep growing.

And most importantly—use what you know to make others better. That's real wisdom.

CHAPTER 31

DIG YOUR TRENCH

THERE'S A SAYING: *WHAT DOESN'T KILL YOU MAKES YOU STRONGER.* It's easy to dismiss as cliché—until life tests you. Because when it does, you realize that adversity, when met with discipline and faith, becomes the fire that forges strength. It doesn't just shape you—it reveals you.

Resilience isn't about having an easy life. It's about building the internal armor to stand firm when everything else crumbles.

Throughout history and scripture, the most revered men were not those who avoided hardship, but those who turned hardship into fuel. They didn't just endure—they emerged stronger, wiser, and more purposeful.

Look to the prophets: men chosen by God, not despite their struggles, but because of their ability to stand tall through them.

- **Prophet Muhammad (PBUH)** faced unimaginable trials: the loss of his beloved wife Khadijah, his protector Abu Talib, public humiliation, persecution, exile. Yet his mission never wavered. Through every storm, he held the line. His resilience changed the course of history.
- **Prophet Moses (PBUH)**, abandoned as an infant, raised in the house of a tyrant, and tasked with leading a stubborn people through the

desert, still carried out his mission with determination and trust in God.
- **Prophet Yusuf (PBUH)** was betrayed by his own blood, thrown into a well, sold into slavery, falsely accused, and imprisoned for years. But through every phase, he kept his faith. And in time, he rose to a position of immense influence—using his wisdom to save an entire nation.

These men didn't crumble in the face of hardship. They built their trench.

The same principle holds true today. One of the greatest examples of modern resilience is Abraham Lincoln. Born into poverty. Rejected countless times. Crushed by personal and political failures. But through it all, he pressed on. His setbacks became stepping stones. His trials became teachers. And in the end, he became the man who would unify a divided nation.

Resilience doesn't require a perfect past. It requires relentless forward motion.

THE SCIENCE BEHIND RESILIENCE

This isn't just spiritual wisdom—it's backed by science.

- **Optimism strengthens the heart.** A study from the University of Illinois found that optimists are 73 percent less likely to develop heart disease.[8]
- **Positive thinking improves emotional regulation.** It buffers the nervous system against the wear and tear of stress.
- **Connection enhances resilience.** According to the American Psychological Association, having even one meaningful relationship significantly boosts your ability to recover from hardship.[9]

---

[8] Sharita Forrest, "Optimistic People Have Healthier Hearts, Study Finds," University of Illinois Urbana-Champaign, January 8, 2015, https://news.illinois.edu/optimistic-people-have-healthier-hearts-study-finds/.

[9] "Building Your Resilience," American Psychological Association, accessed June 23, 2025, https://www.apa.org/topics/resilience/building-your-resilience.

Resilience thrives in community, routine, and meaning. It is a discipline as much as a mindset.

One of the greatest metaphors for resilience is found in the Battle of the Trench. Faced with an overwhelming enemy force, the Prophet Muhammad (PBUH) and the believers didn't rely on strength alone. They turned to strategy. They dug a trench—a defensive barrier that defied conventional tactics.

But more than a physical structure, the trench was a symbol: of unity, preparation, foresight, and most importantly, *faith*.

The Muslims of Medina weren't the strongest. They were the most disciplined. And that made all the difference.

Today, our battles aren't fought with swords and shields—but with temptation, distraction, ego, and fear.

Your trench is not dug with shovels. It's built from habits, values, and actions.

- Waking up early to pray and reflect: **That's a trench.**
- Saying no to distractions that waste your time and energy: **That's a trench.**
- Training your body, nourishing your mind, serving your family: **Each action deepens your trench.**
- Seeking knowledge, staying humble, mentoring others: **That's a fortress of character.**

The trench is discipline in motion. It is built quietly but stands strong in the storm.

ANTICIPATE LIFE'S AMBUSHES

Every stage of life brings new challenges:

- Youth brings impulsiveness.
- Adulthood brings pressure.
- Aging brings uncertainty.

Each phase has its own form of temptation—its own test. Your job is to build your trench *before* the storm hits.

Among the most dangerous threats? **Ego.**

Ego is the internal enemy. It waits for fatigue, stress, and pride to creep in. Like the enemies surrounding Medina, it seeks a weak spot. And when it finds one, it pushes through.

Your defense? **Humility. Reflection. Sincere worship.**

To dig your trench is to train on three levels:

- **Spiritually:** through prayer, fasting, and trust in God's decree.
- **Mentally:** through learning, journaling, and self-awareness.
- **Physically:** through movement, rest, and disciplined health.

This isn't about perfection—it's about preparation. You build strength *before* the test so you're ready *during* it.

The Prophet (PBUH) and his companions didn't wait for battle to begin preparing. They dug their trench long before the enemy arrived.

That's your mission.

Each day, you build—one prayer, one workout, one page, one act of service at a time.

And when life hits—and it will—you'll be ready.

Not because you were lucky. But because you were disciplined. Because you chose preparation over passivity. Purpose over comfort. Faith over fear.

Dig your trench.

Every day.

CHAPTER 32

DISCIPLINE/SELF CONTROL

MASTERING YOURSELF IS ONE OF THE HIGHEST ACHIEVEMENTS A man can pursue. It's not just about resisting temptations or checking boxes on a moral scorecard. It's about aligning your thoughts, actions, and habits with a greater mission—choosing to live intentionally rather than impulsively.

Self-mastery is what turns raw emotion into focused energy. It transforms base desires into building blocks for something greater. It's the difference between living passively and leading with purpose.

The process of mastering oneself is like forging steel—intense, painful, necessary. It takes heat, pressure, and repetition. It's not convenient. It's not comfortable. But it's what makes you unbreakable.

Self-mastery means choosing discipline over indulgence. Patience over haste. Strategy over impulse. It's the daily decision to live for what matters most, not just for what feels good in the moment.

The rewards? Clarity. Confidence. Consistency. Fulfillment. And a strength that others can lean on when life gets heavy.

You can't master what you don't understand.

Desires are not your enemy; they're part of being human. The problem arises when they lead you instead of serving you.

Take ambition. When rooted in values, it builds empires. But when hijacked by greed, it destroys them. Self-mastery is about channeling every desire—whether it's for success, pleasure, or recognition—toward meaningful outcomes. You don't kill your desires. You train them.

Mastery means knowing what drives you, and using that awareness to steer, not crash.

When a man has mastered himself, you can feel it. He moves with intention. He speaks with clarity. He doesn't react—he responds. His presence calms storms.

Self-mastery radiates. It earns trust, commands respect, and builds legacy. A man anchored in discipline becomes a source of strength for his family, his community, and everyone in his orbit.

When your actions are led by principle rather than pressure, you don't just win privately—you elevate others publicly.

At the center of all self-mastery is discipline.

Without it, dreams remain fantasies and potential stays buried. Discipline turns vision into action, action into habits, and habits into identity.

Discipline keeps you consistent when motivation fades. It shields you from distraction and gives you the stamina to finish what you start.

Building discipline isn't about radical transformation overnight. It's about compounding small victories.

- Wake up early.
- Say no when it matters.
- Stick to your word.
- Train your body.
- Guard your tongue.
- Do what's right—especially when no one's watching.

These small wins stack. And over time, they build the foundation of a man who is immovable.

The great scholars of our tradition knew this well.

Imam Al-Ghazali and Ibn al-Qayyim taught that discipline isn't just a means to success—it's the gateway to purification and divine proximity.

In Islam, daily rituals like prayer, fasting, and charity are not only acts of worship. They are exercises in self-restraint. They train the soul to lead the body.

> As for the one who feared the position of his Lord and restrained the soul from lower desires—then indeed, Paradise will be his refuge. (Qur'an 79:40–41)

Discipline is spiritual armor. It protects you from ego, impulsiveness, and self-sabotage. It connects you to your Creator and roots you in your purpose.

The goal of self-mastery is not self-absorption. It's contribution.

The stronger you become, the more others can rely on you. When you take control of your inner world, you free up the energy to lead, love, and lift those around you.

You become the father who is present.

The friend who is loyal.

The leader who inspires.

The husband who honors.

The believer who stands firm.

Self-mastery isn't just about you. It's about what flows from you.

CHAPTER 33

DIVORCE SOCIAL MEDIA

TODAY, ENDLESS SCROLLING HAS BECOME SECOND NATURE. AND in the process, men are quietly surrendering one of their most valuable assets: their focus.

The modern battlefield isn't fought with swords and shields—it's waged through notifications, dopamine loops, and algorithms designed to hijack your mind. And without even realizing it, we've laid down our armor.

Look around. How many men are missing real moments, deep conversations, and life-changing insights—all while hypnotized by a glowing screen?

Connection to God, physical health, family time, intellectual growth—all of it fades into the background as we trade hours of meaning for seconds of distraction.

Social media is packaged as a tool for connection, creativity, and expression. But when unchecked, it becomes a quiet predator—preying on attention, fueling envy, and draining purpose.

We're shown altered bodies, extravagant lifestyles, and highlight reels posing as reality. Over time, we begin to equate happiness with likes, worth with followers, and purpose with virtual validation. We don't just watch other people live—we begin to live *for* them.

Desires blur. Intentions twist. And before we know it, we're scrolling through someone else's life while ignoring our own.

Four years ago, I walked away from social media.

What started as creative expression had devolved into a desperate chase for attention. I traveled to show off. Ate fancy meals for the photo, not the experience. Bought watches, clothes, and cars, not for meaning—but for approval.

Even my charity work—something meant to be sincere—was tainted by the desire to be seen. My life was performative. I was consumed.

When I finally stepped away, it was like waking up. The mask came off. My mind cleared. I started living *for God and myself*—not for a feed or an audience.

In the time I regained—two to three hours a day—I wrote this book, built programs to serve others, strengthened my relationship with God, and became present with my family.

I wasn't just free from social media—I was finally *free*.

According to Common Sense Media, teens spend an average of **nine hours a day** online.[10] In addition, the Pew Research Center on a 2024 study for Teens, Social Media & Technology found that **46 % say they are online "almost constantly."** That means 1 in 2 adolescents are constantly engaged with social media and the internet, leading to a massive disconnect from reality and society. That's a full-time job. And for what?

Viral memes. Reaction videos. Momentary laughs.

Now imagine what could be done with those hours:

- A degree earned
- A business launched
- A body transformed
- A relationship healed
- A book written
- A faith strengthened

---

10 Vicky Rideout and Michael B. Robb, "The Common Sense Census: Media Use by Tweens and Teens," Common Sense Media (2015).

It's not about demonizing technology. Social media has its benefits: it connects, informs, and inspires when used intentionally. But when left unchecked, it deteriorates focus, breeds insecurity, and fragments the soul.

Research from the University of Pennsylvania found that limiting social media use to just **thirty minutes per day** significantly reduces anxiety, depression, and loneliness.

The dopamine hits from likes and notifications are addictive—but they are empty calories for the soul. They leave you hungry for more, but never truly full.

And as misinformation, outrage, and division go viral, trust erodes. Attention spans shrink. People become more reactive, less reflective.

Social media has become a stage for constant performance. Everyone is trying to look more successful, more attractive, more *something* than the next person. And in the process, authenticity dies.

But a "like" is not love. A "share" is not self-worth. A "follower" is not a friend.

You are not your digital persona.

Real value comes from your character, your impact, your faith—not your online presence.

The goal isn't to renounce technology but to master it. Use it intentionally. Draw boundaries. Reclaim control.

Here's how:

- **Set intentions.** Before opening an app, ask: *Why am I here?* If the answer isn't meaningful, log off.
- **Limit your time.** Use tools to track and cap screen time. Try thirty-minute daily limits and use the regained hours to invest in real life.
- **Curate your feed.** Follow those who educate, uplift, and inspire. Mute or unfollow anything that stirs envy, anger, or aimlessness.
- **Engage more offline.** Talk without documenting. Laugh without recording. Be present. Let moments belong to you, not the algorithm.
- **Create before you consume.** Build. Write. Think. Move. Give. Use your energy to create a meaningful life, not just to consume others'.

- **Practice digital detoxes.** Weekly or monthly breaks help reset your nervous system, refocus your goals, and restore your peace.

Your phone is both a tool and a trap.

It connects—but it also distracts. It informs—but it also numbs. It's the most powerful invention of our time—and one of the most dangerous.

The constant pings, beeps, and vibrations pull you away from presence. They inflate your ego, distort your reality, and demand your validation.

But here's the truth: You don't owe the world your every thought, meal, or moment.

Some things are sacred. Keep them that way.

If you want to be a man of discipline, you must control your inputs.

If you want to be a man of peace, you must protect your focus.

If you want to be a man of God, you must be still enough to hear Him.

Here's how to start:

- **Pause before picking up your phone.** Ask: *Am I reaching out of boredom or purpose?*
- **Create tech-free zones.** Dinner. Mornings. Time with family.
- **Protect your sleep.** No phones in bed. Let your mind truly rest.
- **Prioritize in-person connection.** Screens will never replace souls.
- **Spend time with God.** Unplug to reconnect with the One who gave you time to begin with.

A man of character isn't mastered by a device. He masters himself.

He's intentional, focused, and present. He knows the difference between being informed and being consumed.

The digital age doesn't require our surrender. It demands our wisdom.

So use technology—but don't let it use you.

Live your life not for validation but for *value*.

Build offline. Serve others. Strengthen your soul. And embrace the real world—the one with eternal meaning, lasting joy, and limitless depth.

That's where the man you're meant to be is waiting.

CHAPTER 34

THE MIRROR GENERATION

IN THE ANCIENT TALE OF NARCISSUS, A YOUNG MAN BECOMES SO captivated by his own reflection that he loses himself—literally. Enchanted by the image in the water, he stares endlessly, unable to look away, until he withers beside the pool that mirrored his vanity. His story isn't just myth—it's a warning.

Today, we too stand at the edge of a metaphorical pond.

But instead of water, we gaze into screens. Social media feeds, selfie cameras, curated online personas—these are our modern mirrors. We craft images for approval, polish identities for attention, and in doing so, we risk losing something far more valuable: our sense of self.

Welcome to the Mirror Generation, where self-worth is often measured by digital applause, and appearance is elevated above essence.

Caring for your health, appearance, and presentation isn't wrong. In fact, it's a reflection of self-respect. But when external image becomes the priority—when validation becomes the goal—we drift into dangerous territory.

The pursuit of likes can quietly replace the pursuit of virtue.

We begin to live *for* our reflection instead of *from* our values. We exchange authenticity for approval, attention for meaning, and appearance for depth.

But what if we reversed the lens?

What if we gave as much energy to inner reflection as we do to image? What if we trained our minds the way we train our bodies? What if we measured success not in followers but in how faithfully we live our principles?

FROM SELF-IMAGE TO SELF-AWARENESS

True growth starts when we shift our focus inward. The following practices can help realign your relationship with the mirror:

1. **Pause with purpose.** Before snapping a selfie or sharing a post, ask: Why am I doing this? Is this about connection—or validation? Am I capturing a moment—or performing one? This single pause can bring clarity and intention to your actions.
2. **Reclaim the mirror.** Each morning, when you face the mirror, go beyond the surface. Acknowledge a strength of character, a positive habit, or a recent act of integrity. Let your reflection remind you not only of what you look like but who you're becoming.

When you align your inner and outer lives, a powerful transformation happens.

You stop living to be seen—and start living to make a difference. You no longer seek attention—you give it. You become grounded in values rather than lost in impressions. And that groundedness radiates. It uplifts your relationships. It strengthens your leadership. It inspires others to reflect inward, too.

Authenticity isn't loud. It's steady. And it's magnetic.

THE REAL MIRROR IS WITHIN

The key is not to reject the mirror—but to redefine what it reflects.

The reflection that truly matters isn't found in glass or on a screen.

It's the one etched into your character. Shaped by your faith. Revealed in your patience, your honesty, your generosity, and your courage.

> Indeed, Allah does not look at your appearance or wealth, but He looks at your hearts and deeds. (Prophet Muhammad [PBUH], Sahih Muslim)

When you live from this truth, your image becomes a by-product—not a priority. You stop chasing a highlight reel and start building a legacy.

Narcissus teaches us what happens when we fall in love with the image of ourselves instead of the substance. His story reminds us to look past the surface—and into the soul.

Greatness is not found in filters or followers. It's found in how you show up when no one is watching. In how you treat the unseen. In the way you elevate others, even when there's no applause.

True greatness begins when you stop asking, *How do I appear?* and start asking, *What am I becoming?*

So the next time you look in the mirror, don't just check your appearance.

Check your alignment.

Ask yourself:

- Am I chasing attention or living with intention?
- Am I reflecting what I value—or what the world wants to see?
- Am I growing in private—or just performing in public?

The reflection that matters most is the one shaped by purpose, faith, and character. That's the one that lasts. That's the one that leads.

That's the one worth showing to the world.

CHAPTER 35

HANDLING DIVORCE AND BREAKUPS

DIVORCE AND BREAKUPS CAST LONG SHADOWS ACROSS OUR SOCIety. They disrupt families, shatter plans, and leave emotional wreckage in their wake. For many men, it's more than just a legal or financial ordeal—it's a soul-shaking, identity-altering experience.

I know this journey firsthand.

I got married in my early twenties—young, hopeful, full of vision. But that dream collapsed. Divorce didn't just break my heart. It broke *me*. The pain of losing someone I loved deeply—someone I once envisioned forever with—was unlike anything I had known. It felt like drowning in silence. And like many men, I didn't know how to grieve it out loud.

But that pain became a mirror.

It forced me to confront my own shortcomings. To admit where I had failed as a communicator, a partner, and a man. It stripped away the ego and exposed the parts of me that needed work. And through that darkness, I found my way back to God.

Indeed, with hardship comes ease. (Qur'an 94:6)

That verse became my anchor.

It wasn't easy. Healing never is. Some days, it took everything in me just to resist collapsing into bitterness. But I refused to let the pain define me. I chose to let it *refine* me.

Breakups are often seen as failure. But in truth, they're invitations. To rebuild. To examine. To evolve.

Yes, I had to sit with my flaws. But I also learned to develop emotional intelligence, patience, and maturity. I began to redefine what it meant to be a man in a relationship—not just to *love*, but to *lead with love*. To serve. To communicate. To build something that could actually last.

For a while, I was completely antimarriage. I wanted nothing to do with vulnerability again. But deep inside, I knew that marriage was part of my faith. Part of my path to becoming the man I aspired to be. And through prayer, reflection, and surrender to God, I found the courage to try again.

This time, God gifted me a woman of grace, patience, and unwavering character. And though the fear of failure lingered, I chose trust. Not just in her—but in His plan.

He carried me through once. He would carry me through again.

Divorce and heartbreak often come with deep shame, especially for men. Society teaches us to stay stoic, to suppress, to "man up." But silence can be deadly.

According to the National Institute for Healthcare Research, divorced men are **39 percent more likely to commit suicide** than their married counterparts.[11] That statistic isn't about weakness. It's about the crushing isolation men often face when they're emotionally wounded, but too conditioned to reach for help.

And beyond the emotional toll, there's the financial stress—alimony, child support, legal battles. The US Census Bureau reported that in 2019, only 43.5 percent of custodial parents received the full child support owed.[12] That pressure can feel like being trapped with no way out.

---

11 Justin T. Denney, Richard G. Rogers, Patrick M. Krueger, and Tim Wadsworth, "Adult Suicide Mortality in the United States: Marital Status, Family, and the Role of Socioeconomic Status," *Demography* 46(4) (2009): 805–825, https://doi.org/10.1353/dem.0.0071.

12 Timothy Grall, "Custodial Mothers and Fathers and Their Child Support: 2015," (P60–262) (So u2018), https://www.census.gov/content/dam/Census/library/publications/2020/demo/p60-262.pdf.

But here's the truth:
You're not broken. You're being rebuilt.
There is a way forward—and it starts with intentional healing:

- **Faith first.** Prayer, Qur'an, and spiritual grounding give your pain purpose. The Prophet Muhammad (PBUH) endured the loss of his beloved wife Khadijah yet remained steadfast. His resilience reminds us that pain is not punishment—it's preparation.
- **Train the body, sharpen the mind.** Fitness isn't just physical—it's therapy. The discipline of training builds confidence and quiets the mind. When your body becomes stronger, so does your spirit.
- **Grow in emotional intelligence.** Many relationships collapse not from lack of love but lack of understanding. Study yourself. Learn to express, not explode. Practice patience, listen with empathy, and speak with clarity.
- **Rediscover your mission.** Redirect the emotional energy into your goals. Build something. Grow something. Serve someone. Let your heartbreak fuel your highest calling.
- **Lean into brotherhood.** Isolation breeds weakness. Healing happens faster in the company of men who challenge and uplift you. Surround yourself with brothers who won't let you settle or spiral.

PREPARE FOR WHAT'S NEXT

Healing isn't just about recovery—it's about preparation.

You don't want to repeat the same patterns. You want to build a love that lasts. Like a garden, relationships need constant care: communication, intention, patience.

Islam commands us:

And live with them in kindness. (Surah An-Nisa, 4:19)

Modern research backs this. Dr. John Gottman, one of the world's foremost relationship experts, found that emotional intelligence, not romance, is the greatest predictor of relationship success.[13]

So here are a few intentional habits to build a better relationship next time:

- Show affection through consistent, thoughtful gestures.
- Listen—not just to words, but to emotions.
- Celebrate her wins. Be her biggest cheerleader.
- Express gratitude. It strengthens connection.
- Take ownership of your flaws. Growth is attractive.
- Prioritize quality time. It's not just what you do—it's who you become while doing it.

Heartbreak hurts. But it also teaches.

It taught me that growth doesn't happen in comfort—it happens in chaos. That God doesn't waste pain—He repurposes it. That the version of you who emerges from loss can be wiser, stronger, and more aligned with who you're meant to be.

Your story isn't over.

The failed relationship wasn't the end. It was a redirection. A refinement. A reminder.

You are not your mistakes. You are not your divorce. You are not your darkest day.

You are who you choose to become after the fall.

No matter how deep the hurt or how heavy the burden, faith, discipline, and brotherhood will carry you forward. Turn to God. Strengthen your mind. Sharpen your character. Surround yourself with people who remind you of your worth.

Your past pain is not your prison—it's your preparation.

Your best days are not behind you.

They're ahead of you—waiting for the man you're becoming to claim them.

---

[13] John M. Gottman, and Nan Silver, *The Seven Principles for Making Marriage Work* (Harmony Books, 1999).

CHAPTER 36

THE ART OF DOING NOTHING

IN TODAY'S WORLD, BOREDOM, STILLNESS, AND FREE TIME ARE treated like flaws—signs of laziness, inefficiency, or wasted potential. We are conditioned to fill every minute, to move faster, to *do* more.

But in this obsession with activity, we've forgotten how to *be*.

Reframing boredom and free time is essential for mastering the mind. The man who can sit in silence without reaching for distraction is a man who has command over himself. He is not owned by urgency, nor enslaved by stimulation. He is grounded.

Boredom is often misunderstood. It's not a void—it's a space. A doorway. One that leads to creativity, insight, and personal evolution.

Psychologists and neuroscientists have found that boredom, rather than being a passive or negative state, is a launchpad for original thought. A 2024 study in National Geographic proved it: Participants who first engaged in a monotonous, boring task performed significantly better on a creative challenge than those who jumped in immediately.[14] When

---

14 Sandi Mann and Rebekah Cadman, "Does Being Bored Make Us More Creative?" University of Central Lancashire (2013), https://clok.uclan.ac.uk/22263.

the mind is free to wander, it starts making unexpected connections. That's where breakthroughs happen.

Instead of running from boredom, *enter it*. It's in those quiet, idle moments that ideas are born. Solutions surface. Visions expand.

Creativity isn't exclusive to artists. It's essential for innovators, leaders, builders—any man who wants to shape, solve, or elevate. Boredom is not the enemy. It's the training ground.

French philosopher Blaise Pascal once wrote, "All of humanity's problems stem from man's inability to sit quietly in a room alone."

Stillness is uncomfortable because it confronts us with ourselves. That's why so many people run from it—into noise, distraction, addiction, or endless entertainment.

But the man who seeks greatness *doesn't run from himself*. He meets his thoughts. He asks the hard questions:

Who am I?

What do I believe?

Am I living in alignment with my values?

Silence exposes what we often bury. But it also reveals what we most need to face. That's not weakness—it's wisdom.

In a culture that worships busyness, free time is often dismissed as unproductive. But used with intention, it becomes one of the most powerful forces for growth.

A 2021 study in Frontier in Psychology found that individuals who regularly engaged in meaningful hobbies had higher psychological well-being and a stronger sense of agency in their lives.[15]

Free time is not about escaping responsibility. It's about *alignment*—with your priorities, your values, and your mission. What you choose to do when no one is watching defines who you're becoming.

Reading. Training. Learning a new skill. Reflecting. Creating. Time spent here compounds into strength.

A man who wastes his free time weakens his edge.

---

[15] Kathleen Morse, et al., "Creativity and Leisure During COVID-19: Examining the Relationship Between Leisure Activities, Motivations, and Psychological Well-Being," *Frontiers in Psychology*, 12 (2021): doi: 10.3389/fpsyg.2021.609967.

A man who uses it wisely becomes unstoppable.

The Dutch call it *niksen*: the art of doing nothing. In a world obsessed with productivity, choosing stillness is an act of rebellion—and recovery.

Niksen isn't laziness. It's presence. It's a deliberate step back to restore mental clarity, emotional balance, and creative energy. And it's supported by science: Deliberate mental rest improves focus, reduces anxiety, and enhances performance.

This isn't new wisdom. Islam encourages Tafakkur: deep contemplation. Many of history's greatest thinkers, prophets, and warriors sought solitude. They knew:

The greatest insights are not born in noise.

They are born in stillness.

By embracing boredom, cherishing free time, and practicing intentional stillness, you're not falling behind—you're forging depth. These moments of pause are not wasted time. They are foundations for:

- **Heightened creativity:** The wandering mind solves problems structured thought cannot.
- **Greater self-awareness:** In silence, you meet the real you.
- **Replenished energy:** Stillness is fuel. It restores what noise depletes.
- **Purpose-driven living:** Free time used intentionally aligns action with meaning.

The next time you feel the itch to scroll, to fill the quiet, to escape boredom—*pause*. Resist the urge. Let your mind be free. Let your soul catch up.

Stillness won't make you soft. It will make you sharp.

This is where depth is built. Where creativity is sparked. Where clarity is born. And where you begin to rise—not by doing more, but by *becoming more*.

Don't fear the quiet. Step into it.

The man you're meant to be is not found in the noise.

He's waiting for you in the silence.

CHAPTER 37

REMEMBER YOU WILL DIE

"Remember that you are but dust, and to dust you shall return."
—THE QUR'AN 20:55

Thinking about death may feel grim at first. Unsettling. Morbid. But few practices offer greater clarity, purpose, and perspective.

The modern world urges us to ignore mortality. Instead, it tells us to chase pleasure, accumulate wealth, and seek status—*as if we are invincible, as if we will live forever.*

But the wise man doesn't run from this truth. He faces it. He lets it humble him, shape him, and sharpen him into someone who lives with intention.

Across cultures and belief systems, reflecting on mortality is not a practice of despair, but of transformation.

- In Islam, we are taught that this life is a fleeting test before the eternal reality of the Hereafter. Thinking about death pulls us out of distraction and back into alignment—with faith, with values, with what truly matters.
- Stoics embraced death not to dread it, but to *live better because of*

it. Marcus Aurelius wrote, "You could leave life right now. Let that determine what you do and say and think."
- Christianity emphasizes preparing for eternity. Saint Benedict advised, "Keep death daily before your eyes." (RB 4:47) Not to provoke fear, but to inspire virtue.

Across these worldviews, death is not the end of life's meaning—it is the lens that reveals it.

In my own life, I remind myself of death through a simple practice: I lie beneath the earth or submerge underwater and reflect on the three questions every soul will be asked in the grave:

- Who is your Lord?
- What is your book?
- Who is your prophet?

This reflection is not about fear—it's about readiness. It's a way to examine my heart, my actions, and my direction. It reminds me that this life is short, but the next life is forever.

LET MORTALITY REFINE YOU

When we forget death, we become careless—chasing vanity, consumed by ego, addicted to status.

But remembering death grounds us. It makes us honest. It forces us to ask:

- Am I living with integrity?
- Am I treating people with compassion?
- Am I aligned with the purpose I was created for?

Three things follow a deceased person: his family, his wealth, and his deeds. Two of them return, and one remains—his deeds. (Prophet Muhammad [PBUH], Sahih al-Bukhari 6514)

When everything else is stripped away, what will be left standing?

DEATH CREATES URGENCY

Accepting the brevity of life changes how we use our time. We stop wasting it on arguments, shallow pursuits, or meaningless distractions. We stop tolerating what drains us. We start investing in what builds us.

A man who remembers his mortality:

- **Loves without hesitation** and **forgives without pride**.
- **Pursues his mission** with focus, because he knows time is scarce.
- **Serves others** with humility, because he understands legacy is built through impact.
- **Trains his mind, body, and soul**, not for show, but for the journey that lies ahead.

He lives every day with a question at the forefront: If today were my last, would I be ready to meet my Creator?

Ironically, thinking about death doesn't rob life of its joy—it multiplies it.

It doesn't paralyze us with fear. It sets us free from what doesn't matter.

Epicurus once said, "When we are, death is not. And when death is, we are not."

His point wasn't denial—it was freedom. If you stop fearing death, you start living fully.

That's why the concept of *memento mori*—remember you will die—has lasted for centuries. It reminds us that the clock is ticking, not to terrify us, but to wake us up.

The world may teach you to chase what fades. But death reminds you to build what lasts.

Not wealth—but *character*.

Not image—but *impact*.

Not comfort—but *conviction*.

You will not take your followers, bank account, or résumé with you into the grave. You will take your actions. Your intentions. Your service. Your faith.

Contemplating death doesn't diminish life. It amplifies it.

So the question is not *if* death is coming—it is.

The question is not *when*—none of us know.

The question is: **Are you living in a way that prepares you for it?**

Because the man who remembers his mortality lives with urgency, leads with humility, and loves with depth. And when the final moment comes, he will meet it not with fear—but with faith.

Contemplate on this question: If I had one week left to live, what would I do differently today?

CHAPTER 38
―

THE HEALING POWER OF NATURE

THE SIMPLE ACT OF STEPPING OUTSIDE—OF BREATHING IN FRESH air, standing under open sky, and feeling the earth beneath your feet—can restore you in ways no screen, supplement, or stimulant ever could.

In a world dominated by concrete, notifications, and artificial light, nature remains one of the most overlooked yet powerful tools for healing the mind, strengthening the body, and nourishing the soul.

For my wife and me, spending at least an hour in nature each day has become more than a habit—it's a sacred ritual. Away from digital noise, we walk, reflect, and simply *be*. The warmth of the sun, the texture of soil, the rhythm of wind—they reconnect us to the elements from which we were created.

This isn't about leisure. It's about alignment.

Nature reminds us who we are: not machines built for endless output, but human beings—organic, dynamic, and deeply spiritual.

Far from being just a poetic escape, time in nature has measurable, profound effects on health:

1. **Strengthens immunity.** Trees and plants release phytoncides, natural compounds that enhance the activity of natural killer (NK)

cells—critical defenders against viruses and cancer. A 2010 study in *Environmental Health and Preventive Medicine* found that "forest bathing" (Shinrin-yoku) significantly boosted immune function simply by breathing forest air.[16]
2. **Boosts physical fitness.** Nature invites movement—whether it's walking, hiking, or biking. These natural motions enhance cardiovascular health, endurance, and agility. A 2015 Stanford study found that walking in natural environments reduced disease risk and improved overall well-being.[17] It's not just about aesthetics—it's biology.
3. **Delivers vital nutrients.** Sunlight stimulates the production of vitamin D, essential for bone strength, immune function, and mood regulation. Our bodies were designed to thrive under natural light, just as our spirits thrive in its metaphorical warmth.

The stillness of nature is a powerful antidote to modern stress.

The rustle of leaves, the rush of a stream, the vastness of a horizon—all lower cortisol levels, the body's primary stress hormone. They quiet the mind, slow the breath, and anchor us in the present.

Overwhelmed or mentally fatigued? Nature offers more than rest—it rewires the brain.

A 2012 study by Atchley and Strayer showed that participants who disconnected from technology and immersed themselves in nature for four days experienced a **50 percent boost in creative problem-solving**.[18]

Even brief exposure to green spaces has been shown to improve **focus**, **clarity**, and **cognitive function**—echoing the *attention restoration theory*, which suggests that natural environments help reset the brain's ability to concentrate and process.

---

16 Q Li, et al., "A Forest Bathing Trip Increases Human Natural Killer Activity and Expression of Anti-Cancer Proteins in Female Subjects," *Environmental Health and Preventive Medicine* 22(1) (2010): 45–55, https://pubmed.ncbi.nlm.nih.gov/18394317/.

17 Gregory N. Bratman, et al., "Nature Experience Reduces Rumination and Subgenual Prefrontal Cortex Activation," Proceedings of the National Academy of Sciences of the United States of America, 112(28) (2015): 8567–8572. https://doi.org/10.1073/pnas.1510459112.

18 Ruth Ann Atchley, David L. Strayer, and Paul Atchley, "Creativity in the Wild: Improving Creative Reasoning Through Immersion in Natural Settings," PLOS ONE, 7(12) (2012): e51474, https://doi.org/10.1371/journal.pone.0051474.

Biologist E.O. Wilson's biophilia hypothesis suggests that humans possess an innate need to connect with nature. But this connection runs deeper than biology.

Forests, oceans, mountains—these landscapes don't just calm us; they call us.

They remind us of creation. Of simplicity. Of the divine order woven into all living things.

Islam encourages Tafakkur—deep contemplation—and many of the Prophet's most transformative moments came in solitude with nature. Mountains, deserts, and caves weren't escapes. They were sacred spaces of awakening.

In nature, we are reminded not just of life—but of *Who gives it*.

The emerging field of ecotherapy integrates nature into mental health treatment with powerful results. A 2023 study in *Perspectives in Public Health* showed significant reductions in depression, anxiety, and stress among participants engaging in nature-based therapy.[19]

The parallels with spiritual practices are striking.

Prayer, reflection, and immersion in nature all quiet the noise. They ground the mind and guide the heart. When modern life overwhelms, creation itself becomes a sanctuary.

Health isn't confined to gyms or medicine cabinets. It also lives in sunlit trails, ocean air, and mountain silence.

To fully thrive, you must reconnect with the natural world—not as an escape from reality, but as a return to it.

How to begin:

- **Take daily walks.** Even twenty minutes in a park can reset your mood and energy.
- **Disconnect often.** Leave your phone behind. Be fully present.

---

[19] Lilly Joschko, Anna Maria Pálsdóttir, Patrik Grahn, and Maximilian Hinse, "Nature-Based Therapy in Individuals with Mental Health Disorders, with a Focus on Mental Well-Being and Connectedness to Nature—A Pilot Study," *International Journal of Environmental Research and Public Health* 20(3) (2023): 2167, https://doi.org/10.3390/ijerph20032167.

- **Explore variety.** Mountains, oceans, forests, gardens—each offers unique gifts.
- **Be still.** Let yourself *just be* in nature without trying to conquer or capture it.

Engaging with nature is not indulgence. It's *restoration*.

It realigns the body. Refocuses the mind. Reawakens the soul. In its silence, you hear your own thoughts more clearly. In its majesty, you remember your place in something far greater than yourself.

Step outside.

Let the sun touch your skin.

Let the wind remind you that you are alive.

Let the earth beneath your feet remind you of where you came from—and where you'll one day return.

And in those moments, you may find something more than health.

You may find peace.

Because in nature, we don't just find beauty.

We find balance.

We find clarity.

We find God.

LET THE CHILD IN YOU THRIVE

SOMEWHERE ALONG THE ROAD TO ADULTHOOD, MANY MEN BURY a part of themselves. They trade curiosity for caution, wonder for worry, play for productivity. They believe play is for children and that "real men" are measured by how much they carry—not how much they feel.

But in abandoning play, they lose access to one of the most potent sources of strength, creativity, and inner peace.

True mastery of the mind, body, and soul is not built on discipline alone. It also comes from rediscovering joy, spontaneity, and wonder—the forgotten power of play.

Think back to the golden hours of youth—when time moved slowly, and the world was full of mystery. When games weren't scheduled, creativity wasn't judged, and joy came easily. That part of you is still alive. It's not gone. It's just quiet, waiting for permission to reawaken.

Philosophers have long understood the sacredness of wonder. Plato said, "Wonder is the beginning of wisdom." To marvel is to awaken. To play is to explore. And to explore is to grow.

Wonder is not childish—it's *essential*. It cracks open the hardened shell of monotony and reconnects us with what it means to be human.

In *Atomic Habits*, James Clear emphasizes how profound change begins with small, consistent actions. Apply that to play. Try just a few minutes a day of unfiltered fun—sketch something ridiculous, try a goofy dance move, build something just for the thrill of creating.

Over time, joy becomes a practice, not just a reaction.

These microhabits strengthen **cognitive flexibility**, allowing you to see problems differently, think more clearly, and act more creatively.

Dr. Dacher Keltner of UC Berkeley found that moments of awe—watching a sunrise, stargazing, walking through a forest—boost happiness, empathy, and even physical health.[20] Awe is not entertainment. It's alignment. It's a spiritual experience that connects you to something bigger than yourself.

When you nurture your sense of awe, you soften your heart, sharpen your mind, and ground your soul.

PLAY IS MOVEMENT, TOO

Play doesn't belong only in the mind—it lives in the body.

Strength training, martial arts, sports, even dancing—these are physical expressions of play. When movement becomes joyful, not just mechanical, you don't just grow stronger—you become more alive.

The greatest warriors understood this. The samurai, the Spartans, and elite athletes of every generation trained with both discipline and fluidity. Their strength wasn't just in power—it was in adaptability. In creativity. In play.

Modern science confirms this: Movement-based play lowers cortisol, the body's stress hormone, while improving coordination, resilience, and adaptability. This isn't wasted time—it's deep, physical development.

Many spiritual traditions honor the purity of a childlike heart.

In Christianity, Jesus said, "Let the little children come to me…for the kingdom of God belongs to such as these." (Luke 18:16)

In Islam, children are seen as embodiments of innocence and purity.

---

20 Dacher Keltner, *Awe: The New Science of Everyday Wonder and How It Can Transform Your Life* (Penguin Press, 2023).

The Prophet Muhammad (PBUH) played with children, laughed freely, and reminded us that joy has a sacred place in a meaningful life.

This childlike energy is not immature—it's unburdened. It's free from ego, stress, and performance. And sometimes, it's in that lightness that we connect most deeply with the Divine.

The Japanese concept of ikigai—your reason for being—lies at the intersection of what you love, what you're good at, what the world needs, and what can sustain you.

Could play be the missing thread?

When you allow yourself to create without expectation, move without agenda, and laugh without restraint, you reconnect with passions that may have been buried under the weight of obligation.

Sometimes, your truest calling is hiding in the things that make you come alive.

Too often, men believe that seriousness equals significance. But joy is not weakness. Laughter is not wasteful. Fun is not foolish.

Joy is **energy**. It revitalizes the mind. It strengthens relationships. It makes discipline sustainable.

For me, play is nonnegotiable. Whether it's tossing a football at the park, playing tag with my wife, or sprinting across the yard with the dogs—I protect these moments. They anchor me. They refresh me. And they remind me that being a man doesn't mean being rigid.

It means being whole.

PRACTICAL WAYS TO REIGNITE PLAY AND WONDER

1. **Fully engage in the moment.** When's the last time you stared at clouds, watched ants work, or let yourself get lost in the sky? Carve out time for awe. Presence is the doorway to play.
2. **Embrace curiosity.** Ask more questions. Explore new hobbies. Learn about things that have nothing to do with your career. Curiosity keeps the mind young and the heart open.
3. **Seek joy in simplicity.** Return to the simple things: a walk, a silly

game, creating something with your hands. These aren't small moments; they're sacred.
4. **Cultivate playful rituals.** Incorporate joy into your weekly rhythm. Make space for activities that light you up, even if they make no sense to anyone else.

Reclaiming play isn't regression—it's evolution. It's not about reliving childhood; it's about restoring the parts of you that were never meant to be lost.

In a world that glorifies grind, play is an act of rebellion—and a return to balance.

So laugh. Explore. Move. Marvel.

Let joy shape your days, and watch how it transforms your discipline, your purpose, and your presence.

Because the man who plays freely lives fully. And in doing so, he becomes more of who he was always meant to be.

CHAPTER 39

THE SPIRITUMENTAL CRISIS

THE MENTAL HEALTH CRISIS GRIPPING WESTERN SOCIETIES IS often framed by statistics: rising rates of anxiety, depression, and dependence on medication. These figures are real and urgent—but they may only scratch the surface.

Beneath the psychological distress lies a deeper, more pervasive struggle.

It's not just a crisis of the mind. It's a crisis of the soul.

In many Western cultures, identity and happiness are built on impermanent foundations: career success, wealth, beauty, and relationships. These are blessings, but they are not built to carry the full weight of our existence. They are finite. And anything finite can be lost.

When your sense of self is anchored in what can change, you will inevitably feel unstable. Jobs end. Looks fade. Relationships evolve. Fortunes fluctuate. And when they do, many are left feeling unmoored, insecure, and hollow.

We're taught to chase the world, but never taught what to do when it fails us.

Anxiety, depression, and existential despair are often interpreted purely through the lens of biology or psychology. And while these lenses are crucial, they are incomplete.

What's often overlooked is the **spiritual dimension of suffering**—the quiet ache of disconnection from God, the source of all meaning, peace, and permanence.

When the soul is detached from its Creator, nothing in this world feels like enough.

You can achieve your goals, accumulate success, and still feel empty. Why? Because you were never meant to be fulfilled by the created. You were designed to be fulfilled by the **Creator**.

The human soul longs for the eternal. It craves meaning, direction, and connection to something unchanging.

When this longing goes unmet, it manifests in quiet despair: chronic dissatisfaction, emotional fatigue, and a persistent sense of "not enough." We try to numb it with stimulation, silence it with busyness, or mask it with performance. But nothing works for long.

You're not broken. You're homesick.

You were made to know, serve, and draw near to God. Without that anchor, your happiness becomes fragile—tied to things that were never meant to sustain it.

Reframing today's mental health crisis as a **spiritual health crisis** doesn't dismiss the need for therapy, medication, or professional support. These tools are essential, especially in severe cases.

But to stop there is to treat symptoms while ignoring the root.

When you tend to your spiritual health, you create a foundation that doesn't crumble under life's unpredictability. You begin to cultivate peace that is not dependent on circumstances. A sense of self that isn't defined by performance. A happiness that isn't held hostage by the world.

Healing begins when you realign your life with what matters most. Here are pathways to help restore your spiritual foundation:

1. **Cultivate stillness.** Engage in daily prayer or meditation. Even five minutes of intentional silence can ground your soul and quiet the noise.

2. **Serve others.** Helping others lifts your perspective. Service pulls you out of self-absorption and reconnects you with humility and purpose.
3. **Practice gratitude.** Start or end your day by naming three things you're thankful for. Gratitude shifts your focus from what's missing to what's already here.
4. **Reconnect with nature.** Step outside. Walk without your phone. Reflect on the majesty of the natural world. Nature reminds us of beauty, order, and divine design.
5. **Build a faith-based community.** Surround yourself with people who share your values and remind you of your higher purpose. Isolation feeds despair. Brotherhood fuels strength.
6. **Reflect on higher purpose.** Take time to ask life's deeper questions: Who am I? Why am I here? What impact am I meant to leave behind? The answers won't come all at once—but the search itself is transformative.

True healing doesn't just restore mental equilibrium—it brings spiritual alignment.

When we redefine well-being to include the state of the soul, we move beyond coping and toward *clarity*. We begin to live not just for survival or success, but for significance.

This shift changes everything. It teaches us to let go of what's fleeting and hold tightly to what is eternal. It invites us to anchor our worth in something unshakable: our relationship with the One who created us.

Verily, in the remembrance of God do hearts find rest. (Qur'an 13:28)

That's the kind of peace you won't find in possessions, promotions, or public applause. It's the kind that remains when everything else is gone.

The crisis of our time is not just a crisis of the nervous system. It's a crisis of the spirit.

And while therapy and medicine have their place, they are most powerful when paired with spiritual connection, purpose, and faith.

You are not just a body with a mind. You are a soul with eternal significance.

Reconnect with your Creator. Rebuild from the inside out. Let your healing begin not with distraction or numbing, but with reflection and remembrance.

Because real peace doesn't come from escaping the world. It comes from returning to the One who made you for more.

PART III

SOUL

CHAPTER 40

THE HIDDEN THREAT OF SUCCESS

ON THE PATH TO BECOMING THE MAN YOU'RE MEANT TO BE, SUCcess will test you just as much as struggle.

You start with nothing but grit, faith, and ambition. You rise early. You grind harder. You go where most men stop. Eventually, results show. People start noticing. They praise your work ethic. They admire your discipline. Respect follows. Influence builds.

And just as you're climbing highest, a quiet danger creeps in: **hubris**.

THE RISE BEFORE THE FALL

Hubris isn't ordinary pride. It's subtle. It whispers, "You've arrived." It tells you the rules no longer apply. That you're self-made. That you don't need advice, correction, or humility.

It inflates your ego, dulls your self-awareness, and distorts your judgment. Worst of all, it makes you forget.

Forget that every ounce of strength, every moment of clarity, every win you've had was not your right—it was a gift. Mercy. Provision.

History doesn't lie: *Pride always comes before the fall.*

The Greeks understood this deeply. In their myths, hubris was the downfall of great men.

- **Icarus**, who ignored his father's warning, flew too close to the sun—and plummeted.
- **King Xerxes**, drunk on power, led a vast army into ruin, believing he was untouchable.

These weren't just stories. They were signals. Lessons etched in time: *The higher you rise, the more dangerous it is to believe your own hype.*

When hubris takes the wheel, failure isn't just possible—it's *guaranteed*.

In mythology, Nemesis was the force that restored balance. She wasn't cruel; she was justice. Her role was simple: When arrogance tipped the scales, she reminded men of their limits.

She still walks among us.

- The CEO who ignores wise counsel and tanks a billion-dollar company.
- The undefeated athlete who mocks his opponent and ends up humiliated.
- The leader who believes he's untouchable—until scandal strips him bare.

Nemesis doesn't discriminate. She humbles kings and commoners alike.

This isn't just ancient myth—it's divine truth.

Arrogance was the sin that caused Satan to defy God, believing himself superior to Adam.

It was Pharaoh's pride that led him to challenge the Creator—only to be crushed by the very sea he once ruled.

> And do not walk upon the earth exultantly. Indeed, you will never tear the earth [apart], and you will never reach the mountains in height. (Qur'an 17:37)

No one who has an atom's weight of arrogance in his heart will enter Paradise. (Prophet Muhammad [PBUH], Sahih Muslim 91)

Arrogance isn't confidence—it's corruption.

And the moment you stop giving credit to the Source of your success, you start walking toward your own collapse.

Success doesn't have to lead to pride. But staying grounded requires intention.

You need more than strong muscles. You need a strong mirror.

Here's how to keep your soul in check:

1. **Stay humble.** Never forget where you started. You didn't get here alone. Behind every milestone is God's grace and the support of others. Gratitude is your anchor.
2. **Be a student for life.** The moment you think you've "arrived" is the moment you stop evolving. The wisest men keep asking questions. Stay teachable. Stay curious.
3. **Keep truth-tellers close.** Every great man needs people who love him enough to challenge him. Brothers. Mentors. Elders. Their correction isn't criticism—it's protection.
4. **Check your intentions.** Regularly ask: Am I acting from purpose—or from ego? Are my choices grounded in truth—or driven by insecurity? Self-awareness isn't soft. It's survival.
5. **Recognize the source.** You didn't choose your talents. You were entrusted with them. Your gifts are not proof of your greatness—they're reminders of His generosity.

REAL GREATNESS IS ROOTED

The higher you rise, the easier it is to forget. To start believing the applause. To mistake influence for immunity.

But you're not invincible. You're not above correction.

And the moment you start thinking you are, you're already on the way down.

Hubris doesn't shout. It flatters. It feeds your ego. It makes you deaf to feedback, blind to flaws, and numb to gratitude.

That's why you must stay anchored. Stay small before God. Stay grounded in your mission. Let your success make you softer, not louder.

Walk with confidence—but bow with humility.

Celebrate your wins—but keep reverence in your heart.

Chase greatness—but let your character grow faster than your platform.

Because in the end, the measure of a man isn't how high he climbs—It's how deeply he stays *rooted* when he gets there.

CHAPTER 41

GIVE MORE THAN YOU TAKE

WE LIVE IN A WORLD THAT GLORIFIES TAKING.

We're fed mantras like "Take what's yours" or "If you don't, someone else will." Ambition is idolized, and self-interest is repackaged as virtue. The result? A culture that equates success with accumulation—money, power, attention, things—while sidelining values like service, compassion, and humility.

But in the race for *more*, we risk losing something irreplaceable: our connection to meaning.

The more you crave, the more you take, the less satisfied you become. I've seen it in school, in the workplace, in the world—and I've seen it in myself. That insatiable pull to grab more, prove more, display more. It's a game of extraction, not contribution. Of hoarding, not sharing. And it leaves people disconnected, dissatisfied, and spiritually depleted.

This mindset—rooted in unchecked capitalism and competition—creates a world full of takers. It normalizes greed and glorifies self-advancement at the expense of community.

And yet, the most fulfilled people are not the ones who take the most. They're the ones who *give the most*.

ASK YOURSELF THE HARD QUESTION

Take a moment to pause and reflect:

- Do I give more than I take?

True fulfillment doesn't come from taking beyond what you need.
It comes from *giving*—intentionally, quietly, consistently.

History's most impactful figures—the prophets, the visionaries, the builders of nations—were givers. They weren't fueled by applause. They gave from sincerity, not strategy. They didn't serve for optics. They served for truth.

> The best charity is that which is given in secret. (Sahih al-Bukhari, Hadith 1423)

This Hadith isn't just spiritual advice. It's a blueprint for a pure heart. Because when giving is quiet, it becomes sacred. It becomes a direct transaction between you and your Creator, untouched by ego or public perception.

A spiritual mentor of mine, Ustadh Abdelrahman Murphy, once shared a powerful habit:

> For every public good deed, balance it with a private one that only God knows.

That wisdom changed me.

Now, when I close a major deal or see a return on an investment, I give a portion in quiet charity. No captions. No applause. Just gratitude—me and my Lord. I pair it with a silent prayer, reminding myself: This blessing isn't mine. It was entrusted to me.

Those moments realign me. They purify intention. They return me to center.

GIVE WHERE YOU ARE, WITH WHAT YOU HAVE

Giving isn't about grand gestures. It's about consistent sincerity.

It's in the little things:

- Covering the bill without hesitation.
- Ordering food for the group without seeking thanks.
- Sending that message, that gift, that check-in—just because.
- Smiling. Listening. Being fully present.
- Doing good when no one is watching.

The less you need to take, the more abundant your life becomes.

PRACTICAL WAYS TO LIVE AS A GIVER

AT HOME

- Take initiative.
- Do the dishes.
- Handle that task.
- Lighten someone else's load—especially when no one asks you to.

IN CONVERSATIONS

Listen to understand, not just to reply. Offer your full presence. That alone is a gift.

WITH FRIENDS AND FAMILY

Pay the tab. Show up. Send the note. Offer your time. Be the one who gives without keeping score.

IN SPIRIT

Pray for others. Forgive without being asked. Assume the best. Give people grace.

The Prophet (PBUH) taught that the most beloved acts are those done quietly and consistently. A legacy isn't built on viral gestures. It's built on quiet strength. On unseen service. On daily acts of love and integrity.

People may forget your words—but they'll never forget how you made them feel.

And if you live as a giver, that feeling you leave behind? That's your legacy.

This world measures value in transactions. But your soul doesn't.

Give without needing anything in return—not praise, not credit, not favors.

That kind of giving frees you. It anchors you in meaning. It draws you closer to God.

Prophet Muhammad (PBUH) said,

> The most perfect of believers in faith are those with the best character—and the kindest to their families. (al-Tirmidhi [1162])

That's where it starts.

Not with status. Not with power. But with how you treat the people closest to you.

Your greatness will not be measured by what you gained—but by what you gave.

So in a world that pushes you to take, **choose to give**.

Be the one who lifts the room. Who brings warmth. Who leaves light in your wake.

Because when you give with sincerity, you don't just enrich others. You reclaim your soul.

And you walk the path of the man you were always meant to become.

SELF-REFLECTION (MUHASABA)

A MAN'S GREATEST BATTLE IS NOT AGAINST THE WORLD—IT IS against himself.

True strength isn't forged in the gym or on the battlefield. It is forged in the quiet moments of brutal honesty, when a man looks in the mirror and asks:

Am I truly living by my highest values?

Without self-accountability, a man is directionless—chasing illusions of success while neglecting the foundation of his character.

This is where Muhasaba, or the practice of self-reckoning, becomes essential.

Rooted in Islamic tradition and echoed across every path of wisdom, Muhasaba is the intentional act of self-examination: a daily audit of your thoughts, choices, motives, and behavior.

It's not about guilt—it's about growth.

It's not about self-condemnation—it's about realignment.

The early Muslims knew this well. Umar ibn al-Khattab, one of the greatest leaders in history, said: Hold yourselves accountable before you are held accountable.

He understood: Self-reckoning isn't a burden. It's a privilege. It's how you sharpen your soul before the world tests your resolve.

Every great man—every true leader—shares this in common:

He holds himself to a higher standard, even when no one is watching.

Muhasaba is your internal compass. It keeps your ego in check. It exposes hidden weaknesses before they grow. It protects your character from erosion.

You train your body with discipline. You build wealth with precision. Why wouldn't you treat your soul with the same intentionality?

Self-accountability is not passive. It's not vague. It must be practiced with the same focus and consistency you apply to any area of excellence.

PRACTICAL WAYS TO DEVELOP SELF-REFLECTION

Use this six-step framework to build a daily Muhasaba routine:

1. BEGIN WITH GRATITUDE

Before examining faults, acknowledge blessings. Your breath. Your health. Your ability to change. Gratitude grounds you in humility and reminds you: This practice is not about shame—it's about honoring the gift of life.

2. REVIEW YOUR ACTIONS WITH BRUTAL HONESTY

At the end of each day, ask yourself:

- Did I act with integrity?
- Did I control my anger, my lust, my pride?
- Did I honor my word?
- Did I lead with kindness or selfishness?

This is your personal audit. No excuses. No justifications. Just truth.

3. ANALYZE YOUR MOTIVES

Why did you do what you did?

- Was your kindness sincere, or rooted in a desire to be seen?
- Did your mistakes come from ignorance—or ego?
- Were you seeking God's pleasure, or chasing validation?

Muhasaba isn't just about actions. It's about **intentions**.

4. SEEK FORGIVENESS AND MAKE AMENDS

Every day is a chance to reset.

- Ask God to forgive the wrongs no one saw.
- Ask *people* to forgive the wrongs they felt.

A real man doesn't let pride stop him from making peace. Pride is the armor of the weak. Accountability is the weapon of the strong.

5. SET CLEAR INTENTIONS FOR TOMORROW

Reflection without correction is wasted.
Set one or two goals that realign you:

- "I will respond with patience instead of irritation."
- "I will keep my phone down at dinner and be fully present."
- "I will pray with more focus."

Small adjustments. Big transformation.

6. MAKE IT A RITUAL

Don't wait for a breakdown to look inward. Make Muhasaba as consistent as your workouts, your prayers, your meals. The transformation happens in repetition.

A man who holds himself accountable becomes a man others trust—because they know his strength comes from within.

He doesn't wait for the world to correct him.

He corrects himself first.

The Prophet Muhammad (PBUH) was unmatched in wisdom, leadership, and character—and he never stopped reflecting. Never stopped refining. That's the model.

The world doesn't need more men chasing external success.

It needs more men **mastering themselves in private**.

Your bank account won't build your legacy.

Your integrity will.

So ask yourself daily:

- Did I live with honor today?
- Was I faithful to what I claim to believe?
- Am I becoming the man I was born to be?

Self-accountability is not a burden—it's your edge.

It's how you grow into the leader, the protector, the builder, the believer the world needs.

Be the man who wakes before the world.

Kneels in silent reflection.

And rises stronger—because he faced himself first.

Because the man who masters Muhasaba masters his destiny.

CHAPTER 42

PURIFY THE HEART

THE HEART, IN BOTH ITS PHYSICAL AND SPIRITUAL STATES, SITS at the center of our existence. It does more than circulate blood. It carries our emotions, directs our intentions, and reflects our connection with God. In Islam, the heart is not simply an organ; it is the seat of sincerity, faith, and purpose. A person's character, actions, and nearness to the Divine all stem from the condition of his heart.

A man is only as healthy as his heart. (Sahih al-Bukhari, Hadith 52) That health is not just measured by beats per minute, but by purity, humility, and remembrance. The heart is always searching, aching for meaning, yearning for peace, and it finds stillness only in God.

I used to believe a hardened heart was necessary for survival. The music, media, and culture around me praised emotional detachment and numbness. Strength was portrayed as stoic. Cold. Unfeeling. I took that message to heart, and in doing so, lost mine.

As time passed, I felt the effects. It became harder to love, to cry, even to pray. Worship felt robotic. Charity felt forced. My heart, once alive with light, began to dim. And the more I fed this performance of "toughness," the more spiritually starved I became.

The healing wasn't instant. It took repentance. Remembrance. Tears.

Solitude. Moments of brutal honesty with God. Slowly, light returned. I discovered that a strong heart isn't cold; it's one that reflects its Creator: full of mercy, sincerity, and grace.

The Prophet Muhammad (PBUH) said:

> Truly, there is a piece of flesh in the body which, if sound, the whole body is sound. And if corrupted, the whole body is corrupted. Verily, it is the heart. (Sahih al-Bukhari, Hadith 52; Sahih Muslim, Hadith 1599)

THE STATES OF THE HEART

Islamic scholars describe the heart in three conditions. Understanding these can help us diagnose where we are, and where we need to go.

1. THE SOUND HEART

A heart free from arrogance, hypocrisy, and excessive attachment to the Dunya. It surrenders fully to God, moves with humility, and is guided by light.

> The Day when neither wealth nor children will benefit [anyone], but only one who comes to God with a sound heart. (Surah Ash-Shu'arā' 26:88–89)

2. THE DISEASED HEART

This heart is conflicted—it holds both faith and darkness. Pride, doubt, or insincerity cloud its clarity. But it can still be healed through intention, discipline, and remembrance.

3. THE DEAD HEART

A heart that has turned away from God. It feels nothing. It seeks nothing. But even this heart can be revived by the mercy of God if repentance is sincere.

Ibn al-Qayyim said:

The heart is either sick, healthy, or dead. If it is sick, it can be treated. If it is healthy, it can be nourished. If it is dead, it needs resurrection. (Ibn Al Qayimm, Ighāthat al-Lahfān)

PRACTICAL WAYS TO PURIFY THE HEART

Purifying the heart isn't complex in theory, but it demands sincerity, self-awareness, and effort. The goal is to uproot spiritual toxins and cultivate divine qualities. Here's a roadmap you can implement today; many of these have been discussed in greater detail throughout the book.

1. TAWBAH (SINCERE REPENTANCE)

Return to God often. Not just with words, but with real remorse and humility.

> O you who believe, turn to God in sincere repentance… (Qur'an 66:8)

2. DAILY QUR'AN CONNECTION

One verse a day can shift your entire heart—if read with reflection.

> We send down the Qur'an as healing and mercy… (Qur'an 17:82)

3. DUA: ASK FOR A STEADFAST HEART

The Prophet (PBUH) frequently prayed:

> O Turner of hearts, keep my heart firm upon Your religion. (Tirmidhī)

4. GUARDING THE SENSES

What you look at, listen to, and speak about enters your heart. Guard the gates.

5. DHIKR (REMEMBRANCE OF GOD)

Regular remembrance softens the heart and brings tranquility.

> Verily, in the remembrance of God do hearts find rest. (Surah Ar-Ra'd 13:28)

6. QIYĀM AL-LAYL (NIGHT PRAYER)

Even two Rak'āt before Fajr can change you. It's the time hearts are most exposed to Divine mercy.

7. RIGHTEOUS COMPANY

Your environment shapes your heart. Surround yourself with those who remember God—not just those who chase the Dunya.

8. HIDDEN GOOD DEEDS

Give. Serve. Help others—quietly. Sincerity lives in what no one sees.

9. MURAQABAH (WATCHFULNESS)

Ask often, "Is this for God?" If it's not, either fix your intention or walk away.

10. PATIENCE AND CONSISTENCY

You will slip. You will forget. Keep going. The path to purity is not about perfection—it's about persistence.

Purifying the heart is the greatest struggle you'll ever face, but it's also the most rewarding. A clean heart forgives. It seeks truth. It reflects light and most importantly it draws near to its Creator.

> Verily, God does not look at your appearance or your wealth, but He looks at your hearts and your deeds. (Sahih Muslim)

Polish your heart the way you would polish a mirror: gently, consistently, and with care. Let it reflect the light of God back into the world. And never believe the lie that your heart is too far gone. Every heart can return. Every heart can shine again.

For a deeper dive, *Purification of the Heart* by Shaykh Hamza Yusuf is a powerful resource rooted in classical Islamic wisdom. Let it guide you further.

CHAPTER 43

IHSAN

AT THE HEART OF EVERY GREAT MAN LIES A COMMITMENT TO excellence, not just in appearance, wealth, or status, but in character, integrity, and purpose. True mastery of self demands more than discipline and strength; it requires an internal alignment with the highest virtues and a determined dedication to something greater than oneself. This is where the concept of Ihsan comes into play.

Ihsan, an Islamic principle deeply embedded in the pursuit of excellence, extends beyond faith alone. It offers a timeless framework for personal mastery, one that transcends religious boundaries and applies to men of all walks of life. To embody Ihsan is to strive for moral, intellectual, and physical refinement in every aspect of existence. It is the ultimate standard of living with virtue, mindfulness, and integrity.

The path to Ihsan unfolds in three progressive stages, mirroring the journey of mastering mind, body, and soul. By integrating these stages into daily life, a man cultivates the qualities necessary to lead, protect, and serve with honor and purpose.

1. ACQUIRING KNOWLEDGE OF VIRTUE

Excellence begins with awareness. Just as a warrior studies combat before entering battle, a man must seek wisdom before attempting to refine his character. This stage requires:

- Learning the virtues that define strong, noble men like integrity, patience, discipline, humility, and courage.
- Studying the lives of great men who led with honor, fought for truth, and left legacies of righteousness.
- Understanding the moral and ethical principles that form the foundation of a life worth living.

A man cannot act with wisdom if he does not first seek it. By consuming knowledge from religious teachings, philosophy, history, and personal mentors, he builds the blueprint for his own excellence.

2. ACTIVE PRACTICE OF PRINCIPLES

Knowing what is right is only the beginning. The second stage of Ihsan requires the action of applying virtues in daily life with commitment. This is where discipline is forged and character is tested.

- **Integrity in action:** A man must align his behavior with his values, standing firm in truth even when it is inconvenient or costly.
- **Strength through adversity:** Living with Ihsan means responding to hardship with resilience, viewing every challenge as an opportunity to refine oneself.
- **Serving others:** True greatness is not measured by personal success alone, but by the ability to uplift, protect, and inspire those around you.

This stage is where most men falter. It is easy to know what is right; it is far harder to live it. Yet, this is the battleground where the weak are separated from the strong.

3. NATURAL INCLINATION TOWARD RIGHTEOUSNESS

The highest level of Ihsan is when virtue becomes second nature. A man no longer forces himself to act with honesty, courage, or kindness because these qualities flow effortlessly from his being. This is the embodiment of true mastery.

- **Warrior's instinct:** Just as a trained fighter does not hesitate in battle, a man who reaches this stage responds to life with immediate integrity and wisdom.
- **Internal harmony:** There is no contradiction between who he is in private and who he is in public. His actions align perfectly with his principles.
- **Spiritual presence:** He does not merely perform religious or ethical obligations out of duty but out of sincere devotion and mindfulness.

A man who lives with Ihsan radiates confidence, strength, and purpose. He does not chase ephemeral pleasures or external validation; he is at peace with himself because he has conquered his desires and aligned his life with higher ideals.

A man without spiritual grounding is like a ship without navigation: drifting aimlessly, easily swayed by desires, distractions, and worldly temptations. Ihsan in the soul is the highest and most critical level of mastery, for it dictates the direction of both mind and body. It is the anchor that keeps a man steadfast in his values, connected to his Creator, and aligned with his divine purpose.

QUALITIES OF A MAN OF IHSAN
1. A HEART FILLED WITH MINDFULNESS

A man of Ihsan is constantly aware of the presence of God in every thought, decision, and action. He does not act merely out of obligation, but from a deep consciousness of the Divine. His heart is filled with sincerity, seeking not just to appear righteous, but to be righteous in the eyes of his Creator.

- **Prayer as a discipline:** He does not pray mechanically; he prays with deep focus, feeling the weight of his words and the connection they create.
- **Gratitude as a way of life:** Instead of constantly chasing more, he pauses to appreciate the countless blessings he already has, knowing that contentment is the key to true peace.
- **Repentance and reflection:** He understands that perfection is unattainable, but striving for continuous self-improvement is mandatory. He holds himself accountable, regularly reflecting on his shortcomings and seeking ways to refine his character.

2. THE MASTERY OF DESIRES

A man ruled by his desires is a man enslaved. True freedom comes from self-control and the ability to say no to temptation, to delay gratification, and to prioritize long-term growth over momentary pleasure.

- **Fasting as a tool for mastery:** Fasting teaches a man to control his urges, proving to himself that he is greater than his hunger, his impulses, and his worldly cravings.
- **Avoidance of toxic influences:** He does not allow harmful relationships, distractions, or indulgences to corrupt his soul. He guards his heart as fiercely as a warrior guards his kingdom.
- **Purity of intentions:** Every action he takes, whether in work, relationships, or personal endeavors, is rooted in sincerity and purpose.

3. SERVICE AS THE ULTIMATE EXPRESSION OF IHSAN

The highest manifestation of Ihsan is to live not just for oneself, but for the betterment of others. A man of true spiritual excellence understands that his strength, knowledge, and influence are not meant for selfish gain, but to uplift those around him.

- **Charity and compassion:** He gives freely, not just of his wealth, but of his time, attention, and kindness.
- **Leading by example:** He does not lecture others about morality while failing to embody it himself. He is a walking example of the principles he preaches.
- **Protecting the weak:** He stands against oppression, defends the vulnerable, and ensures that his strength is always used in service of righteousness.

Ihsan is not for the weak. It is not for the man content with mediocrity or comfort. It is a call to rise, to refine, and to elevate every aspect of life.

To live with Ihsan means to commit to:

- **Daily reflection:** Holding yourself accountable for your actions, thoughts, and intentions.
- **Discipline in all areas:** Training the body, sharpening the mind, and fortifying the soul with relentless commitment.
- **Serving a higher purpose:** Leading with integrity, protecting those in need, and leaving behind a legacy of righteousness.

The road to Ihsan is not an easy one. It demands effort, sacrifice, and an unshakable commitment to excellence. But for the man who walks this path, the reward is a life of true strength, deep fulfillment, and eternal significance.

CHAPTER 44

MASTER YOUR DESIRES

GENUINE FREEDOM COMES IN SURRENDERING YOURSELF TO YOUR Creator and not to your desires, social expectations, or the distractions of this world. This is the paradox of freedom: By submitting to something higher, you release yourself from the shackles of everything lower. You free yourself from the chains of others' opinions, the lure of material possessions, and the addictive pull of temporary pleasures that leave you emptier than before.

Society sells a false narrative, packaging indulgence as liberation. We are told that more drinking, more casual encounters, or more mind-numbing distractions will lead to a life of meaning. But what is the reality? The morning after the party, the silence after the noise, the emptiness that lingers when the thrill fades. These so-called freedoms are not liberating; they are enslaving. They dull your instincts, weaken your will, and keep you addicted to cycles of short-lived pleasure.

Ask yourself: If something controls you, is it really freedom?

Imam Al-Ghazali, in *The Alchemy of Happiness*, describes the world as an illusion cloaked in silks and treasures, a deception that dissolves the moment we try to hold onto it. The high wears off. The applause fades. The possessions decay. And in that moment, your mortality hints at a sobering truth: If your sense of worth is tied to what can be taken away, you are not free.

We have explored the concepts of discipline, fighting the devil, and conquering the desires (Nafs) thoroughly throughout this book, but I'd like to add in a different perspective on how our society uses these desires to control us and enslave with the false allure of freedom. I thought doing anything I wanted at any moment meant true freedom; in reality, it meant a dependence on desires to feel free. Nowadays, people go to the ends of the earth to find freedom. I've heard stories of people sleeping in the grass, going on weeklong psychedelic retreats, experimenting with drugs to find true freedom, and everything in between. It's an endless hamster wheel of seeking external freedom while the internal is enslaved. You have to attain freedom from within, and the only way to do that is to master yourself. Real freedom is not about indulging every craving, but about controlling them. It's about standing firm in your values, resisting the need for outside approval, and rejecting indulgences that pull you away from your deeper purpose.

This is not an easy path. It will require introspection, self-discipline, and sacrifice. But what is the alternative? A life dictated by short-term emotions? A reality where your identity is shaped by external forces?

When you shift inward, when you seek clarity instead of distraction, when you align your will with your Creator's, you gain something that no external force can take away: an unshakable sense of purpose. No longer do the highs and lows of this world define you, because you are anchored in something eternal.

This journey to real freedom demands that you confront the hardest parts of yourself, including your insecurities, fears, and temptations. It's uncomfortable. But growth always is. Modern distractions like entertainment, excess, and instant gratification often serve as coping mechanisms, helping people escape from unresolved wounds and an unfulfilled life. But escaping is not the same as being free.

When you face yourself, armed with wisdom and divine guidance, you become clear, grounded, and unburdened by the superficial. You start living a life of substance where freedom means being true to who you are and why you're here, not running after the next quick thrill.

Reject the false promises of freedom that lead nowhere. Turn inward. Ask yourself: What am I running from? What am I truly seeking?

Nurture your connection with your Creator and commit to the journey of self-discovery and spiritual mastery. By doing so, you will rise above the noise of the world and experience a peace that is not dependent on external circumstances.

The choice is yours: Will you continue chasing illusions, or will you step into the freedom that only a life of meaning can bring?

CHAPTER 45

COURAGE

WHEN YOU THINK OF COURAGE, DO YOU PICTURE LEGENDARY warriors, men who stood unshaken in the face of adversity? Or, like me, does the image of the Cowardly Lion from *The Wizard of Oz* come to mind as an apt symbol of many men today? Outwardly, we have the potential to be lions, standing tall and fearless. Yet, internally, many wrestle with self-doubt, shrinking into the role of timid sheep.

Courage is not just a virtue; it is the cornerstone of character, shaping how you show up in every aspect of life. It is the force that frees your best self, but it's not merely about facing physical danger. True courage is deeper than what is presented on the surface. It is the quiet resolve to stand firm when the world pushes back, the internal fortitude to confront life's challenges, and the steadfast commitment to truth in an age that rewards compromise.

But let's go beyond the surface. Real courage isn't about bravado, aggression, or dominance; it is a reflection of the heart. It means taking action in the face of fear, pushing forward even when the path ahead is uncertain. More importantly, at its highest level, courage is rooted in spiritual conviction. To be truly courageous is to move beyond ego and align yourself with higher principles, ideals, and the will of your

Creator. This kind of courage is not about seeking recognition, power, or validation. It is about surrendering personal desires and living a life guided by divine purpose.

Submission to God is not weakness. It is the source of ultimate strength. When you commit to something greater than yourself, you tap into a power beyond human limitations. This is where courage finds its deepest roots, not in self-image or external validation, but in a soul fortified by faith.

I heard a story of a man who came to my teacher and said, "I wish I could give more to charity; here is all I have," and handed him a five-dollar bill, which is all he had in this world, money-wise. That's true courage. Standing for what is right and against injustice, even at the expense of your worldly well-being, is true courage.

The greatest example of courage comes from the Prophet Muhammad (PBUH). When he first received revelation, he faced ridicule, persecution, and relentless opposition. The leaders of his tribe sought to bribe him, threaten him, and silence him, but he stood firm. He said, "By God, if they were to put the sun in my right hand and the moon in my left on condition that I abandon this mission, I would not abandon it until God has made it victorious or I perish therein." Standing for truth in the face of overwhelming adversity is true courage.

As men, we are constantly engaged in an internal battle between our higher selves and our baser instincts. Courage grants the strength to win these battles, to conquer the impulses that lead to self-destruction, and to rise as a champion of righteousness. But courage is not just raw strength and power; it is the fusion of wisdom and power. Wisdom grants discernment, the ability to know what is right. Strength grants the ability to act upon that knowledge. If either is lacking, the foundation collapses: Strength without wisdom is reckless, like a tyrant, while wisdom without strength is powerless, like a just king without an army. But when these forces unite, they create an extraordinary man who commands respect not because he seeks it, but because he has become worthy of it.

Your mission is twofold: Develop both strength and intellect. Sharpen your mind, refine your body, and cultivate wisdom. A man who embodies these qualities naturally stands out through his presence, his integrity, and his unshakable commitment to truth.

Here's the reality: To be truly courageous, you must first understand submission. That is the paradox. By yielding to God, you gain an unbreakable foundation. This is not a surrender to weakness, but a mastery over self. When your will is aligned with your Creator's, your courage is no longer limited by fear, doubt, or the opinions of others. You become the man you were destined to be.

Let courage be your foundation. Let it shape your presence, so that when you walk into a room, you radiate strength, dignity, and light. Carry confidence in your gaze, steadiness in your steps, and conviction in your heart. True masculine excellence is not about dominance, but about embodying divine submission. Face life's trials with courage, and you will rise to your greatest heights.

CHAPTER 46

BRAVERY

WHEN WE THINK OF BRAVERY, MODERN CULTURE OFTEN CONJURES up images of extreme sports, adrenaline-fueled risks, or acts of physical endurance. Skydiving, cliff diving, and running into burning buildings are often celebrated as the pinnacle of bravery. But is that truly bravery? Or is it merely recklessness disguised as valor?

Real bravery isn't about thrill seeking. It isn't about jumping out of airplanes or chasing temporary highs. True bravery is about standing firm in your values, even when the entire world pushes back. It is about integrity, faith, and conviction in the face of opposition.

Muhammad Ali, one of the greatest athletes of all time, exemplified this kind of bravery. At the height of his career, when fame and fortune were at their peak, he made a decision that would cost him everything. On April 28, 1967, he refused to be drafted for the Vietnam War, standing by his religious beliefs and moral convictions. As a result, he was stripped of his heavyweight title, barred from boxing, and faced imprisonment. Yet, he remained steadfast, refusing to compromise his beliefs for the sake of comfort or societal approval. That is true bravery. Know it might not be the kind that makes headlines for its spectacle, but it is the kind that requires immense personal sacrifice.

Bravery is not always found in battlefields or political stances. Sometimes it is found in the quiet acts of devotion that defy societal norms. I remember a moment when I was traveling with a colleague at an airport. As prayer time approached, I put down my prayer mat and began my Salah in the middle of the terminal. When I finished, my colleague looked at me in astonishment. He admitted, "I have so much respect for you after seeing your devotion to God and your faith."

He was surprised not because he doubted my beliefs but because he had never seen someone practice them so openly in a public space. That moment taught me something incredibly important. That bravery is sometimes as simple as being unapologetically yourself. It is the fearlessness to worship in a world that wants you to conform, to hold onto faith when it is easier to let go.

Many people hesitate to express their faith publicly out of fear of judgment, fear of ridicule, or fear of standing out. But true bravery is choosing to honor God regardless of who is watching. It is recognizing that the opinions of others pale in comparison to the weight of your relationship with the Divine.

Another often-overlooked form of bravery is the self-awareness and strength to keep your mouth shut when the world tempts you to speak. Nowadays it feels like gossip and drama are currency in society. People trade in secrets and scandals, using them to gain social status or momentary attention. But it takes true strength to resist that temptation, to protect the dignity of others rather than exploit their mistakes for entertainment.

We all have the opportunity to stir the pot by spreading the rumors we hear or exposing secrets we hold. But every time we choose to remain silent, every time we protect someone's honor rather than tarnish it, we exercise a rare kind of bravery. It is easy to join the crowd, to laugh at someone's misfortune, to tear others down for the sake of fitting in. It is far harder to walk away, to shut down negativity, and to hold fast to integrity even when no one else does.

Bravery is choosing what is right over what is easy. It is the ability to stay silent in a world addicted to noise, to withhold judgment in a culture that thrives on condemnation.

Make no mistake though; true bravery comes with a price. Muhammad Ali lost years of his prime and suffered public backlash. People who pray in public risk side glances, judgment, and discomfort. Those who refuse to gossip might be ostracized from social circles. But bravery is not about comfort. It is about character. It is about standing firm when the storm rages, when the pressure mounts, when the world demands you compromise who you are.

Bravery is the resolute belief that doing the right thing is worth any sacrifice. It is the quiet strength to live with conviction, even when you stand alone.

If you want to be brave, start small. Start by speaking the truth when it is inconvenient. Start by praying when others expect you to remain silent. Start by refusing to indulge in gossip, even when everyone around you does. Real bravery isn't about impressing the world. It is about honoring your soul. The man you are meant to be is one who stands for what he believes in without apology, without hesitation, and without fear. That is the kind of bravery that changes lives and builds legacies.

CHAPTER 47

CHIVALRY

THERE'S AN OLD SAYING THAT "CHIVALRY IS DEAD." IF I HAD A dollar for every time I heard that, I could probably retire and stop writing altogether. With gender roles continuing to evolve and individualism often taking precedence over collective values, it may seem like respecting women has faded into obscurity. But if you're reading this, it means you care about what it truly means to be a modern gentleman who embodies respect, integrity, and honor in every interaction.

Respecting women is not about grand gestures or outdated customs; it's about living with intense principles. It's about safeguarding those who are vulnerable, treating others with dignity, and contributing to a just society. From the legendary Knights of the Round Table to faith-based traditions that emphasize honor and responsibility, the virtues of a real man like protection, respect, and integrity are echoed throughout history and are more relevant today than ever.

Perhaps the most profound truth about being a modern gentleman is that it is not about dominance but about responsibility. At its core, respecting women means recognizing their equal worth and understanding our role not as rulers, but as protectors and allies. Women are not fragile beings in need of saving, but neither should they be subjected to the predatory tendencies of those who mistake power for control.

The spirit of respecting women has been immortalized in storytelling for centuries. The gallant Knights of the Round Table swore an oath to protect the innocent and uphold justice, personifying an enduring code of honor. From the valor of Lancelot to the wisdom of Galahad, these knights embodied courage, respect, and duty. But this concept is not confined to medieval tales or literary figures; it finds deep resonance in faith traditions as well. The teachings of the Prophet Muhammad (PBUH) place a strong emphasis on honoring and protecting women. His acts of kindness and respect serve as a lasting example, offering lessons in compassion and reverence that have inspired generations. One well-known story recounts how the Prophet (PBUH), upon seeing a woman struggling under a heavy load, immediately offered his assistance. His love and respect for his wife, Khadijah, further underscore the significance of respecting women in Islamic teachings. He valued her intellect, strength, and independence, showing that true respect means recognizing wisdom and leadership.

Being a protector is not just about physical defense; it is about emotional and spiritual guardianship as well. It is about ensuring that women are safe from harm in the streets and more importantly in their homes, workplaces, and communities. It means using our voices to challenge degrading language, speaking up against harassment, and cultivating a culture where respect is the baseline, not the exception.

True protection means building an environment where women feel safe, valued, and heard. This responsibility is not about exerting control but about standing against injustice, challenging abuse, and creating a culture of dignity. When embraced sincerely, this role cultivates empathy, emotional depth, and a stronger sense of purpose. A man who upholds these values sets a standard of behavior for others, creating a ripple effect where respect and honor become the norm.

Being a protector enriches the lives of women as well as your own. It builds trust and deepens your relationships, whether romantic, familial, or platonic. More importantly, it cultivates emotional resilience, self-discipline, and a higher sense of purpose.

Respecting women isn't just about how you treat others; it's about who you become in the process. A man who embraces respect develops patience, humility, and strength of character. He does not seek validation but finds fulfillment in upholding his values, regardless of recognition.

Here are some ways to embody respect:

Listen and Believe—When a woman shares her experiences, whether about harassment, discrimination, or personal struggles, listen without dismissing or invalidating her perspective. Create an environment where her voice is valued.

- **Speak up.** Don't be a passive bystander. Challenge sexist comments and behaviors when you witness them. By speaking up, you set a precedent for respect and integrity.
- **Educate yourself.** Expand your understanding of gender equality, women's rights, and the challenges women face. Read, watch, and engage in meaningful discussions to become a more informed advocate.
- **Reflect and unlearn.** Recognize your own biases and be willing to challenge outdated beliefs. Growth requires introspection and the courage to change.
- **Support women's initiatives.** Whether through financial contributions, volunteering, or spreading awareness, support efforts that uplift and empower women.
- **Advocate in the workplace.** Push for gender equality in professional settings. Advocate for fair pay, equal opportunities, and a culture of respect.
- **Hold others accountable.** Engage in conversations with fellow men. Challenge disrespectful behavior and encourage others to uphold the same values.

How you treat your significant other falls into this as well. I consult my wife on major decisions, elevate her, and treat her with respect and care no matter what. Even in tough situations when tempers rise, it's your job to remain calm, cool, and collected. Never, ever should a man lay his hands on a woman or use physical force in any way. Never should a man try to exert dominance through control or false submission, which only reveals a deep insecurity in self.

Much of my understanding of respecting women comes from the incredible example set by my mother. Lila Igram is a powerful, compassionate woman who has dedicated her life to empowering women and girls across the world. Islam has been her foundation, a faith that truly protects and uplifts women, and through her, I learned the importance of standing alongside women, not above them. Yet, growing up in the West, I also had to battle the constant bombardment of hypersexualization and objectification of women as mere objects, an agenda that seeks to manipulate men's perception of women. It has been a struggle, one I continue to navigate, but through these lessons, I have worked to rewire that conditioning.

This book is part of that process to teach men how we can shift our mindsets, challenge the toxic narratives we've been fed, and return to a model of manhood that is rooted in strength, dignity, and respect. The journey is not just about changing how we see women but about reshaping ourselves into men who lead with honor, protect with sincerity, and live with dedicated principles. The world needs men who don't just speak of respect but who embody it in every action. That's the man I strive to be, and that's the man I hope you choose to become.

CHAPTER 48

LOVE

A MAN OF EXCELLENCE IS NOT DEFINED BY DOMINANCE OR STOicism but by the depth of his heart, the mercy he extends, and the love he embodies. To lead with love is to embrace the most powerful and undefeatable force in existence. Love is not weakness…it is strength in its purest form. It conquers not by force, but by transforming the hearts of those it touches. A man who truly understands this walks with purpose and security in his identity and is devoted to a higher calling.

A man of true character and integrity cultivates an expansive heart, overflowing with love, mercy, and forgiveness. Before he can extend love outward, he must first cultivate love for himself and for his Creator, which is the most essential and transcendent form of love. From this divine source, an endless wellspring of love flows, enabling him to embrace humanity with boundless compassion.

Loving yourself is not an act of arrogance, nor is it self-indulgence. It is a recognition of the value God has placed in you. To love yourself means to honor the gift you have been given of your body, mind, and soul. It means treating yourself with kindness, nurturing your well-being, and refusing to engage in self-destructive habits. A man who truly loves himself is not consumed by ego but walks in gratitude, using his gifts to serve others and fulfill his purpose.

True self-love begins with faith. When a man acknowledges that he is a creation of the Most High, he understands that his worth is inherent, not dictated by external validation. This knowledge frees him from the endless chase of status, wealth, and approval. He no longer seeks love in temporary things because he has found it in its eternal source of God Himself.

A man rooted in love does not hoard it to himself, but he gives it freely. Love is the currency of the soul, and when given without conditions, it multiplies rather than diminishes. The Prophet Muhammad (PBUH) taught that "None of you truly believes until he loves for his brother what he loves for himself." This is not just an ideal but a way of life. A man who leads with love uplifts, supports, and protects those around him. His love is not based on temporary emotions, but on sincere devotion to the well-being of others.

Love is reflected in actions such as in the way a man treats his spouse, his children, his friends, and even strangers. It is in his patience, in his ability to listen, and in his willingness to serve without expecting anything in return. It is choosing to forgive when wronged, choosing to uplift rather than tear down, and choosing to be present in the lives of those who need him. The strongest men are those who are unafraid to show kindness, tenderness, and empathy. These are not traits of weakness but of immense strength.

LOVE MANIFESTS IN MANY FORMS

- **Eros:** the natural attraction that draws people together.
- **Philos:** the bond of brotherhood and shared experiences.
- **Agape:** a selfless, unconditional love that knows no boundaries.

When these forms of love are interwoven into daily life, they cultivate resilient children, construct strong communities, and elevate one's character to new heights. Love can be reflected in grand gestures, but also in the way we speak of others. When we view our fellow human beings as brothers and sisters, gossip loses its allure, and we choose to uplift and defend one another. Speaking well of others, both in their presence and absence, strengthens bonds and sets an example of integrity, which creates a culture of love and unity within our communities.

Too often, society equates masculinity with emotional suppression, as though to love deeply is to be weak. But true strength lies in having vulnerability and the courage to express love, to admit fears, to be open about struggles, and to connect on a human level. A real man does not hide behind a hardened exterior; he stands firm in his emotions, allowing love rather than fear to guide him.

The greatest leaders in history were those who led with love. Nelson Mandela's commitment to justice was rooted in his love for humanity. The Prophet Muhammad (PBUH) conquered hearts not with the sword but with compassion, patience, and mercy. The legacy of great men is not built on dominance, but on the depth of their love for their people, their principles, and their Creator.

PRACTICAL WAYS TO CULTIVATE LOVE IN YOUR DAILY LIFE

1. **Love yourself through discipline and care.** Treat your body with respect through proper nutrition, exercise, and rest. Guard your mind from negativity and cultivate a spiritual routine that nourishes your soul.
2. **Extend love to others through action.** Tell the people in your life that you love them. Give hugs. Speak well of others both in their presence and absence. Offer your time, attention, and support freely.
3. **Practice gratitude daily.** Reflect on three things you are grateful for each day. Gratitude shifts your perspective and fills your heart with appreciation for life's blessings.
4. **Be present and listen with an open heart.** Love is in the simple act of truly listening, understanding, and being there for someone in need.
5. **Forgive quickly and love unconditionally.** Holding onto resentment

diminishes love. A strong man forgives not because the other person deserves it, but because his heart is too expansive to be weighed down by bitterness.
6. **Strengthen your connection with God.** Love for the Divine is the ultimate love that fuels all others. Through prayer, reflection, and acts of worship, deepen your relationship with the One who is the source of all love.

When you lead with love, you leave behind a legacy that outlives you. People will remember how you made them feel, the kindness you extended, and the warmth you shared. True masculinity is not about being feared; it is about being revered for the love, wisdom, and integrity you embody.

Love is the force that transforms, uplifts, and conquers. A man who chooses love chooses a life of purpose, peace, and fulfillment. Love yourself, love others, and above all, love God. In doing so, you will become the man you were meant to be and inspire others to do the same.

CHAPTER 49

REFLECTION ON GRATITUDE

GRATITUDE IS MORE THAN A FEELING OF APPRECIATION; IT'S AN essential force that transforms a man's heart, mind, and soul. A man who masters gratitude possesses an unshakable foundation, one that keeps him humble in success and resilient in hardship. True gratitude isn't just about acknowledging your blessings; it's about recognizing the Source of those blessings and understanding that even the ability to be grateful is a gift from the Almighty.

One of the most profound lessons on gratitude comes from the narration about Prophet Dawood (PBUH). When he said, "O Lord, how can I be grateful to You when my gratitude itself is a blessing from You?" he wasn't merely expressing thanks; he was unveiling an ethereal truth: Even our ability to recognize and express gratitude is granted by God. To this, God responded, "Now you have truly thanked Me, O Dawood." This moment teaches us that gratitude is not just in words but in the deep realization of our dependence on divine mercy.

In Surah Ibrahim (14:7), God promises, "If you are grateful, I will surely increase you [in favor]; but if you deny, indeed, My punishment is severe." This verse isn't just about material wealth; it speaks to spiritual blessings as well. The more we recognize and express gratitude, the more God opens our hearts to His guidance and wisdom. Similarly, Surah An-Nahl (16:53) reminds us, "And whatever you have of favor it is from God." Every good thing we have, like our talents, our health, our opportunities, our family. They are all gifts from the Creator, not products of our own making alone.

This life celebrates self-sufficiency and personal achievement, making it easy to attribute success solely to hard work and intelligence. But a real man understands that even his strengths are not entirely his own. They are blessings entrusted to him. Recognizing this doesn't diminish his effort; rather, it roots his accomplishments in humility and deepens his connection to God.

I try to say thanks to God and express gratitude one hundred times during the day. This can be thanking Him and appreciating everything you have in the moment or just dwelling on the simple blessings you have been given. Gratitude is a key part of maintaining a healthy, positive mindset, and from the aspect of the soul, if you are not grateful for what you have, that's how you can invite envy in, especially as ungratefulness basically means you disagree with what God has provided for you and others. There could always be more, but there could always be less. The Prophet (PBUH) also encourages spending time with those less fortunate to truly appreciate and understand what you have and need to be happy. Don't neglect your blessings by focusing on others' blessings while losing your own blessings in the process.

I also like to express gratitude to others. Friends, family, and loved ones should be appreciated, and we should be grateful for these blessings as well. So, nurture your blessings the same way you would tend to your business, home, and self.

You choose gratitude every single day. You can choose to focus on the positives and be grateful or drag yourself into the pits of an ungrateful, pessimistic mindset. You truly cannot lose, as whatever happens is what God had meant for you, regardless of the outcome.

What would your life be like if you faced challenges with this mindset? Instead of reacting with frustration, a grateful man asks, "What lesson or hidden blessing does this moment hold for me?" This shift in perspective turns hardships into opportunities for growth and spiritual refinement.

Gratitude, when truly embodied, is a way of life. It's in how a man treats others, how he responds to trials, and how he carries himself in moments of both abundance and scarcity. Prophet Dawood's realization invites us to see every breath, every opportunity, and every moment of peace as a divine gift worthy of recognition.

So the next time you say, "Thank God," pause for a moment. Don't just acknowledge the blessing, but acknowledge the One who gave you the ability to recognize that blessing. In that awareness lies the essence of true gratitude. It is the key to contentment, the foundation of inner peace, and the mark of a man who walks with both strength and humility.

CHAPTER 50

CHARITY

SOME OF THE MOST WORTHLESS THINGS IN THIS LIFE HOLD PRICEless value in the afterlife. Committing a portion of your wealth to improve the lives of others isn't just an act of generosity; it's a discipline that reshapes your character, refines your relationship with wealth, and strengthens your connection to your community. By dedicating at least 2.5 percent of your annual income to philanthropic efforts, you are not just helping the less fortunate. You are rewiring how you view money and wealth, allowing you to dismantle materialism and build a richer sense of fulfillment.

Beyond the required 2.5 percent charitable contribution, or Zakat, I strive to give more through donations, time, and sharing knowledge. My former principal and I embraced this philosophy to launch a leadership program at my high school and across the district. With his guidance and the support of trustee Alex Okafor, we scaled the program to nearly five hundred students per month. When you view everything you have as a trust or blessing from God, your thoughts on gratitude and generosity shift. What we possess is not truly ours. Your name may appear next to that bank account or paycheck, but in reality, these are gifts bestowed upon you by the Almighty.

Wealth is a tool, not a trophy. Left unchecked, the desire for more becomes insatiable, leaving even the richest feeling empty. The Qur'an warns of this trap: "If I were to grant mankind abundance, they would surely transgress in the land." Accumulation without purpose leads to an endless cycle of greed rather than fulfillment. The solution? Give.

Generosity isn't a one-time act; it's a way of life. It draws you closer to the Divine, leading to a paradise that eclipses anything this world can offer. Contrarily, miserliness chokes the soul, keeping you shackled in fear and leading to a barren existence. True generosity isn't about throwing money at problems or seeking recognition, it's about giving with a pure heart, knowing that wealth means nothing unless it's used for good.

If you feel discomfort when donating, take it as a sign to give even more. That discomfort is detaching you from materialism. The goal is to give so freely that you don't even remember what or when you gave. My father embodied this principle. He picked up trash at the mosque every Sunday, installed gym equipment and speed bumps for the community, and gave his time to teach Sunday school and organize events. He never hesitated when asked to help. My parents even took in a Palestinian child and family for heart surgery and rehabilitation. They always gave more than they took, and their generosity was boundless.

The Prophet Muhammad (PBUH) exemplified this reality. His generosity was quiet but relentless, done solely for the pleasure of God. He taught that being content with little while praying for others to receive more is true kindness and nobility. Wealth isn't measured by your bank account but by how freely you give. To share without expectation is the highest form of strength.

History echoes this truth. Andrew Carnegie, one of the wealthiest men of his time, believed that "the man who dies rich dies disgraced." He spent the last years of his life giving away his fortune, building libraries and institutions that still benefit the world today. His story proves that charity isn't just a moral duty; it's the only real legacy we leave behind.

In Islam, charity isn't optional; it's one of the five pillars of faith. Zakat purifies your wealth, proving that what you own is never truly yours. The same principle exists across faiths and philosophies. Buddhism teaches dana, which means selfless giving. Christianity commands charity as a reflection of love and service. Across history, the message remains the same: Give, and you will grow.

Even science supports this. Studies show that people who give regularly are happier, healthier, and more resilient. Generosity builds empathy, strengthens relationships, and gives a deeper sense of purpose. Giving doesn't just help the receivers; it transforms you.

Generosity also creates real change. Providing food, shelter, education, or mentorship can alter the course of someone's life. In 2019 alone, Americans donated nearly $450 billion to charity, demonstrating the power of collective generosity to reshape society.[21] If the ultrarich gave 2.5 percent of their wealth in charity, we would solve world hunger and eradicate poverty.

But generosity isn't just about money. Volunteering, donating goods, and even offering a kind word or helping hand all count. The Prophet Muhammad (PBUH) said, "Even a smile is charity." Every act of kindness, no matter how small, makes a difference. The key is the intention behind your giving. When you give without expecting anything in return, you turn generosity into a source of strength and joy.

Make this a nonnegotiable in your life. Dedicate at least two hours every week to charitable work. Mentor someone. Feed the hungry. Clean up your community. Use your skills to serve others. Start small if necessary, but be consistent, and over time generosity will become second nature.

Dr. Hawa Abdi is a perfect example. A Somali physician and human rights activist who turned her family's land into a refuge for thousands during the Somali civil war, her selflessness saved lives and restored dignity to those in desperate need. Her story proves that giving isn't just about helping others but about becoming the person you're meant to be.

Charity sets off a chain reaction, transforming both the giver and the

---

[21] Giving USA Foundation, "Giving USA 2020: The Annual Report on Philanthropy for the Year 2019," June 16, 2020, https://givingusa.org/giving-usa-2020-charitable-giving-showed-solid-growth-climbing-to-449-64-billion-in-2019-one-of-the-highest-years-for-giving-on-record/.

receiver. When you commit to sharing your wealth, time, and energy to uplift others, you become part of a force greater than yourself. Recognizing your blessings and using them to help others rewires your entire existence, making generosity, gratitude, and purpose the foundation of your life.

CHAPTER 51

GUARD THE TONGUE

ALONG THIS PATH TOWARD EXCELLENCE, BE MINDFUL OF THE pitfalls that can divert you, especially the seemingly minor habits of gossip, dishonesty, and negative speech. These habits are like silent toxins, slowly poisoning your character and relationships before you even realize the damage they've done.

Gossip, for example, may offer a quick sense of connection or superiority, but it slowly erodes relationships, damages reputations, and undermines trust. I've seen careers stall or fall apart because someone couldn't control their words. One former colleague of mine who was an incredibly talented salesman at a high-growth startup at the time struggled with gossip. Within six months, strained relationships and dwindling productivity forced him to look for another job. No matter how skilled or ambitious a man may be, his ability to lead, inspire, and be trusted is directly tied to the integrity of his words.

Studies confirm this reality. According to ResumeLab, 50 percent of employees admit to engaging in workplace gossip.[22] It may seem harm-

---

[22] Agata Szczepanek, "What Makes a Nightmare Coworker?" ResumeLab, August 9, 2023, https://resumelab.com/career-advice/terrible-coworkers.

less at the moment, but the consequences are often severe. Instead of focusing conversations on others' shortcomings, use those moments to discuss ideas, growth, and self-improvement. As the Prophet Muhammad (PBUH) taught, "Whoever believes in God and the Last Day should speak good or remain silent." (Sahih al-Bukhari 6018)

If you have nothing good to say, say nothing at all. When drawn into negativity, recognize it for what it is, an invitation to evil, and avoid it at all costs. And if someone speaks poorly about others to you, think about what they might say about you in your absence. Reevaluate such relationships and distance yourself from unproductive dialogues. My life transformed when I learned to recognize gossip and walk away.

Acknowledging the destructive impact of negative speech is just the first step. True character transformation requires the courage to own your words and actions. The most powerful antidote to gossip is empathy. Strive to understand others' struggles and challenges rather than judging or speaking ill of them. A circle built on trust, respect, and positivity leaves no room for harmful chatter.

Think of your words as currency. If you had $100 to spend each day, would you waste it on meaningless purchases, or would you invest it wisely? Similarly, before speaking, ask yourself: Does this word serve me? Does this conversation help me grow? Could my words be used more productively? Treat your words with the same level of scrutiny.

SWEARING

Swearing and negative language are like verbal litter. Growing up, I used to think swearing was SO COOL. The rappers I idolized swore, you'd get in trouble for it so it seemed edgy, and every cool kid at school or on TV would swear. It's part of the athletics culture too, as both athletes and some of my coaches swore more than a drunken sailor, and it started to get out of hand the older I got. I didn't even realize it and just casually would swear like it was nothing, F-bomb after every sentence; it became part of my speech, and the people I was around spoke the same way.

I knew this weakness was holding me back, and as I started to remove the blindfold on what "cool" was, I realized negative speech was draining my battery and soul. I made a commitment to myself: stop swearing altogether. I had my wife and friends call me out if I did. I'd use my Muhasaba (self-accountability) each day to think about the words I said and if I swore. It took years, but those words are no longer part of my vocabulary and even hurt to hear nowadays.

A mentor once told me, "Swear words are what people use when they can't think of something more meaningful to say." Reflect on your daily content consumption, including the music and podcasts you listen to, the shows you watch, and work conversations you have. All these influence your speech. If vulgarity fills your ears, it will inevitably seep into your habits. Just as standing near garbage makes you reek, consuming toxic language shapes your communication.

The Prophet Muhammad (PBUH) taught, "If you have nothing good to say, then don't speak." Confucius echoed this wisdom: "He who speaks without modesty will find it difficult to make his words good." And as the Arabs say, "Speech is silver, but silence is golden." Malcolm X put it bluntly: "A man curses because he doesn't have the words to say what's on his mind."[23]

HONESTY

Though bending the truth might seem like an easy escape, it eventually forms a web that entangles you. A study from the University of Notre Dame found that honesty correlates with better mental and physical health.[24] When you're honest with others and yourself, you gain peace of mind and a stronger sense of self-worth.

Lying has become so normalized that its damage often goes unnoticed. We lie to avoid trouble, protect our image, or spare someone's feelings. But each lie, no matter how small, chips away at integrity. Over

---

23 Malcolm X and Alex Haley, *The Autobiography of Malcolm X* (Ballantine Books, 1992).

24 Anita E. Kelly and Lijuan Wang, L., "A Life Without Lies: How Living Honestly Can Affect Health," American Psychological Association, 2012, https://assets1.cbsnewsstatic.com/i/cbslocal/wp-content/uploads/sites/15/16066/2012/08/kelly-a-life-without-lies.pdf.

time, it makes you appear untrustworthy and furthers internal conflict, guilt, and anxiety.

The Prophet Muhammad (PBUH), known as Al-Amin ("the trustworthy one"), upheld the highest standards of honesty. Following his example means valuing truth, even when it's inconvenient.

COMMUNICATION

One of the most overlooked aspects of powerful communication is active listening. The difference between merely hearing and truly understanding someone is profound. To develop this skill, practice these strategies:

- **Show empathy:** Acknowledge the speaker's perspective. Simple phrases like "I understand why you feel that way" make others feel heard.
- **Paraphrase and summarize:** Ensure you've captured their message correctly by paraphrasing and asking for confirmation.
- **Ask open-ended questions:** Encourage deeper discussions by replacing yes/no inquiries with open-ended ones.

It's in difficult conversations that we discover the essence of others and ourselves. Throughout history, religious teachings and philosophy have emphasized the power of righteous communication. Islam stresses the moral quality of speech, while philosophers like Socrates highlight dialogue as a path to truth.

The Qur'an advises, "And speak to people with good words..." (Qur'an 2:83). Even in disagreement, maintain kindness and constructiveness. Embrace Socratic principles like seeking truth through thoughtful questioning rather than heated argument.

By practicing mindful communication you become a better version of yourself while also inspiring those around you. Gossip, dishonesty, and negative speech may provide short-term gratification, but they erode long-term integrity and growth. Approach communication with empathy, honesty, and clean language to build a foundation of self-excellence.

Your words and actions are reflections of your character. Choose them wisely, and you will become a source of inspiration to those around you.

CHAPTER 52

TRANSFORMING ANGER INTO STRENGTH

THE PROPHET MUHAMMAD (PBUH) SAID, "THE STRONG MAN IS not the one who can physically overpower others, but the one who can control his anger."

We've all been there. Those moments when you red-out and blind rage surges like wildfire, consuming the mind, clouding judgment, and leaving behind destruction. Anger, when left unchecked, becomes a force that dictates our actions, hijacks our emotions, and erodes our character. I know this because I've lived it.

For years, my anger controlled me. A potent mix of testosterone, suppressed rage, childhood bullying, and rejection compounded into an uncontrollable temper. My father, seeing the damage it was causing, called me out on it frequently, which only fueled my fury further. It wasn't until I grew older, reflecting on the fractured relationships and self-inflicted wounds caused by my unchecked anger, that I understood its true cost. Anger is not just an emotion that you are born with; it is a force that can build or destroy, depending on how it is wielded.

Anger is not just an emotional reaction; it triggers profound physiological changes in the body. When anger takes over, your body enters a heightened state of arousal as your heart rate spikes, blood pressure soars, and cortisol floods your system, impairing rational thought. A mentor once described it best: "When you get angry, your body swells up like a balloon, and all it takes is one prick to blow up."

Science backs this up. Studies show that frequent anger and hostility significantly increase the risk of heart disease, stroke, and even certain cancers. The mental toll is just as severe. Anger feeds anxiety, depression, and addiction. Socially, it isolates and alienates. One heated argument can fracture a relationship beyond repair, and one rash decision made in anger can alter the course of a lifetime.

The key to mastering anger is mastering the pause. Mindfulness is more than a trendy buzzword. It's a tool that can rewire your brain's response to anger. The moment you feel your temper rising, take a breath. Step back. Reset.

I recall one heated argument with my wife; I wanted to lash out, but instead, I stepped back, laid down on the floor on my back, and breathed deeply. Within minutes, my anger subsided, and we could talk things through rationally instead of igniting a war. Within minutes, my anger subsided, allowing me to communicate rationally rather than escalate the conflict. That single pause changed everything.

By interrupting anger's momentum, you reclaim control, choosing a response instead of allowing rage to dictate your actions.

Anger is often a mask for deeper emotions such as fear, insecurity, frustration, or sadness. I worked closely with a passionate entrepreneur who erupted whenever his ideas were challenged. Over time, he started to realize his anger was rooted in a fear of rejection and failure. By addressing these insecurities, he transformed his anger into resilience, using criticism as a tool for growth rather than a personal attack.

Self-awareness is the first step to dismantling anger. Ask yourself: What am I really angry about? What's the deeper wound? Often, anger is just the symptom and you'll need to find the root cause to find clarity.

It's like gripping a burning coal with the intent of throwing it at someone. In the end the only person who ends up suffering is you. Holding onto grudges stokes the flames of anger, while forgiveness extinguishes them.

Lewis B. Smedes put it perfectly: "To forgive is to set a prisoner free and discover that the prisoner was you." Forgiveness isn't about letting others off the hook; it's about releasing yourself from the shackles of past pain.

Mastering anger isn't about suppressing the anger and eventually blowing a gasket, it's about transforming and managing the emotion. Here's how to channel it constructively:

When anger flares, your body enters fight mode. Shift your physical state to influence your emotional state. The Prophet Muhammad (PBUH) advised, "If you become angry while standing, sit down. If you are still angry, lie down." This advice underscores the importance of altering physical and spiritual states to master emotions. Deep breathing activates the parasympathetic nervous system, calming the storm within.

Words spoken in anger are like deadly poisonous arrows that you cannot retrieve once released. If you struggle with verbal outbursts, bite your tongue when you're angry. Literally. This physical reminder creates space for reflection before speaking. Silence often carries more wisdom than a hasty retort.

Exercise is a powerful outlet for pent-up rage. The gym is my sanctuary for any anger or emotion and gives me a place to transform my aggression into power, where every rep and every drop of sweat purges toxicity from my system. Running, lifting weights, or engaging in combat sports strengthens the body and also disciplines the mind.

For those with faith, prayer and meditation provide unparalleled peace. Surrendering anger to a higher power shifts perspective, dissolving ego-driven reactions.

Bottling up anger leads to explosive outbursts. Find a healthy outlet. For example, talk to a trusted friend, journal, or seek guidance from a mentor. Expressing emotions in a controlled environment prevents collateral damage.

Anger is raw energy and can be channeled. Some of history's greatest achievements were born from frustration redirected into innovation. Use anger to propel you forward, not consume you. Let it sharpen your focus, drive, and determination.

Mastering anger is not about eradicating it, because that will never happen. It's about understanding its power, respecting its force, and learning to wield it with intention. Anger, when controlled, fuels motivation and drives us toward justice. When unchecked, it wreaks havoc on our lives.

True strength is not in overpowering others, but in conquering yourself. As you practice mindfulness, unravel the deeper emotions behind your anger, and embrace forgiveness, you will transform this volatile force into a source of resilience and wisdom.

CHAPTER 53

FORGIVE AND FORGET

TO ERR IS HUMAN, BUT TO FORGIVE IS DIVINE.

Forgiveness is the foundation of our humanity, a divine quality that elevates the soul. No one is more forgiving and merciful than our Creator, and it is through His mercy that we, too, have the capacity to forgive even the greatest transgressions. True strength lies in showing mercy when we have the power to condemn.

Some may see forgiveness as weakness, mistaking it for powerlessness. They may say you are soft or that you lacked the strength to retaliate. But do not be swayed by their words, as true power is not found in vengeance but in restraint. Allah is always with those who are connected to Him and those who uphold a higher standard.

Being harsh and unforgiving leads to an emotional landfill filled with the discarded remains of envy, rage, hatred, and animosity. Every unprocessed emotion piles up, piece by piece, until what was once the sanctuary of your heart becomes a dark, desolate wasteland.

Life, with its inevitable heartaches and turmoil, often brings us to a crossroads. One path is an emotional roller coaster fueled by anger and resentment; the other, the road less traveled, is marked by patience, love, mercy, and, ultimately, inner peace.

At twenty-eight, I found myself standing at that very crossroads. My world crumbled in an instant as my first marriage dissolved unexpectedly and I lost an executive position with millions in stock options at stake. It felt as though the universe had conspired against me, stripping away the love and security I had relied upon. I had two choices: I could let bitterness consume me, or I could navigate those turbulent waters with patience and faith, believing that life had something greater in store.

Though my circumstances were uniquely mine, the struggle to forgive is universal. We all encounter betrayal, disappointment, and loss. These trials were more than just painful experiences; they were profound lessons in humility, forgiveness, and the art of letting go. I learned that holding onto resentment only burdens the soul.

Forgiveness is difficult and it demands courage, a willingness to release self-righteous pride, and, above all, an open heart. Yet, it is often our own arrogance that chains us to bitterness, trapping us in a prison of pain. And for what? Choosing not to forgive doesn't grant us a gold medal or a million-dollar bonus. Our Creator forgives billions upon billions of people for their sins and atrocities, yet we hesitate to forgive someone we love for the simplest of things.

Here's the truth: Forgiveness is not about excusing those who have wronged us. It is about liberating ourselves from the emotional shackles that keep us tethered to past wounds. Research from the *Journal of Cognitive Psychotherapy* confirms that those who practice forgiveness experience lower levels of anxiety and depression, leading to improved mental health.[25] In essence, forgiveness does not just free us from the actions of others; it releases us from our own internal struggles with resentment and hurt.

Think of forgiveness as a detox for the spirit, flushing out the toxins of vengeful thoughts and clearing the way for peace, clarity, and happiness. Each act of forgiveness becomes a master key, undoing locks to personal growth and self-actualization, freeing us from the burdens of the past.

---

25 Giacomo Bono and Michael E. McCullough, "Positive Responses to Benefit and Harm: Bringing Forgiveness and Gratitude Into Cognitive Psychotherapy," *Journal of Cognitive Psychotherapy: An International Quarterly*, 20(2) (2006): 147–158, https://doi.org/10.1891/jcop.20.2.147.

Moreover, a study published in the *Journal of Health Psychology* shows a strong correlation between forgiveness and stress reduction.[26] Letting go of past grievances is not just a spiritual exercise; it is in fact a psychological necessity. Much of our daily stress and anxiety stem from our unwillingness to release old wounds.

By embracing forgiveness, you unchain yourself from the past and lighten your emotional load. The barren landfill of your heart transforms into a thriving oasis, where seeds of contentment, joy, and peace take root.

Forgiveness is not a sign of weakness, nor is it surrender. It is divine strength. When you let go of yesterday's pain, you open yourself to the limitless potential of tomorrow. Forgiveness is the rain that washes away the debris of resentment, allowing a lush garden of peace and purpose to grow in its place.

Before moving forward, I urge you to reflect on all those you harbor resentment toward, as well as those who have wronged you. Look deeply, reflect, and forgive each of them. You cannot move forward in attaining the nature of this book until you have a heart free of resentment and ill will.

ENVY: POISON OF THE SOUL

Throughout history, men have battled not only external forces but also the inner demons of envy and arrogance. These emotions, though subtle at times, have the power to erode character, destroy relationships, and blind a man to his own blessings. If left unchecked, they become a corrosive force that undermines the very foundation of success, peace, and fulfillment.

Envy is not a new affliction. It was the very first sin committed by Satan himself. When God created Adam and granted him honor, Satan, once a noble worshipper, was consumed with envy. He could not accept that another being was receiving a favor he did not. His jealousy led him

---

[26] Loren L. Toussaint, Grant S. Shields, and George M. Slavich, "Forgiveness, Stress, and Health: A 5-Week Dynamic Parallel Process Study," *Journal of Health Psychology*, 21(6), (2016): 1151–1164, doi: 10.1007/s12160-016-9796-6.

into a blind rage, ultimately causing his downfall. Instead of recognizing his own blessings, he fixated on another's, turning his envy into rebellion.

Envy operates the same way in a man's life today. It makes him resentful of others' success while ignoring his own potential. It shifts focus from self-mastery to destructive comparison. Rather than using another man's accomplishments as motivation, an envious heart seeks to diminish, undermine, or even sabotage. Envy is a thief that steals joy, contentment, and ambition, leaving behind only bitterness.

The Prophet Muhammad (PBUH) warned, "Beware of envy, for it consumes good deeds like fire consumes wood." When we allow jealousy to dictate our thoughts, we lose sight of gratitude, a key ingredient in true strength and fulfillment.

Where envy is rooted in comparison, arrogance is rooted in delusion. It is the false belief that one is inherently better than others. Arrogance is a mask for insecurity, a fragile ego's attempt to validate itself through superiority.

The dangers of arrogance are profound. A man consumed by arrogance refuses to learn. He stops growing because he believes he already knows everything. He alienates those around him, mistaking dominance for respect. He resists humility, which is the foundation of wisdom. In the Qur'an, God warns, "Do not turn your cheek in arrogance, nor walk upon the earth exultantly. Indeed, God does not like the arrogant and boastful." (Qur'an 31:18)

The greatest leaders in history, men who built legacies that transcended their lifetimes, shared one thing in common: humility. They understood that true power is not about appearing superior but about lifting others, about service, and about continuous self-refinement.

Scholars have identified four destructive traits that create misery and suffering in the world:

1. **Arrogance:** the belief that one is above correction or growth.
2. **Jealousy:** the resentment of another's blessings.
3. **Lying:** the erosion of integrity, which poisons all relationships.
4. **Gossip:** the act of tearing others down instead of building oneself up.

These vices do not just harm others; they weaken the man who possesses them. A man dominated by these traits is not truly strong; he is brittle and easily shattered by challenges and insecurity.

Excessive bragging is a by-product of arrogance. While there is value in recognizing one's achievements, boasting often stems from a need for validation. If you are doing things solely for the sake of God, with pure intention, there is no need to boast or brag about accomplishments. Actions speak for themselves. My teacher used to say, "I can't hear you; your actions are too loud."

A study published in the *Journal of Experimental Social Psychology* found that boastful individuals tend to lose respect and damage relationships.[27] Others naturally distance themselves from those who flaunt their success rather than share it with humility. The more a man seeks validation through boasting, the more fragile his confidence actually is. True excellence is quiet, focused, and steady.

Many cultures acknowledge the concept of the evil eye. The idea that harm can come from being envied. This belief is not mere superstition but a recognition of the psychological and spiritual effects of unchecked jealousy.

The Prophet Muhammad (PBUH) said, "The evil eye is real. If anything were to overtake destiny, it would be the evil eye." This emphasizes the need to protect oneself from envy cast by others and from within.

The best antidote? Gratitude. The more we focus on our own blessings, the less we are affected by what others have.

To combat envy and arrogance, a man must cultivate two essential traits:

1. **Humility:** A real man knows that strength is not found in proving superiority but in self-improvement. He listens more than he speaks. He seeks wisdom rather than validation. He acknowledges that his

---

[27] Irene Scopelliti, George Loewenstein, and Joachim Vosgerau, "You Call It 'Self-Exuberance'; I Call It 'Bragging': Miscalibrated Predictions of Emotional Responses to Self-Promotion," *Journal of Experimental Psychological Science*, 26(6) (2015): 903–914, doi: 10.1177/0956797615573516.

success is not self-made but the result of effort, divine blessings, and support from others.
2. **Gratitude:** Instead of fixating on what he lacks, a strong man counts his blessings. Every morning he wakes up, he has something to be thankful for like health, opportunities, and the ability to grow. Gratitude transforms envy into contentment and arrogance into purpose.

The world does not need more men consumed by arrogance and envy. It needs men of substance who uplift rather than diminish, who strive for greatness without tearing others down, and who lead with both confidence and humility.

By rejecting envy and arrogance, and instead embracing gratitude and humility, you carve a path to true inner peace and fulfillment. You become a man who commands respect not through intimidation but through wisdom and virtue.

Your journey to becoming the man you were meant to be begins with mastering yourself. Let go of resentment, dispel jealousy, and walk forward with strength, wisdom, and grace.

CHAPTER 54

CHECK YOUR EGO AT THE DOOR

THE EGO, OUR SENSE OF SELF-IMPORTANCE AND IDENTITY, IS LIKE a double-edged sword. On one side, it fuels our ambition, confidence, and drive to achieve. But when left unchecked, it mutates into arrogance, pride, and self-absorption, thus blinding us, weakening our character and damaging our relationships. The path to true greatness is not about inflating the ego but mastering it.

Lao Tzu once said, "He who conquers others is strong; he who conquers himself is mighty." Mastering the ego is one of the hardest, yet most essential, battles a man will ever face. This chapter explores the nature of the ego through the lenses of Stoicism, Islam, philosophy, and history, drawing lessons from great minds and leaders who wrestled with its power.

Stoicism, an ancient Greek philosophy, teaches discipline, virtue, and self-awareness. For Stoics like Marcus Aurelius, humility was the antidote to an overgrown ego. Despite being the most powerful man in the Roman Empire, he constantly reminded himself, "A man's worth is no greater than the worth of his ambitions." True ambition is directed inward toward self-improvement and service, not external validation.

Stoicism reminds us that we control very little in this world, especially how others perceive us. If we are ruled by the need for approval, our ego will drive us into insecurity, comparison, and reckless decision-making. Instead, we must focus on what we can control: our thoughts, actions, and integrity.

Seneca warned of ego-driven desires, arguing that wealth, power, and status are impermanent. A man who chases them at the expense of his character is not truly strong; he is enslaved. Epictetus, a former slave turned philosopher, reinforced this wisdom, teaching that external achievements mean nothing if one lacks inner peace.

Stoic principles, though practiced thousands of years ago, are more powerful than ever in our current world of excess. We must train ourselves to detach from the noise, find worth in our actions, and resist the pull of ego-driven validation.

In Islam, the ego (Nafs) is considered a barrier to spiritual growth. Left unchecked, it breeds pride, arrogance, and self-worship. The Qur'an warns, "Do not walk upon the earth exultantly. Indeed, you will never tear the earth [apart], and you will never reach the mountains in height." (Qur'an 17:37)

The Prophet Muhammad (PBUH) embodied humility, despite being a leader of nations. He lived simply, mended his own clothes, and reminded his followers that no man is superior to another except in righteousness. Islam categorizes the ego into three levels:

- **Nafs al-Ammara (The Commanding Self):** The lowest form, ruled by desires and arrogance.
- **Nafs al-Lawwama (The Self-Reproaching Soul):** The stage of self-awareness, where a man recognizes his flaws.
- **Nafs al-Mutma'innah (The Tranquil Soul):** The highest state, where a man conquers his ego through discipline, faith, and humility.

Through prayer, fasting, and acts of charity, a Muslim trains himself to control his ego, ensuring it serves him rather than enslaves him.

Friedrich Nietzsche warned against the "will to power," a manifestation of the ego that, if left unchecked, leads to destruction. Chasing dominance and self-glorification can blind men to wisdom and morality. History proves this time and again.

Carl Jung further believed the ego should not be destroyed but integrated. True self-mastery comes from balancing our strengths and weaknesses, facing our darkness, and refining ourselves into complete men.

Sigmund Freud's psychological model echoes this concept: The ego mediates between primal desires (*id*) and higher moral consciousness (*superego*). When the ego is overinflated, it leads to narcissism; when weak, it results in self-doubt and insecurity. The goal is to balance confidence without arrogance and ambition without recklessness.

History is a graveyard of men destroyed by unchecked egos. Napoleon Bonaparte, one of the greatest military strategists in history, fell victim to his pride. His invasion of Russia in winter, which was a reckless decision fueled by overconfidence, eventually led to catastrophic defeat and his eventual downfall. His ego blinded him to reality, proving that even the mighty can fall when arrogance takes the reins.

Modern examples also illustrate this struggle. Our current president is a great example of this, allowing unchecked ego to spawn into a Thanos-esque megalomania that could lead to catastrophic worldwide war and destruction.

Steve Jobs, once known for his arrogance, learned humility through failure. His return to Apple was marked by a transformed leadership style that valued collaboration and empathy. His story teaches us that recognizing and correcting our ego's faults can lead to even greater success.

Understanding the ego's pitfalls is the first step; actively working to master it is the next. Here are some battle-tested strategies:

1. **Practice humility.** Regularly remind yourself of your limitations. No man is invincible. Acknowledge the contributions of others and express gratitude.
2. **Embrace constructive criticism.** Seek honest feedback from those who will hold you accountable. Listen more than you speak.
3. **Cultivate mindfulness and self-awareness.** Engage in daily intro-

spection, prayer, or meditation. Are your thoughts driven by pride or purpose?
4. **Adopt a growth mindset.** See challenges as opportunities to refine yourself. A man who believes he has already "arrived" stops growing.
5. **Detach from external validation.** Social media, wealth, and status mean nothing if your character is weak. Measure success by your discipline, integrity, and impact.
6. **Serve others.** True strength lies in lifting others, not just yourself. A man who serves is a man who is in control of his ego.

The ego is a deceptive beast. It tricks you with beautiful lies telling you that you are superior, entitled, or beyond reproach. It urges you to chase status, to seek revenge, to refuse correction. But a real man of strength masters it before it masters him.

So ask yourself: Who is in control? Are you leading your ego, or is it leading you?

The battle against the ego is lifelong, but victory is possible for those willing to fight it.

CHAPTER 55

CONFIDENCE

IN THE JOURNEY TO BECOMING THE MAN YOU WERE MEANT TO be, confidence is a foundational element. It is not an act of bravado displayed for the world's approval but a quiet, unshakable force that governs a man's thoughts, decisions, and actions. Confidence, when rooted in integrity, purpose, and discipline, becomes a compass for self-actualization. Unlike the momentary highs of external validation, authentic confidence does not waver in the face of hardship; rather, it flourishes in solitude, where character is tested without an audience.

I have realized that confidence is mainly about being right with God, knowing He has your back and is in control of every single outcome in life. Second, it is about being secure in yourself and who you are, what you stand for, and practicing what you preach. I used to think confidence was this hard, alpha, egocentric presentation and force that had to be on at all times. In reality, that is just an insecurity or a sign of an unchecked ego. When you are right with God and the self, your light and confidence will shine, and you will be able to live knowing that you are only accountable to the Most High and no one or nothing else.

This world often equates confidence with outward dominance like loud voices, unchecked ambition, and an insatiable hunger for recognition. But true confidence is best measured in private moments, when no one is watching. It is found in the man who adheres to his principles even when the world tempts him to compromise. It is displayed in the father who wakes before dawn to provide for his family, in the leader who makes the difficult choice aligned with justice rather than convenience, and in the man who controls his desires rather than being controlled by them.

One of the greatest historical examples of this principle is found in the life of Prophet Yusuf (Joseph). Betrayed by his brothers, sold into slavery, and unjustly imprisoned, he never abandoned his principles. His patience and steadfast faith allowed him to rise from captivity to leadership, not because he sought power but because he was worthy of it. This is the essence of true masculine confidence. It is an inner strength that is independent of external circumstances, forged through faith, resilience, and purpose.

At the core of masculine confidence is self-mastery. Without the discipline to control one's thoughts and actions, confidence is nothing more than arrogance waiting to collapse. The Stanford Marshmallow Experiment, which studied delayed gratification, revealed a critical truth: Those with the ability to resist immediate temptations in favor of long-term rewards achieved greater success in life.[28] This principle extends beyond childhood psychology and right into masculine resilience.

A man who can prioritize purpose over pleasure, legacy over indulgence, and discipline over distraction is a man who commands his own destiny. This is why the world's most respected men—leaders, warriors, scholars—were not slaves to their impulses but masters of their actions. They understood that confidence is built through consistency, through the quiet repetition of right choices over time.

Confidence is not a static trait; it is an evolving force, strengthened through knowledge, experience, and self-improvement. Whether in professional development, physical health, or spiritual refinement, growth

---

28 Walter Mischel, Yuichi Shoda, and Philip K. Peake, "The Nature of Adolescent Competencies Predicted by Preschool Delay of Gratification," *Journal of Personality and Social Psychology*, 54(4) (1988): 687–696, doi: 10.1037//0022-3514.54.4.687.

is a nonnegotiable component of confidence. A man who refuses to learn is a man who stagnates, and stagnation is the death of confidence.

Strength is cultivated through discipline, resilience, and lifelong learning. It is not enough to just exist. You must push beyond comfort, challenge limiting beliefs, and pursue excellence in all aspects of life. Confidence grows in the discomfort of effort, in the sharpening of skills, and in always becoming better than yesterday.

Beyond self-discipline and external refinement, the deepest and most enduring confidence comes from spiritual grounding. Research by the Pew Research Center has shown that individuals with strong spiritual practices often exhibit higher levels of confidence and resilience.[29] When a man recognizes that he is part of something greater he becomes unshakable.

Faith provides an anchor, a guiding principle that keeps a man steady through the storms of life. When a man is right with God, he is right with himself. This alignment creates an unshakable confidence, which you carry in quiet assurance, knowing that you are moving with divine purpose.

Confidence is not the absence of hardship but the ability to persevere through it. The strongest men are not those who have avoided failure but those who have learned to rise from it. Psychological resilience, or the ability to view setbacks as opportunities rather than defeats, is a defining trait of true confidence.

This mindset shift is lifesaving. Life will present obstacles, betrayals, losses, and challenges. A confident man does not crumble in the face of adversity; he adapts, learns, and grows stronger. Every challenge becomes fuel, every hardship a lesson, and every setback a stepping stone.

Physical well-being plays a critical role in confidence. A strong body contributes to better mental clarity, sustained energy levels, and improved decision-making. We've discussed several times in this book

---

[29] Report, "Religion's Relationship to Happiness, Civic Engagement and Health Around the World," *Pew Research Center*, January 31, 2019, https://www.pewresearch.org/religion/2019/01/31/religions-relationship-to-happiness-civic-engagement-and-health-around-the-world/.

that physical training is not about vanity; it is about honoring the body through which purpose is executed. Strength is a reflection of discipline, and a disciplined man exudes confidence not because of how he looks but because of how he carries himself.

Confidence does not develop in comfort zones. It requires the risk of stepping into the unknown, embracing failure, and facing challenges head-on. Whether in public speaking, entrepreneurship, or personal relationships, confidence is a skill honed through repeated experiences of overcoming obstacles.

A man who avoids challenges will always be haunted by his own doubts. But a man who confronts his fears, who dares to fail and rise again, becomes untouchable. Every challenge he conquers adds another layer to his confidence, making him stronger, wiser, and more capable.

Building true masculine confidence is not a destination, but a lifelong journey. It requires self-awareness, resilience, continuous self-improvement, and a commitment to a higher purpose. Confidence is earned, not given; it is developed through consistent introspection, disciplined effort, and faith in a greater plan.

In the end, the reward is not just personal success, but a deep sense of fulfillment and authenticity. The man who cultivates true confidence becomes a force of stability, leadership, and inspiration for himself and those around him.

You will embody purpose, legacy, and the highest version of yourself. And that is the essence of true masculine confidence.

HUMILITY/HUMBLENESS

It's easy to believe that success is about recognition and worldly awards. The trophies, the titles, the applause. Society teaches us that greatness is measured in accolades, that power is displayed through dominance, and that influence is built on the ability to command attention. But if you've ever met a man who is truly great, you'll notice something different. He isn't the one shouting his own name or demanding attention. He walks with quiet confidence, his actions speaking louder than his words.

Humility is the mark of real strength. It is the trait that separates the men who build legacies from the ones who merely chase status. It is the difference between power that corrupts and power that serves. The world has seen many men rise to positions of influence, yet only a few are remembered with reverence—those who led not for personal gain, but for a greater purpose.

I will never forget July of 2024. My brother and dear friend, Jaylen Brown, had just won an NBA championship and was crowned Finals MVP. He had reached the pinnacle of his career. The moment most athletes dream of from childhood. If there was ever a time to bask in glory, this was it. And yet, what did he choose to do?

Rather than indulging in the noise of fame, he sought the peace of his Creator. Instead of parades and parties, he made his way to Mecca to perform Umrah with a close group of companions. In that sacred place, he wasn't "NBA Champion Jaylen Brown" or "Global Leader Jaylen Brown." He was just "Brother Jaylen."

One moment in particular made me smile. As we walked together in the sacred mosque, some Indonesian travelers spotted us and rushed over excitedly. They wanted a picture with our friend Tacko Fall. They handed their camera to Jaylen without realizing who he was. Did he get offended? Did he remind them of his achievements? No. He smiled warmly, took the picture, and carried on.

Later, as we circled the Kaaba together, my Ihram, the simple white cloth worn by pilgrims, slipped from my shoulders. Before I could adjust it, I felt a hand fixing it back into place. It was Jaylen. A small moment, but a profound one. A reminder that true leadership is service, that greatness is found in the simplest acts of care.

The world teaches men to be loud about their success, to make sure everyone knows their name. But the strongest men in history, the ones who shaped the world, built empires, and changed lives, were not defined by arrogance. They led with humility.

The Prophet Muhammad (PBUH), the greatest leader to walk this earth, never sat above his people. He ate with them, served them, walked among them as an equal. He mended his own shoes, helped with household chores, and never used his status to belittle anyone. He was a leader not because he sought power, but because he sought to serve.

Jaylen's actions reminded me of this. True strength isn't about being above others, but about lifting them up. Whether it's fixing a brother's Ihram, taking a photo for a stranger, or treating every person with respect, the smallest acts of humility reveal the greatest strength.

This is the kind of man we should all strive to be. The one whose greatness is not measured by his titles but by his character. The one who understands that real power is not about what you take from the world, but what you give back to it.

In the end, the loudest voices fade, but the impact of a humble man echoes for generations. The question is: What kind of legacy will you leave?

CHAPTER 56

YOUR "STARTING FIVE"

THE PROPHET MUHAMMAD (PBUH) SAID:

> The example of a good companion and a bad companion is like that of the perfume seller and the blacksmith's bellows. The perfume seller might either gift you perfume, or you may buy some from him, or at the very least, you'll enjoy a pleasant fragrance from him. As for the blacksmith's bellows, he will either burn your clothes, or at the very least, you'll breathe in an unpleasant odor. (Sahih Al-Bukhari and Sahih Muslim)

One of the most important lessons I've learned is that the company you keep shapes the man you become. Your "starting five," the core people in your circle, either push you toward greatness or pull you toward mediocrity. Just as being around a perfume merchant inevitably leaves you smelling pleasant, surrounding yourself with virtuous company enhances your character, spirituality, and morals. Conversely, being around negative influences (symbolized by the blacksmith's bellows) inevitably harms or negatively impacts you, whether immediately or subtly.

The people I admire most are those who keep their faith at the center of their lives, no matter how much success they achieve. They are the ones who remind me that a man's worth isn't in his wealth, his fame, or his achievements but in his character.

Ask yourself:

- Who are the five people closest to you?
- Do they inspire humility, discipline, and faith?
- Do they challenge you to be better, or do they feed your ego?
- Would your Creator be pleased with the company you keep?

If you want to be a man of true greatness, surround yourself with brothers who remind you of what truly matters. Build friendships that are rooted in purpose, not just convenience. Love each other for the sake of God, and you will find a bond that no success or failure can break.

In the end, titles fade. Trophies collect dust. Money comes and goes. But the way you treat people and the humility with which you carry yourself will be your true legacy.

A real man understands this: The more he is blessed, the more he serves. The higher he rises, the more he lowers himself in gratitude. And the closer he gets to his dreams, the closer he walks toward his Creator.

Because humility isn't weakness. It's the highest form of strength.

Have you ever paused to really think about who your "starting five" are? If life were a basketball game, your starting five would be the key players surrounding you. They are the ones who influence, inspire, and challenge you to evolve into the best version of yourself. These aren't just casual friends but the people who mold your thoughts, impact your emotions, and guide your decisions. The quality of this circle is critical, and that's what we explore in this chapter.

The ancient Greek philosopher Euripides once said, "The company you keep reveals your character." Similarly, Jim Rohn, a renowned entrepreneur and motivational speaker, famously stated, "You're the average of the five people you spend the most time with." These powerful insights highlight the importance of carefully curating the individuals in your inner circle. Your starting five can be a springboard to success or an anchor that drags you down.

Psychological studies back this up. Research on social influence demonstrates that habits, aspirations, and even emotions are contagious within close-knit groups. In a 2007 study published in *The New England Journal of Medicine*, scientists found that obesity spreads through social circles.[30] Meaning if a close friend becomes obese, your own risk of obesity rises by 57 percent. This principle applies to every area of life: ambition, self-discipline, and even integrity are shaped by the people we spend time with.

You need to surround yourself with people who push you beyond your comfort zone, who inspire you to take risks, to keep learning, and to pursue your dreams relentlessly. The right circle consists of individuals who radiate positivity, embody a growth mindset, and align with your values, beliefs, and aspirations. These are the people who genuinely care about your well-being and success.

Conversely, negative influences can derail your growth. Toxic people with bad energy consumed by jealousy, insecurity, or a misalignment with your values will drain your energy and cloud your focus. It's like trying to row a boat while someone on board constantly pulls against the current; you'll end up going nowhere.

I faced this firsthand. Multiple times in my life, I found myself hanging around the wrong crowd. These were people obsessed with chasing women, flaunting status, and partying hard. Over time, I started mirroring their behavior. Like a frog slowly boiling in water, I drifted further from the man I was meant to be, allowing negative influences to shape my path.

I reached my breaking point when I got into a straight-up brawl with my dad in the kitchen. I had become an unrecognizable version of myself, succumbing to my ego and abandoning my values. At that moment, I stepped back and reflected on who I had become and why I had attracted these acquaintances. That period of introspection led me to rebuild my true self.

---

30 Nicholas A. Christakis and James H. Fowler, "The Spread of Obesity in a Large Social Network over 32 Years," *The New England Journal of Medicine*, 357(4) (2007): 370–379, doi: 10.1056/NEJMsa066082.

Through prayer and self-work, God began facilitating amazing people into my life in ways I couldn't have imagined. I started focusing deliberately on the qualities I wanted to see in myself such as faith, integrity, character, love, and I made these nonnegotiables in my circle. My greatest blessing and example from this came in college when I chose to room with Mohammad Rahman. We had nothing in common on the surface: He was a nerdy math major from New York, and I was a football player from Texas. But we shared one thing that mattered most: faith. That decision led to a lifelong brotherhood that has shaped me into the man I am today.

At first, we struggled to understand each other. He was detail oriented, calculated, and focused on his studies, while I thrived on competition, physical intensity, and camaraderie. Yet, over time, our differences became our greatest strengths. He taught me discipline in academics, the power of deep thinking, and how to approach life with patience and strategy. In return, I helped him break out of his shell, build confidence, and embrace leadership beyond the classroom. We held each other accountable in faith, prayed together, fasted during Ramadan side by side, and engaged in deep discussions about purpose and legacy.

One defining moment was during a particularly rough time in my life when I was battling injuries and personal struggles. Mohammad sensed my frustration and, instead of offering empty encouragement, he sat me down and reminded me why I started this journey in the first place. He challenged me to see beyond the present hardship and focus on the bigger picture. That moment solidified our bond. He wasn't just a friend; he became a brother in every sense of the word.

Years later, we've traveled the world together, stood beside each other through life's greatest triumphs and hardest losses, and remained each other's closest confidants. His presence in my life has been a divine gift, reinforcing the truth that the greatest friendships are those founded on shared values, faith, and an unwavering commitment to making each other better men.

Establishing brotherhood and community is integral. A man's journey is not meant to be a solitary one. Across cultures and throughout history, community, companionship, and brotherhood have been central to a man's well-being and growth.

- **The Spartans** trained together, fought together, and relied on each other with unshakable loyalty. Their strength wasn't just in their individual abilities but in their collective bond.
- **Medieval guilds** ensured craftsmen had the mentorship, discipline, and community to thrive in their trade and in life.
- **Prophet Muhammad (PBUH)** built a community of men who supported each other in righteousness, emphasizing that true strength lies in unity and shared purpose.

This power of camaraderie is evident in military units, sports teams, and fraternal organizations. These groups create a sense of belonging, unity, and shared purpose, promoting deep trust and mutual support. But these relationships don't develop overnight. They require consistent effort, patience, and time. Here are key steps to building and maintaining a strong brotherhood:

- **Show genuine interest.** Ask thoughtful questions and listen attentively.
- **Embrace vulnerability.** Share openly to build trust.
- **Create shared experiences.** Plan activities to strengthen bonds.
- **Communicate transparently.** Address concerns respectfully and be open to feedback.
- **Express appreciation.** Celebrate achievements and show gratitude.
- **Offer support in triumph and adversity.** Be present through highs and lows.
- **Build trust.** Be reliable, honest, and respectful of confidentiality.
- **Listen actively.** Pay attention to words, tone, and body language.

Your starting five isn't just about having a few friends around. It's about deliberately choosing people who push you to grow, hold you accountable, and support your journey toward excellence. A strong brotherhood provides more than companionship; it offers a sanctuary where you can be challenged, encouraged, and uplifted.

Take stock of your starting five. Are they empowering you or draining you? Are they pushing you to strive for excellence or holding you back? Your community shapes you, whether you realize it or not, so choose your team wisely. And remember, just like any team, relationships require commitment, effort, and the willingness to build each other up.

By surrounding yourself with the right influences, building meaningful connections, and committing to a life of brotherhood, you'll create an unbreakable support system that propels you to grow, thrive, and become the best version of yourself.

CHAPTER 57

HEAVEN IS AT THE FOOT OF YOUR MOTHER

ONE OF THE MOST DEFINING MEASURES OF A MAN'S CHARACTER is how he treats his parents. A man who lacks gratitude and respect for those who gave him life is a man who has lost sight of himself. The way you honor your parents reflects your humility, discipline, and capacity for love. It is not just a moral obligation; it is a blueprint for personal growth and success in life.

Momma, I love you. I am endlessly grateful for your light, your sacrifices, and the love that has shaped me into the man I am today. You carried me for nine months, protected me, and instilled in me the values of compassion, optimism, and authenticity. To anyone reading this book, never forget the immense blessing of your mother. Whether she is here or has returned to the Almighty, pray for her daily.

The saying "Heaven is at the feet of your mother" is a profound reminder of the weight of our duty to honor and cherish our parents. In a world that often prioritizes individualism over family, we must realign ourselves with this fundamental truth: Respecting and caring for our parents is a source of immense blessings, both in this life and the next.

A man of integrity does not wait until his parents are old and frail to acknowledge their sacrifices. He cultivates a bond with them through communication, gratitude, patience, and time.

1. COMMUNICATION: LISTEN AND SPEAK WITH RESPECT

Good communication is at the core of any relationship, and the parent–child bond is no exception. Active listening or truly paying attention to what your parents say builds understanding and trust. Too often, we are quick to dismiss their advice, thinking that times have changed, but wisdom is timeless. Speak with respect, even in disagreement. The Qur'an instructs:

> And your Lord has decreed that you not worship except Him, and to parents, good treatment. Whether one or both of them reach old age [while] with you, say not to them [so much as], "uff," and do not repel them but speak to them a noble word. (Qur'an 17:23)

A real man exercises emotional control and patience, knowing that one day, he too will seek understanding from his children.

2. GRATITUDE: ACKNOWLEDGE THEIR SACRIFICES

A grateful heart is the foundation of strength. Your parents sacrificed sleep, finances, and personal comfort to provide for you. Show appreciation not just in words, but in actions through kindness, service, and thoughtfulness. Whether it's a phone call, a simple "thank you," or taking them out for a meal, never let them feel unappreciated.

3. TIME: THE MOST VALUABLE GIFT

Time is the most precious currency, and spending it with your parents is one of the greatest expressions of love. It doesn't take extravagant gestures like fancy trips or lavish gifts. It can be doing things as simple as sharing a meal, watching a game, or going for a walk that can deepen your bond.

4. CONFLICT RESOLUTION: PATIENCE OVER PRIDE

Disagreements are inevitable, but they must be handled with wisdom. A mature man understands that winning an argument with his parents is never truly a victory. Instead of reacting with frustration, seek to understand their perspective. If deep-rooted conflicts exist, seeking guidance from a counselor or trusted advisor can help navigate these challenges while maintaining respect.

A key indicator of character is how a man treats the parents of others including his friends, his wife's family, or even strangers. Showing respect to the parents of those you care about is a sign of genuine consideration and emotional intelligence. It demonstrates an understanding that our upbringing shapes who we become.

Many ancient traditions emphasize the importance of honoring one's parents:

- **Islam:** The Prophet Muhammad (PBUH) said, "He is not of us who does not have mercy on young children, nor honor the elderly."
- **Stoicism:** Epictetus taught that gratitude and humility toward parents are essential for self-mastery.
- **Confucianism:** Filial piety (孝, xiào) is considered one of the highest virtues, stressing that respect for parents leads to a harmonious society.

The decline of these values in modern times, fueled by entitlement and defiance, has weakened family structures. By returning to these principles, we strengthen not just our families but our communities and ourselves.

Honoring your parents should never come at the expense of your own well-being. A strong man takes care of his mind, body, and soul so that he can be present and supportive without burning out. Set healthy boundaries when necessary, and practice self-care to maintain balance in your life.

How you treat your parents today is the example you set for your own children. One day, you will be in their position, seeking love and respect from those you raised. By embodying gratitude, patience, and kindness, you uplift your parents and also pave the way for future generations to do the same.

A life built on respect, gratitude, and love for our parents leads to a richer, more fulfilling existence. Honor them while you have the chance. Pray for them, cherish them, and let them see the man you've become. A man who understands that true strength begins with the simple act of saying, "Thank you."

CHAPTER 58

BUILD STRONG FAMILY

THE STRENGTH OF OUR RELATIONSHIPS AND BONDS, PARTICULARLY with family and friends, is a reflection of our character. These bonds form the foundation of our lives, offering solace, support, and guidance. A man who values his kinship with family and friends understands the paramount importance of connection, trust, and mutual respect. He does not view relationships as secondary to his aspirations but as the cornerstone upon which his legacy is built.

Equally significant is the ability to prioritize the needs of others, embodying the essence of selfless service. A real man understands that service is not weakness; it is strength in its highest form. This commitment to altruism does more than build strong connections; it creates unity and belonging. It cultivates empathy and compassion, qualities indispensable to personal and spiritual growth. Acts of service vary, from dedicating time to a charitable cause to offering a listening ear. Even the smallest gestures like being present, providing emotional support, or extending a helping hand can carry a profound impact.

However, serving others should not come at the expense of our own well-being. There's a reason airline attendants instruct us to secure our oxygen masks before assisting others. The glorified world-savior who sacrifices himself entirely for others is a facade. You cannot uplift others without ensuring your own foundation is secure. Family relationships profoundly influence our overall well-being. They shape our attitudes, behaviors, and resilience in the face of adversity. Society often pressures men to prioritize careers, finances, and personal aspirations, but the strength of familial bonds is equally important. Research consistently shows that individuals with strong family connections are generally happier, healthier, and more resilient. These relationships provide a sense of belonging, purpose, and emotional support, helping us navigate life's challenges. To cultivate these bonds, we must prioritize them, whether through weekly calls, shared meals, or just making time for one another. Small acts of connection can profoundly strengthen familial ties.

Clear and open communication is the heart of any thriving relationship, especially within families. While we may assume our loved ones know us best, dialogue remains essential for deepening understanding. Meaningful conversations including asking open-ended questions, listening without judgment, and sharing our own thoughts can strengthen the bonds that hold us together.

Conflict is inevitable in any family, but unresolved resentment can create lasting rifts. Forgiveness, while challenging, is essential to maintaining strong relationships. It requires acknowledging mistakes, empathizing with others, and freeing ourselves from the burdens of past grievances. Forgiveness isn't about forgetting; it's about choosing peace over prolonged conflict.

My own family has faced its share of trials. I remember nights when my dad waited at the doorstep until 3:00 a.m. after my late-night music sessions or the time I packed a bag to run away after getting caught with a fake ID. Growing up in a strict Muslim household, each of us had our rebellious phases via financial strain, reckless living, or unfortunate accidents. A few years ago, we faced a situation that nearly broke us. In that moment, we relied on the Islamic teachings of maintaining family ties, practicing forgiveness, and exercising patience. By sticking together, communicating, and living for a higher purpose, we weathered the storm.

I have no doubt that life will throw more challenges our way, but what matters is how we ride the waves together and emerge stronger.

A special tribute must be given to my father, a man who embodied everything I aspire to be. He built a beautiful and righteous family, always putting us before himself. He never missed a game, a graduation, or a birthday. He taught our Sunday school classes and lived by the principles he instilled in us. He was an exemplary father and husband, proving that true strength is found in service, sacrifice, and unwavering love. His legacy is not in material wealth but in the character he shaped within his children and the love he infused into our home.

Strong men don't sever ties at the first sign of difficulty, nor do they allow brief desires to dictate their relationships. They understand that maintaining family bonds requires effort, patience, and resilience. True strength lies not in abandoning relationships when they become difficult, but in working through challenges to emerge with deeper, stronger connections. The road to fulfilling relationships is undoubtedly difficult, but the rewards are immeasurable.

The strength of family relationships is fundamental to a man's overall well-being. These bonds provide a deep sense of belonging, purpose, and emotional support, fortifying resilience and happiness. By prioritizing family, practicing effective communication, and embracing forgiveness, we build a foundation that endures life's trials. Strengthening family ties is a decree from God and a journey that defines our character and shapes our legacy. The effort required is immense, but the rewards are boundless.

CHAPTER 59
———

DIVINE ENERGY

ALL POWER AND ENERGY FLOW FROM THE DIVINE CREATOR, GOD. When we align ourselves with this Source, we tap into an endless well of strength, clarity, and purpose. The most successful and fulfilled people are not those who merely manage their time well but those who manage their energy, especially their spiritual energy.

I've experienced this firsthand. I recently attended a retreat in Panama with high performers from multiple fields. Despite minimal sleep and intense activity, I felt more energized than ever before. It was as if we were all beams of light, charging each other just by being in alignment with divine energy. The presence of high-energy individuals, all spiritually connected and mission-driven, created an environment of pure vitality.

Contrast this with days when I've slept ten hours, taken all the right supplements, and yet still struggled to keep my eyes open. The difference? Energy protection. On those drained days, I had allowed my energy to be scattered and leaked through distractions, meaningless interactions, and low-frequency environments. Just as the right people can recharge you, others can deplete you.

WE ARE ALL ATOMS FROM ADAM

Every individual radiates a unique energy and force that influences how we engage with the world and how the world responds to us. Think of it as a personal broadcast, constantly transmitting our emotions, attitudes, and spiritual state. This energy, shaped by our mindset, lifestyle, and faith, leaves a profound mark on everything we do.

Our energy constantly shifts between positive, negative, and neutral states, directly impacting our physical, emotional, and mental well-being. Negative energy acts like quicksand, pulling us into stress, anxiety, and even depression. Furthermore, positive energy elevates our spirit, creating joy, peace, and clarity. Put yourself in the mind-state of walking into a room where laughter fills the air, you feel warmth, and the energy is uplifting everyone present. Now picture stepping into a space heavy with tension and negativity. It drains you instantly. This illustrates the profound power of energy in shaping our experiences.

To truly master our energy, self-awareness is critical. Recognizing the energy we exude, and how it ripples out to influence others, is the first step toward transformation. Cultivating positive energy requires conscious effort through prayer, meditation, movement, and a balanced lifestyle. These practices boost our well-being and also uplift everyone we encounter.

In Islam, energy is deeply tied to one's spiritual state and connection with God. Living in alignment with divine principles becomes a powerful conduit for sustaining positive energy. This spiritual link acts like a divine generator, radiating light that attracts blessings and cultivates happiness, not just for ourselves but for everyone around us. As the Qur'an states:

Verily, in the remembrance of God do hearts find rest. (Qur'an 13:28)

When we are spiritually aligned, our energy is purified and amplified, transforming us into beacons of light. It's as though we tap into an infinite source of divine goodness, enabling us to embody joy, peace, and purpose.

Our energy is profoundly shaped by the company we keep. Just as a tuning fork vibrates in harmony with surrounding frequencies, we unconsciously sync with the people around us. Surrounding ourselves with optimistic, supportive, and spiritually grounded individuals increases our positive energy. Conversely, toxic relationships and negative influences act like energy vampires, draining our vitality and joy.

Science supports this. A study published in the *Journal of Consumer Research* explores "emotional contagion," the phenomenon where people absorb and mirror the emotions of those around them.[31] This means the energy we allow into our space directly shapes our mood, thoughts, and actions. Think back on a time when you were around someone radiating enthusiasm and positivity. Chances are, their energy was contagious, leaving you uplifted. The same holds true for negativity.

Acknowledging that our energy is a powerful and shifting force, one that shapes our lives and the world around us, is the foundation for change. By consciously nurturing positivity through spiritual connection, personal growth, and intentional choices, we become the builders of our own joy and beacons of divine light.

A spiritually connected life, grounded in faith and positive intention guides us toward the best version of ourselves. When we align with divine energy, protect our light, and surround ourselves with the right influences, we don't just exist. We radiate. And in doing so, we uplift, inspire, and transform the world around us.

Protecting your energy is just as important as cultivating it. Without boundaries, your spiritual energy can be depleted by toxic environments, negative people, and daily distractions. Here are three essential strategies to guard your divine connection:

1. **Daily spiritual recharge:** Begin and end each day with practices that align you with divine energy. This can include prayer, Qur'an recitation, meditation, or even sitting in silence to reflect and express gratitude.

---

[31] Daniel J. Howard and Charles Gengler, "Emotional Contagion Effects on Product Attitudes," *Journal of Consumer Research*, 28(2) (2001): 189–201, https://doi.org/10.1086/322897.

2. **Selective exposure:** Be intentional about who and what you allow into your energy field. Limit time with negative influences and increase interactions with those who elevate and inspire you.
3. **Mindful consumption:** The content you consume impacts your energy. Choose uplifting books, lectures, and media that reinforce your faith and positive mindset, rather than draining distractions.

When you master your spiritual energy, you operate at a higher frequency where clarity, strength, and divine guidance become your norm. In this state, you are unstoppable, filled with purpose, and deeply connected to the Source of all power.

CHAPTER 60

GOOD MANNERS

THINK ABOUT A WORLD WHERE PEOPLE GREET EACH OTHER warmly, show genuine respect, and approach every interaction with kindness. Unfortunately, today's social interactions are often rushed, and genuine respect for others can feel like an afterthought. Yet, good manners are far from outdated; they remain the foundation of strong relationships, a harmonious community, and personal success.

Manners are not just a set of social niceties; they are a reflection of one's character. They shape our interactions, influence perceptions, and determine the quality of our relationships. A man who embodies discipline and integrity must also embody respect for others. Schools and families must prioritize etiquette as a fundamental life skill, teaching individuals how to navigate the world with grace, humility, and integrity. A society that values good manners furthers mutual respect and cooperation, creating an environment where people feel valued and understood.

Politeness, kindness, and consideration for others are the hallmarks of good manners. They dictate how we treat family, friends, colleagues, and even strangers. From showing gratitude to practicing patience, these small yet meaningful actions create a culture of respect and dignity. Good manners are an investment in relationships, both personal and professional, and can open doors to opportunities that would otherwise remain closed.

Throughout history, good manners have been recognized as the foundation of civilized societies:

- **Islamic teachings:** The Prophet Muhammad (PBUH) said, "Nothing is weightier on the Scale of Deeds than one's good manners." (Al-Bukhari) Respect for others, humility, and kindness are central to leading a life of virtue.
- **Confucianism:** The principle of *li* emphasizes proper behavior, reinforcing values like respect for elders, loyalty, and social harmony.
- **Western chivalry:** Originally a code for knights, chivalry evolved into a broader expectation of politeness, courtesy, and honor.
- **Ancient Greek virtues:** The Greeks valued *arete* (excellence in character), which included respectful speech and honorable behavior.

Regardless of culture or tradition, the universal message remains the same: Good manners are the key to a harmonious and successful life. They serve as the glue that binds communities together, promoting empathy, cooperation, and a deeper sense of connection among people.

Simple gestures like saying "please" and "thank you," holding the door for others, or offering a seat to someone in need demonstrate respect and kindness. These small acts create an environment of mutual appreciation and consideration. Expressing gratitude, no matter how small the favor, builds positive connections and reinforces the importance of thoughtfulness in everyday life.

Good manners extend beyond words; they include respecting physical and emotional boundaries. A courteous individual is mindful of personal space, refrains from intrusive questions, and understands the importance of tact and discretion. This is particularly important in professional settings, where respecting boundaries contributes to a healthier and more productive work environment.

Being on time is a simple yet powerful way to show consideration for others. Whether attending meetings, social events, or family gatherings, arriving on time conveys reliability and appreciation for the time of others. If delays are unavoidable, a sincere apology and clear communication demonstrate accountability.

Punctuality is often an indicator of one's overall sense of responsibility and discipline. People who respect others' time are perceived as dependable, professional, and considerate, which are all qualities that contribute to success in both personal and professional spheres.

I remember my time playing football at Harvard under Coach Tim Murphy. We followed what was known as "Murphy Time," which meant that being seven minutes early was the expectation. If you showed up only five minutes early, you were late. This discipline strengthened character and reinforced the importance of reliability, a habit that has served me well beyond the football field.

Manners extend to how we behave in public. Being mindful of noise levels, waiting patiently in lines, and keeping shared spaces clean reflect an awareness of others and a commitment to community harmony. Public spaces are shared by all, and simple acts such as keeping one's phone volume down, cleaning up after oneself, and offering assistance to those in need contribute to a more civilized and pleasant environment for everyone.

Exemplifying good manners does more than boost personal interactions, but it sets a standard for others to follow. When one person consistently practices respect and kindness, it encourages those around them to do the same. Families, workplaces, and entire communities benefit when individuals prioritize etiquette.

Leading by example is one of the most effective ways to inspire others. When children observe their parents practicing good manners, they internalize those behaviors and carry them forward. Similarly, colleagues in professional settings who practice kindness and consideration create a more respectful and cooperative work culture.

Good manners are more than just a social expectation; they are a way of life. By consistently practicing politeness, thoughtfulness, and respect, we contribute to a more compassionate and dignified world. Achieving good manners requires intention and effort, but the rewards such as stronger relationships, a positive reputation, and a meaningful impact on society are well worth it.

A society that upholds good manners creates an environment where individuals feel valued and respected. Your actions should be a demonstration to the power of manners, inspiring others to uphold the same standard of excellence. In a time where self-interest often takes priority, choosing to prioritize kindness, respect, and etiquette is a powerful statement.

CHAPTER 61

KNOWLEDGE OF SELF

THE JOURNEY TO TRUE SELF-AWARENESS IS NOT MARKED BY EXTERnal success or social status. It is an introspective epic, an unfiltered examination of your essence, your convictions, and how you navigate the world. Afdal al-Din Kashani eloquently states, "To know oneself is to know the everlasting reality that is consciousness, and to know it is to be it."[32] This wisdom compels you to pause. Not to see yourself through the lens of society's expectations but to see yourself in the reality of your inner consciousness, the eternal force that defines you.

What if you could look into a mirror that reveals the depths of your soul. Self-awareness is not a one-off moment of reflection; it is the deliberate practice of mapping your strengths, weaknesses, and hidden potential. It is a paradox: The deeper you explore inward, the more connected you become outward, to others, to nature, to the cosmos, and ultimately, to the Divine.

At its core, self-awareness is not a checklist of traits or ambitions. It is the foundation upon which you build authenticity, purpose, and

---

[32] William C. Chittick, *The Heart of Islamic Philosophy: The Quest for Self-Knowledge in the Teachings of Afdal al-Din Kashani* (Oxford University Press, 2001).

a life of unwavering integrity. To truly know yourself, you must strip away societal expectations, transient desires, and external pressures to uncover your core values. This kind of self-knowledge is not static; it is an ongoing refinement that aligns your actions with the man you are meant to become.

As you deepen your understanding of yourself, you begin to perceive your connection to something far greater. Ancient wisdom holds that "He who knows himself, truly knows his Lord." The journey inward is also a journey upward. It is not merely an intellectual experience but a spiritual awakening and an alignment with the cosmic rhythm that governs existence.

Ralph Waldo Emerson said, "The soul is the perceiver and revealer of truth. We know the truth when we see it, let skeptic and scoffer say what they choose."[33] Curiosity urges you to explore the uncharted territories of your inner world while simultaneously seeking universal truths. With each realization, you refine your understanding of yourself and deepen your relationship with the world and the Creator.

As self-awareness blossoms, transformation unfolds: Life is no longer measured by comparisons or external validation but by gratitude and growth. Challenges, setbacks, and even your flaws become milestones of progress rather than sources of shame. Gratitude begins to fuel generosity when you appreciate your own journey and you recognize the shared humanity in others. Compassion becomes a guiding principle, inspiring you to uplift those around you while continuing to grow yourself.

This is the essence of personal evolution. The deeper you descend into self-discovery, the greater your capacity to be a transformative force in the lives of others. True transformation is not merely introspective; it is holistic. It reshapes your perception of yourself, your relationships, and your Creator, grounding your actions in a framework of unwavering virtue.

True self-love is not indulgence, nor is it hollow affirmations. It is the active practice of nurturing your body, mind, and soul. It involves

---

33 Essay titled "The Over-Soul," first published in 1841 as part of his collection Essays: First Series.

honoring your achievements, setting and respecting your boundaries, and embracing lifelong growth. Intrinsic worth is the internal gold that remains untouched by external markers of success. It is the quiet assurance that regardless of wealth, accolades, or social status, you possess an irreplaceable, God-given dignity.

The Stoics understood the power of self-mastery. Epictetus taught that it is not circumstances that trouble us, but our judgments of them. Marcus Aurelius emphasized that our minds are shaped by what we dwell upon. When you cultivate self-love and discipline your thoughts, you build an inner fortress that becomes an impenetrable stronghold that shields you from external turmoil and negativity.

Islam upholds self-worth as divinely bestowed. Every individual is sculpted by God, endowed with inherent goodness and value. The Prophet Muhammad (PBUH) emphasized full-faceted well-being, reminding us that our bodies have rights over us. In Islam, self-worth is not measured by material success but by faith, virtue, and service to others.

Immanuel Kant spoke of the inherent dignity within every human being, a dignity that no external force can diminish. Meanwhile, Jean-Paul Sartre argued that we define our essence and value through our actions. Together, these perspectives reveal a profound truth: We hold both the responsibility and the power to shape our self-worth, not according to society's shifting standards but by our principles and choices.

To know oneself is to commit to a lifelong journey that touches every facet of existence. It is an invitation to jump into consciousness, align with the Divine, and live a life rooted in virtues that uplift both yourself and those around you. Let gratitude, generosity, and kindness shape your interactions. Let self-awareness guide your path.

In the end, the journey of knowing oneself is the journey of becoming a man who stands firm in faith, resilient in challenges, and luminous in every sphere of life. Be that beacon. Be that transformation. Let your legacy be one of profound purpose, deep connection, and unwavering authenticity.

CHAPTER 62

SUBMIT TO GOD

FREEDOM IS IN SUBMISSION. THAT IS THE ENTIRETY OF OUR EXIStence. The journey toward true peace begins with surrendering to a higher power. Becoming a man of excellence is not merely about accumulating accolades or achieving societal success. Instead, it requires a journey of self-discovery and alignment with the divine. The first step in this spiritual odyssey is recognizing and submitting to the Creator, the Divine Being, God.

I'll never forget that first moment I saw the Kabaa, the holy site in Mecca. It was ethereal. To see the location I've prayed toward my entire life, to see hundreds of thousands of people worshipping their one true God. I immediately wept. It felt like I had been transported into an alternate universe. I could feel the presence of the divine and at that moment my heart felt full. Knowing God is not just about religious customs or rituals; it is about understanding your Creator. The source of life and the architect of the universe. It means recognizing the divine presence within and embracing the interconnectedness of all things. To truly know God is to understand the boundless love and grace He bestows upon us, guiding us through life's trials and tribulations.

Through submission, we cultivate humility, acknowledging that we are not the center of the universe but part of a larger cosmic plan. We surrender our egos, our desires, and our illusions of control, seeking instead to align with divine will. This surrender is not weakness but strength, wisdom, and liberation. It frees us from narrow perspectives, allowing us to experience life in its fullest form.

One evening, I stared into the mirror after a spree of designer shopping and lavish parties. The reflection looking back at me was unfamiliar. I didn't recognize a face of fulfillment, but one of emptiness. That moment of superficial pleasure masked a deeper void. I had redirected the love and reverence meant for God toward the alluring glow of materialism. When happiness is placed in worldly gains, we inevitably lose sight of our true selves and our connection to the Divine.

That night, I realized I needed to rebuild my foundational relationship with my Creator to regain self-love and true fulfillment. Strengthening this connection is like nurturing any relationship. It requires intention, time, and effort. Often, we prioritize careers, relationships, and ambitions over our spiritual bond. Yet, neglecting the most essential relationship, the one with our Creator, only deepens the spiritual void.

I began my journey by talking to God, engaging in honest communication, and being actively present in my faith. This relationship asks for nothing but sincerity and presence, yet its impact is profound. Knowing God enables us to understand ourselves better, to see our strengths, weaknesses, aspirations, and fears. It instills a sense of purpose, direction, and meaning, equipping us to navigate life's challenges with wisdom and grace. Our true worth is not found in external validation but in the purity of our hearts, the nobility of our actions, and the sincerity of our intentions.

An unchecked ego leads to destruction, diverting us from justice and divine alignment. The pursuit of proving oneself right, acquiring material wealth, or fulfilling selfish desires often clouds our sense of purpose. Grounding ourselves in God's teachings and surrendering our ego allows us to discover a deeper, more authentic sense of self and manhood.

Life may not always seem fair by our standards, and justice may not always be immediately visible. But by trusting in God's flawless wisdom, we gain resilience and patience. Our focus shifts from seeking validation in this transient world to finding peace in eternal truths.

When facing difficulties, our instinct is often to turn to social media, friends, or colleagues for solace. Yet, true fulfillment and lasting peace are found in our relationship with the Source of all existence. Instead of venting frustrations publicly or seeking external validation, we should first turn to God, pouring out our hearts and leaning on His infinite wisdom. This direct engagement creates greater love, resilience, and inner peace.

I think about the day I was let go from my executive position at WHOOP, now a multibillion-dollar technology company. I had a role with significant stock options and financial security. With a family to feed and minimal savings, I could have succumbed to despair. However, rather than allowing external circumstances to define my inner state, I turned to God. I thanked Him for His mercy, acknowledged my blessings, and trusted that something better was in store.

Islam teaches Istikhara, which is a prayer seeking divine guidance, asking God to bring what is best in this life and the next. This practice embodies surrender, trusting in the Creator's infinite wisdom. How often do we question, "Why me?" only to realize years later that an apparent loss was, in fact, a hidden blessing? God's perspective is vast, beyond our comprehension, and His justice is flawless.

Character and strength develop when we recognize accountability to a higher power. Understanding that our actions and choices have consequences in the sight of God guides us toward righteousness and compassion. The realization that our time on Earth is limited encourages us to live with gratitude, humility, and empathy, which are key traits for any man striving for excellence.

Submission to God strengthens our spiritual connection. By surrendering to divine will, we draw strength, guidance, and comfort from His wisdom and grace. This submission equips us to face life's challenges with resilience and purpose. The path to becoming a man of character is illuminated by this profound love and accountability to the Creator.

As we grow into men of excellence who embody humility, compassion, integrity, and responsibility, we become beacons of virtue for those around us. Our actions reflect our inner strength, our connection with God, and our commitment to justice. This journey is not solely about self-improvement but about being a living example of the values we uphold.

By integrating spiritual practices into daily life, prioritizing accountability, and living with humility and justice, we create a legacy that extends beyond ourselves. Every challenge faced and every act of goodness performed becomes a building block for a more harmonious world.

To know God is to know yourself, and to know yourself is to walk the path toward excellence. By anchoring life in spiritual connection, nurturing a relationship with the Creator, and living justly, we cultivate strength, peace, and fulfillment. Every action, decision, and interaction becomes aligned with a higher purpose, empowering us to live with honor, authenticity, and wisdom.

CHAPTER 63

LOVE GOD

IN A WORLD OFTEN CLOUDED BY ILLUSIONS AND TRANSITORY desires, one truth remains unshaken: God is the ultimate source of love, guidance, and fulfillment. We chase after love, success, and validation, believing that these will make us whole, yet these pieces often leave us longing for something deeper. The cultural narratives surrounding love, achievement, and self-worth can obscure the completeness we already possess through our connection with the Divine. Understanding this truth is essential for attaining true fulfillment.

The notion of finding "my other half" suggests that we are inherently incomplete, as if our wholeness depends on another person or external success. But this is a falsehood. God has created each of us as complete beings. Relationships and accomplishments can enrich our lives, but they are not the essence of who we are. The most profound relationship we must cultivate is our bond with God. In this divine connection lies the key to fulfillment, wholeness, and purpose.

Throughout history, faith has provided a blueprint for balanced living. Islam, for example, offers timeless examples through the life of the Prophet Muhammad (PBUH) and his companions. They engaged fully with the world, forming strong relationships, pursuing knowledge, contributing to society, and striving for excellence, all while keeping their spiritual foundation intact. Their lives demonstrate that it is possible to be present in this world without losing sight of our ultimate purpose.

PRACTICAL STEPS TO DEEPEN YOUR LOVE FOR GOD

1. **Regular prayer and meditation:** Establishing a consistent routine of prayer and meditation strengthens your connection with God and furthers self-awareness. These practices anchor you in peace, reflection, and divine presence.
2. **Community and service:** Engaging in acts of service allows you to practice compassion, build meaningful relationships, and see every act of kindness as an extension of divine love. Serving others uplifts your soul while benefiting those around you.
3. **Balanced living:** Pursue personal and professional goals while remaining anchored in your spiritual values. When your ambitions align with divine purpose, success becomes more meaningful and fulfilling.
4. **Study and reflection:** Deepening your understanding of religious texts and reflecting on their teachings provides wisdom for daily decisions. A regular habit of studying the Qur'an and other sacred writings shapes your character and strengthens your faith.
5. **Mindfulness in relationships:** View relationships as divine blessings, treating each connection with gratitude and respect. Cherishing bonds with family, friends, and others enriches your spiritual journey while keeping your ultimate fulfillment rooted in God.

Modern society often reduces our existence to consumerism, personal gain, or temporary pleasures. We are bombarded with messages that equate happiness with possessions, status, or superficial relationships. Yet, these temporary gratifications never truly satisfy the soul.

To love God is to reclaim your wholeness, to rise above distractions, and to seek a life of true purpose. Recognize that you are already complete, created with divine intent. God's love is the source of true contentment and peace. It is a love that is unwavering, undiminished by external circumstances. When your soul finds its anchor in God, your perspective shifts. Life's challenges become opportunities for growth, deepening your connection with the Divine.

When you align your life with God's love and wisdom, you naturally inspire others. Your words, actions, and character become reflections of divine grace, drawing people toward a higher purpose. Your life becomes a testimony to faith, resilience, and unwavering trust in God.

True freedom is not found in material wealth or human validation but in complete submission to God. Let every decision you make, every relationship you nurture, and every challenge you face be guided by divine love. With God as your guiding light, you transcend worldly limitations, cultivating a legacy of integrity, peace, and boundless love.

Embrace God as the center of your existence and the One who completes and guides you. In a world filled with illusions, let divine love be your truth, illuminating your path with purpose and joy. When you seek God wholeheartedly, you discover a fulfillment that resonates beyond this temporary world. Let His love be the light that leads you to unparalleled heights of peace and wholeness.

CHAPTER 64

PRAYER

PRAYER IS A BEACON OF SPIRITUAL LIGHT, ILLUMINATING THE believer's path five times a day. More than a ritual, it is an intimate encounter with God. A blessing that grounds the soul, disciplines the mind, and fortifies the heart. Just as physical training strengthens the body and knowledge sharpens the mind, prayer fortifies the soul, providing an unshakable foundation upon which a man can build his character and purpose.

To fully understand the depth of Islamic prayer, we must distinguish between its two pivotal forms: Salah and Dua. Salah, the obligatory act of worship, is the structured rhythm that defines a Muslim's day. Fajr at dawn, Dhuhr at midday, Asr in the afternoon, Maghrib at sunset, and Isha at night. This disciplined cycle is more than just routine; it is a reminder that amid the chaos of the world, there is always time to realign with one's purpose and connect with your Lord. Dua, on the other hand, is the unscripted outpouring of the heart. It is a personal dialogue with the Creator that can be uttered anytime, anywhere. Together, these forms of prayer establish a framework for both spiritual resilience and personal growth.

At its core, Salah is an act of connecting with God. With each movement and recitation, standing in humility, bowing in submission, prostrating in surrender, you are reminded of your true position in the universe. It is a practice that instills presence, silencing the noise of the world and anchoring the believer in divine connection. Each prayer is a checkpoint, ensuring that no matter how far one strays, there is always a moment to return, realign, and submit.

Discipline is the backbone of success in every area of life. Just as an athlete adheres to a strict training regimen or an entrepreneur commits to unwavering work ethic, a man committed to prayer strengthens his spiritual discipline. Salah demands punctuality, focus, and self-awareness. All qualities that, once mastered, extend into all aspects of life.

Prayer refines character by stimulating gratitude, patience, and humility, which are the very traits that define a man of strength and integrity. A man who consistently prays builds resilience; he learns to withstand hardship, knowing that adversity is but a test, and relief is promised. In moments of struggle, Salah is not merely an obligation but a lifeline, a source of clarity and fortitude in the face of trials.

While Salah's spiritual benefits are immeasurable, its impact is also affirmed by science and psychology. Studies reveal that regular prayer and meditation contribute to:

- **Reduced stress and increased longevity.** Research published in the *American Journal of Epidemiology* links consistent prayer with lower stress levels, improved immune function, and decreased risks of heart-related conditions.[34]
- **Mindset transformation.** Studies in *Cognitive Therapy and Research* indicate that prayer builds optimism, resilience, and a strengthened sense of purpose.[35]
- **Balanced masculinity.** The *Journal for the Scientific Study of Religion* finds that men who engage in consistent prayer exhibit greater

---

[34] Janice Bell Meisenhelder and Emily N. Chandler, "Frequency of Prayer and Functional Health in Presbyterian Pastors," *Journal for the Scientific Study of Religion*, 40(2) (2001): 323–329, https://doi.org/10.1111/0021-8294.00059.

[35] Amy L. Ai, et al., "Types of Prayer, Optimism, and Well-Being of Middle-Aged and Older Patients Undergoing Open-Heart Surgery," *Mental Health, Religion & Culture*, 11 (2008): 131–150, doi: 10.1080/13674670701324798.

emotional intelligence and a more balanced, authentic masculinity.[36] Contrary to the hypermasculine archetype of dominance and aggression, a praying man cultivates strength through self-restraint, wisdom, and service to others.

If you are committed to optimizing your mind, body, and soul, Salah must be a nonnegotiable pillar in your daily life. Here's how to ensure it enhances your journey of self-mastery:

- **Discipline through consistency:** Establish a structured prayer routine and allow Salah to serve as your anchor. Just as you wouldn't neglect your physical training, don't neglect the training of your soul.
- **Mindful presence in prayer:** Treat Salah as more than a habitual motion; immerse yourself in its meanings. Focus on the verses you recite, reflect on their depth, and let the experience cultivate self-awareness and mental clarity.
- **Gratitude as a power source:** Approach prayer with a heart full of gratitude. Gratitude shifts your mindset, making you more resilient to life's trials. When you stand before God, you are not just asking, you are acknowledging, thanking, and realigning with a higher purpose.

Think of yourself as a structure. Without a solid foundation, you are vulnerable, easily swayed by desires, distractions, and hardships. Salah forms the pillars that hold your character upright. It is not a burden; it is a gift, a built-in opportunity to pause, realign, and fortify yourself daily.

A man who neglects his prayer is like a warrior entering battle without armor. He is ill-prepared for the inevitable struggles of life. In a world filled with noise, distractions, and pleasures on every corner, Salah provides clarity. It reminds you of who you are, why you are here, and where you are headed.

In moments of adversity, instead of seeking temporary escapes

---

36 Matthew Bradshaw and Blake Victor Kent, "Prayer, Coping, and Health: A Conceptual Framework and Empirical Review," *Journal for the Scientific Study of Religion*, 57(4) (2018): 664–685.

through social media, vices, and external validation, decide to turn to the One who truly understands your struggles. True power is not found in excess wealth, status, or control; it is found in submission to the Divine. Through prayer, you cultivate unshakable inner strength, ensuring that no trial can break you.

Salah is more than an act of worship. It is the key to full-scale self-development. From both a spiritual and scientific lens, its benefits are undeniable. As you continue refining yourself into the man you were meant to be, let Salah be your foundation, guiding you to strength, purpose, and lasting fulfillment.

THE POWER OF DUA

"Nothing can change the Divine decree except dua."
—JĀMI' AL-TIRMIDHĪ, HADITH 2139

Amid life's relentless challenges, there lies a secret weapon that every great man has carried throughout history: Dua. More than a mere request, Dua is an intimate dialogue with God, an act of surrender, and a declaration of unwavering trust. It is the moment you raise your hands to God in absolute certainty that the One who created you is listening. Dua is a direct connection, free of intermediaries, barriers, or pretense. It is where faith meets action and where resilience is forged.

When life's struggles rage, and trials seem insurmountable, doubt may creep in. Impatience may create the idea that your prayers have gone unheard. But understand this: God's timing is perfect. Every request you make is recorded, every plea is valued, and every Dua is answered, though not always in the way or time frame you expect. The righteous predecessors, the Salaf, understood this truth. They prayed with unshakable faith, convinced that no supplication was ever in vain. Even after years of unanswered prayers, they remained hopeful, knowing that what God withholds is often as much a mercy as what He grants.

A real man does not view Dua as an act of desperation but as an act of leadership over his own soul. It is not passive; it is powerful. It is the intentional act of handing over your burdens, fears, and aspirations to the One who controls all outcomes. Dua is the heartbeat of reliance on God (Tawakkul), an exercise in humility that roots a man in divine wisdom rather than the illusions of self-sufficiency. To neglect Dua is to allow Satan to deceive you into believing you are self-made. A man who truly understands his purpose knows that his strength does not lie in mere willpower but in the One who fuels it.

The Qur'an reminds us:

> ...Call on Him with both fear and hope; indeed, God's mercy is close to those who do good. (Qur'an 7:56)

The Prophet Muhammad (PBUH) reinforced this, saying:

> God is as you think He is. If he remembers Me in himself, I too remember him in Myself; if he remembers Me in a group, I remember him in an even better gathering. Approach Me walking, and I rush towards you.

A man who understands this principle carries an unshakable mindset. He knows that his efforts, discipline, and ambition mean nothing without divine guidance. He embraces Dua as both a source of peace and an engine for transformation.

PRACTICAL STEPS TO MASTERING DUA

1. **Cultivate sincerity.** Approach Dua with an open and honest heart. Speak to God as you would in your most vulnerable moments, without pretense and without pride.
2. **Consistency over quantity.** A man of discipline does not wait for hardships to turn to God. Make Dua a habit, embedding it in your daily routine, even in moments of ease.
3. **Praise before plea.** Before asking, glorify God. Acknowledge His greatness, His mercy, and His control over all things. This shifts your mindset from desperation to gratitude.

4. **Invoke His names.** God has ninety-nine names. Use them with intention. Seek provision by calling upon *Ar-Razzaq* (The Sustainer), seek guidance from *Al-Hadi* (The Guide), and seek mercy from *Ar-Rahman* (The Most Merciful).
5. **Be present and focused.** Remove distractions. Dua is a spiritual discipline, not a hurried wish list. Find moments of solitude where your heart is fully engaged.
6. **Express gratitude.** Recognizing what you already have opens the doors to even greater blessings. Gratitude in Dua reinforces faith in God's plan.
7. **Have patience in response.** Trust that God answers Dua in the best possible way, whether by granting your request, delaying it for a better time, or replacing it with something greater.

A man of faith does not measure success by what is in his hands but by the strength of his connection to the Divine. Dua is a shield, a weapon, and an anchor. Use it. Master it. Live by it.

DHIKR

Among all the tools available for cultivating your divine connection and strengthening your soul, Dhikr, which translates as the remembrance of God, is one of the **most powerful weapons a man can tap into**.

Think of Dhikr as a divine force field that guards you from negativity, repels darkness, and serves a beacon of light that strengthens your soul. Dhikr is not just a ritual but an elixir-divine medicine for the heart and mind. Whether subtly under your breath or declared with conviction, Dhikr includes phrases like:

- **Allahu Akbar (God is great)**
- **Alhamdulillah (All praise is due to God)**
- **Astaghfirullah (Forgive me, God)**

These prayers refocus your heart on what truly matters, stripping away stress, pride, and distraction, and replacing them with clarity, gratitude, and peace.

Dhikr is not confined to moments of solitude or prayer. You reach an ethereal level of existence when it belongs everywhere. At the gym, on a walk, during your morning commute, while waiting in line, even at dinner with your family. The Prophet Muhammad (PBUH) was constantly engaged in the remembrance of God, whether in the marketplace, on the battlefield, or in the stillness of the night. When you make Dhikr a constant companion, you elevate even the most mundane moments into acts of worship.

Modern life is designed to keep us distracted. Screens demand our attention, social media feeds us comparison, and entertainment dulls our senses. Dhikr cuts through all of it. Instead of mindlessly scrolling your phone, repeat **SubhanAllah (Glory be to God)**. Instead of wasting time watching another empty TV show, engage your tongue and mind with **La ilaha illa Allah (There is no god but God)**.

God loves when a man prioritizes His remembrance over the temporary pleasures of the world. And the more you do it, the more you'll feel the shift: our mind clears, your soul brightens, and your connection with the Divine strengthens.

The world is not just physical; it is deeply spiritual. Just as we guard our homes with locks and security systems, we must guard our souls with Dhikr. The Prophet Muhammad (PBUH) taught that Dhikr repels the whispers of Satan, prevents sin, and serves as a fortress of protection. When a man neglects Dhikr, his soul becomes exposed, making him vulnerable to negativity, anxiety, and temptation. When he engages in Dhikr, he builds an impenetrable shield, one that deflects the harmful influences of the world and strengthens his inner resilience.

The spiritual benefits of Dhikr extend beyond just personal peace as it **attracts the company of angels**. The Prophet Muhammad (PBUH) said that when a person remembers God, the angels surround him, mercy descends upon him, and tranquility fills his heart.

What if everywhere you went, instead of being alone, you are accompanied by divine beings recording your good deeds, interceding for your success, and lifting your heart in moments of struggle. This is the unseen power of Dhikr. It invites the presence of God's angels into your life, making you feel lighter, stronger, and more spiritually fortified.

When I made Dhikr a priority in my daily routine, everything changed. My mind became sharper, my anxieties faded, and I felt an overwhelming sense of calm and clarity. It strengthened my connection with God, acting as both a refuge and a source of empowerment. It is a habit that elevates every aspect of life.

Dhikr requires no equipment or perfect setting, just a willing heart and a moving tongue. You can use prayer beads or your fingers to keep count, or simply track mentally. I recommend aiming for **three hundred repetitions per day**, similar to getting your reps in at the gym. Over time, it becomes second nature, flowing effortlessly through your day, fueling your spirit like oxygen fuels the body.

Every man who seeks strength—true, lasting strength—must commit to Dhikr. This is your challenge:

- **Start with one hundred repetitions daily.** Whether it's **Allahu Akbar**, **SubhanAllah**, or **Alhamdulillah**, make it a nonnegotiable part of your day.
- **Incorporate it into your routine.** Say it while driving, lifting weights, walking, or before bed.
- **Reflect on its power.** Notice how it shifts your mindset, calms your heart, and strengthens your faith.

This simple habit will redefine your life, turning everyday moments into spiritual victories. It is not just a practice; it is a weapon, a shield, and a guiding light that will transform you into the man you were always meant to be.

CHAPTER 65

PURIFYING AND STRENGTHENING THE ESSENCE WITHIN

TAKE A PAUSE TO LOOK AROUND YOU. THE WORLD RACES FORWARD with people aspiring, achieving, and acquiring at breakneck speed. Yet amid this hustle lies a part of us often overlooked: the soul. Rooted deep within, the soul, as articulated by scholars like Ibn Qayyim al-Jawziyyah, is like a ceaselessly churning millstone. This metaphor offers profound insight into mastering ourselves and living with purpose and clarity.

To truly grasp the soul's power, envision a millstone perpetually spinning, grinding everything fed into it. Our psyche operates in much the same way. Day and night, whether awake or asleep, it processes every thought, emotion, and experience. Just as a millstone transforms seeds into flour, our soul continuously churns, shaping our inner world and influencing how we perceive and interact with the outer world.

WHAT ARE YOU FEEDING YOUR SOUL? WHEAT OR GRAVEL?

If thoughts and emotions are seeds, the question arises: What are you feeding your soul? Positive, life-affirming thoughts are akin to wheat. They are nourishing and wholesome. Just as wheat is ground into flour to sustain the body, nurturing thoughts enrich the soul, furthering wisdom, clarity, and a radiant spirit. They provide the essential "flour" of our mental and emotional state, strengthening relationships and deepening self-awareness.

Furthermore, negative or toxic thoughts resemble gravel and stones. While wheat nourishes and sustains, grinding stones yields nothing but dust. A dust that clouds our vision, chokes our spirit, and prevents us from realizing our true potential. This negativity erodes mental health, diverts us from the path of righteousness, and leaves the soul malnourished and weak.

THE JOURNEY OF PURIFICATION: STRENGTHENING THE SOUL

The journey of purifying the soul begins with a conscious choice to feed it the "wheat" it needs to thrive. Just as one selects the best grains for a millstone, we must intentionally choose positive, healthy thoughts and emotions to sustain our soul. Though distractions abound, purification is possible through mindfulness, meditation, and consistent self-reflection.

STEPS TO PURIFY AND STRENGTHEN THE SOUL:

1. **Awareness:** Begin by observing your thoughts. Recognize the patterns, both positive and negative, that influence your mood, decisions, and actions. Awareness is the first step to change.
2. **Reflection:** Set aside time daily to reflect on your thoughts, actions, and experiences. Just as a millstone separates grain from chaff, self-reflection helps retain valuable insights and discard negativity.
3. **Mindful meditation:** Ground yourself in the present through med-

itation. This practice calms the mind and prevents the dust of past regrets and future anxieties from clouding your soul.

4. **Affirmations:** Replace self-defeating thoughts with constructive beliefs through positive affirmations. These affirmations serve as the high-quality "wheat" that nurtures your soul and builds resilience.
5. **Inspiration:** Read spiritual and philosophical teachings from scholars like Ibn Qayyim al-Jawziyyah. Their timeless wisdom offers guidance on how to nourish and sustain your soul.

Once purification begins, the next step is fortification or making the soul resilient against life's inevitable adversities. Strength is nurtured through continual learning, seeking enriching experiences, and cultivating authentic relationships. Purpose-driven actions and meaningful connections deepen the soul's roots, making it resilient against challenges.

To travel outwardly with clarity, one must journey inwardly with depth and consistency. Think of your soul as a burning flame. Left unattended and unfueled, it will quickly burn out, leaving you to traverse life in darkness and confusion. However, when nourished properly, it becomes a guiding flame, illuminating your path with clarity and purpose and keeping you aligned with God. This inner light requires constant attention and nourishment, for when neglected, you risk losing sight of your true path.

By understanding the ceaseless activity of the soul and choosing to feed it with positivity, gratitude, and purpose, you set the millstone of your inner life to work in your favor. A well-nurtured soul transforms your entire existence, making life richer, more meaningful, and deeply fulfilling.

CHAPTER 66

REFLECTIONS AND REMINDERS

"Leave that thing that has nothing to do with you."
—JĀMIʿ AL-TIRMIDHĪ, HADITH 2318

This simple yet profound reminder underscores the art of selective focus. Every day, countless distractions compete for our attention. Engaging with these drains our mental peace and adds unnecessary stress.

Selective engagement is not merely about ignoring the unimportant; it is about actively choosing to invest our time and energy in what aligns with our values, goals, and well-being. Think about encountering a heated debate that neither concerns you nor contributes to your personal growth. You have a choice: to be consumed by the noise or to walk away, preserving your energy for what truly matters.

By consciously filtering where we direct our focus, we maintain clarity and purpose amid the chaos of daily life. A simple yet powerful question can guide us: Is this worth my time, energy, and peace?

Interact with God in a positive manner and see Him in the highest light.

Our perception of God shapes the way we experience life. When we approach Him with love, hope, and trust, our faith becomes a source of strength and resilience. Challenges are no longer obstacles but stepping stones, guiding us toward personal and spiritual growth.

Hardships often test our patience, but trusting in God's wisdom and mercy allows us to navigate life's trials with grace. Think about the person who faces adversity yet remains steadfast, knowing that every struggle is an essential piece of a greater design. This mindset enhances spiritual resilience, helping us transform setbacks into opportunities for reflection and renewal.

To cultivate this connection, engage with God positively through gratitude, sincere supplication, and a steadfast belief in His divine plan. Your relationship with Him is a mirror; how you perceive Him reflects how you interpret life's unfolding journey. When you choose to see Him in the highest light, you illuminate your path with faith, courage, and unwavering peace.

CHAPTER 67

PATIENCE

PATIENCE IS NOT MERELY THE ACT OF WAITING; IT IS THE FOUNdation of resilience, discipline, and spiritual strength. It is the quiet force that fortifies a man's ability to endure hardship, resist temptation, and remain steadfast in your journey toward greatness. In a world that glorifies speed, instant gratification, and impulsive action, patience is a rare and invaluable virtue. One that distinguishes the men who lead from those who follow.

The esteemed scholar Ibn Taymiyyah emphasized patience as the glue that binds faith together, highlighting its essential role in promoting clarity, fortitude, and unwavering commitment to personal and spiritual growth.[37] He categorized patience into three essential dimensions: patience in obedience to God, patience in avoiding sin, and patience in enduring trials. These dimensions serve as a roadmap for developing inner strength and maintaining integrity.

---

[37] Ibn Taymiyyah, *A Principle Concerning Patience and Gratitude*, trans. Abu Rumaysah (Daar Us-Sunnah Publishers, 2006).

1. PATIENCE IN OBEDIENCE: THE PATH TO CONSISTENCY

Obeying God requires perseverance, particularly in a world filled with distractions and temptations. True discipline lies not in momentary bursts of motivation but in consistent devotion. Acts of worship, such as prayer, fasting, and acts of kindness, demand patience. They require a man to show up, even when it is inconvenient, even when his mind is restless, and even when the world tempts him to stray.

A real man does not worship based on convenience; he worships based on conviction. The test of patience in obedience is remaining steadfast in faith and commitment, regardless of external circumstances. The man who wakes before dawn to pray, who fasts with resolve, and who commits to self-improvement in the face of difficulty is the man who fortifies his soul against weakness.

2. PATIENCE IN AVOIDING SIN: MASTERING THE DESIRES

Temptation is relentless. The allure of wealth, status, and instant pleasures often presents itself as an appealing shortcut to satisfaction. But a man ruled by his impulses is not a true man; he is a slave to his desires. Patience in avoiding sin is the ability to say no when the world pressures you to say yes. It is self-restraint in moments of weakness, the strength to walk away when others indulge, and the discipline to remain steadfast when compromise seems easy.

Patience, in this sense, acts as a shield, protecting the heart from spiritual erosion. Every great man in history mastered his desires, channeling his strength toward purpose rather than pleasure. By exercising restraint and making deliberate choices to stay on the straight path, you guard yourself against moral compromise and stand unwavering in faith.

3. PATIENCE IN TRIALS: STRENGTH IN ADVERSITY

No man is exempt from hardship. Life is unpredictable and full of illness, loss, failure, and personal struggles that test emotional and spiritual endurance. Patience during trials is not about passive endurance but about actively seeking growth through hardship. It is about using setbacks as stepping stones, transforming pain into strength, and trials into lessons.

The men who leave a legacy are not those who had an easy path; they are the ones who embraced difficulty and refused to break under pressure. When you view challenges as opportunities for refinement rather than punishment, you unlock a level of resilience that makes you unstoppable. Hardship is inevitable, but how you respond defines your character.

THE POWER OF PATIENCE IN SHAPING A MAN

Patience is not a passive virtue but an active force that fuels growth, resilience, and unshakable faith. It is what separates the ordinary from the extraordinary, the weak from the strong, the misguided from the wise. A man who embodies patience builds an unshakable foundation in every aspect of his life.

1. **Developing inner strength:** Patience builds mental and spiritual fortitude, allowing you to endure difficulties without being overwhelmed. It transforms obstacles into lessons and challenges into opportunities. Every great leader, warrior, and scholar cultivated patience because they understood that true power lies in the ability to remain composed and focused under pressure.
2. **Deepening faith:** Trusting in God's timing, even when circumstances seem unclear, strengthens faith. Through patience, you cultivate reliance on His wisdom and divine plan, finding peace in the understanding that every event in life unfolds with purpose. This trust nurtures a sense of calm and resilience, even in times of uncertainty.
3. **Maintaining positive character:** A patient man does not react impulsively; he responds thoughtfully. Patience prevents frustration from turning into anger, bitterness, or despair. It aids emotional intelligence, preserves dignity, and nurtures healthier relationships by allowing you to engage with others with wisdom and grace.
4. **Achieving excellence:** Success, be it in faith, personal growth, or

professional aspirations, requires dedication over time. Excellence is never achieved overnight. The road to self-improvement is paved with obstacles, but patience ensures that you stay committed despite setbacks, ultimately leading to lasting fulfillment.

CULTIVATING PATIENCE: PRACTICAL STRATEGIES

Developing patience is a daily practice, requiring conscious effort and strategic approaches. Here's how you can strengthen this virtue in your life:

1. **Practice introspection and mindfulness.** Self-reflection helps identify moments of impatience and emotional triggers. By becoming aware of your reactions, you can consciously practice calmness and self-control, allowing you to handle challenges with greater composure.
2. **Set long-term goals.** Patience thrives when you maintain a long-term perspective. Breaking larger aspirations into smaller, achievable steps creates motivation and prevents discouragement. Recognizing progress, even in small increments, reinforces perseverance.
3. **Seek spiritual support.** Turning to God through prayer and Dua (supplication) provides comfort and strength. Expressing your struggles and seeking divine guidance promotes resilience, reminding you that no hardship is faced alone.
4. **Build a strong support network.** Surrounding yourself with patient and wise individuals encourages growth. Family, friends, and mentors offer guidance, reassurance, and a broader perspective, helping you remain patient during difficult times. Their support reminds you that struggles are temporary and growth is always possible.
5. **Reframe challenges as growth opportunities.** Instead of viewing obstacles as setbacks, see them as chances to develop resilience and wisdom. Every difficulty carries a lesson, and each challenge refines your strength, patience, and faith.

Patience is not a weakness; it is a manifestation of inner strength, discipline, and faith. Ibn Taymiyyah's teachings remind us that patience in obedience, patience in avoiding sin, and patience in trials are interconnected virtues that shape our character and refine our spiritual journey.

By embracing patience, you develop resilience, deepen your connection with God, and nurture a life rooted in steadfast faith and excellence. A man of patience is a man of power. Be that man.

CHAPTER 68

THE ULTIMATE BLUEPRINT FOR MASCULINITY: LESSONS FROM THE PROPHET MUHAMMAD (PBUH)

NO MAN IN HISTORY EMBODIED FAITH, DISCIPLINE, INTEGRITY, and service better than the Prophet Muhammad (PBUH). He was the ultimate example of strength with humility, power with compassion, and leadership with service. To follow his path is to strive for excellence (Ihsan) in all aspects of life including spiritual, personal, social, and professional.

1. STRENGTHEN YOUR FAITH AND SPIRITUAL CONNECTION

A real man is grounded in faith. Without it, even the strongest mind and body are directionless. Prophet Muhammad (PBUH) prioritized his connection with God above all else. His life teaches us that true strength comes from submission to God.

- **Pray with presence.** Perform the five daily prayers on time with Khushu' (deep focus). This is your foundation. No excuses.
- **Wake up for Tahajjud (night prayer).** The Prophet (PBUH) sought strength and guidance in the stillness of the night. If you want to be exceptional, rise when others sleep.
- **Recite and reflect on the Qur'an daily.** The Qur'an is the ultimate guide to life. Don't just read it; understand and apply it.
- **Make Dhikr (remembrance of God).** Keep your heart alive by constantly remembering God.
- **Fast regularly.** The Prophet (PBUH) fasted on Mondays and Thursdays. Fasting sharpens willpower, purifies the heart, and strengthens self-control.
- **Trust in God (Tawakkul).** Take action, but leave the results to God. Real strength is knowing that you don't control everything. He does.
- **Purify your intentions.** Every action should be for God's sake. Success without sincerity is meaningless.

2. DEVELOP STRENGTH OF CHARACTER AND LEADERSHIP

A man's true worth is in his character. The Prophet (PBUH) said, "The best among you are those with the best character." Strength is not in arrogance or dominance, but it is in self-control, honesty, and humility.

- **Be truthful.** Speak the truth even when it's hard. Lies weaken your soul.
- **Be trustworthy (Amanah).** Keep your word. If you say you'll do something, do it. Reliability is a mark of true masculinity.
- **Stay humble.** The Prophet (PBUH) was the most powerful leader, yet he lived simply. Arrogance is weakness in disguise.
- **Control your anger.** A strong man is not the one who fights but the one who restrains his anger. Master your emotions.
- **Show gratitude.** The more grateful you are, the more God gives you. Appreciate everything including your health, family, and even hardships.

- **Forgive easily.** Holding grudges is a sign of weakness. The Prophet (PBUH) forgave those who wronged him. Be bigger than your ego.
- **Greet people with a smile.** A smile is an act of charity. It radiates confidence, kindness, and positivity.

3. STRENGTHEN YOUR RELATIONSHIPS (FAMILY AND BROTHERHOOD)

How you treat others, especially your family, defines you. Prophet Muhammad (PBUH) was a devoted husband, loving father, and loyal friend. If you aspire to be a real man, prioritize your relationships.

- **Be a loving husband.** Show affection, patience, and care. The Prophet (PBUH) helped with household chores and treated his wives with the utmost respect.
- **Be an engaged father.** Spend time with your children. Teach them, guide them, and lead by example.
- **Honor your parents.** No matter how successful you become, if you neglect your parents, you've failed. Serve them with love.
- **Maintain strong brotherhood.** Surround yourself with good company. A man is shaped by his friends, so choose wisely.
- **Be generous and charitable.** Give freely, expecting nothing in return.
- **Help the weak and oppressed.** Stand for justice. A real man protects, defends, and uplifts others.

4. PURSUE EXCELLENCE IN WORK AND LEADERSHIP

A man's legacy is built through his work and contributions. The Prophet (PBUH) led with service, fairness, and wisdom. Be excellent in all that you do.

- **Work with integrity.** Be honest in business and work. Don't cut corners.

- **Strive for excellence (Ihsan).** Never settle for mediocrity. Whether at work, in your fitness, or in worship, always give your best.
- **Lead by example.** True leadership is through action, not just words.
- **Seek counsel (Shura).** The Prophet (PBUH) consulted others before making decisions. Don't let pride keep you from learning.
- **Stay productive.** Avoid laziness. Your time is your most valuable asset, so don't waste it.

5. STRENGTHEN YOUR BODY (PHYSICAL FITNESS AND HEALTH)

Your body is an Amanah (trust) from God. The Prophet (PBUH) emphasized physical strength and fitness, not for vanity but for resilience, self-discipline, and the ability to serve others.

- **Eat in moderation.** Follow the Sunnah: one-third food, one-third water, one-third air.
- **Exercise and stay active.** The Prophet (PBUH) encouraged archery, swimming, running, and horseback riding. Train for strength, endurance, and agility.
- **Prioritize sleep.** A well-rested mind and body perform better.
- **Practice personal hygiene.** Stay clean, groomed, and presentable.

6. LIVE WITH SIMPLICITY AND GRATITUDE

True success is not in wealth or status. True success is in contentment. The Prophet (PBUH) lived simply, despite having the means for luxury.

- **Avoid materialism.** Don't chase money or status at the expense of your soul.
- **Be content with what you have.** Trust that God provides what is best.
- **Give more than you take.** Be generous in wealth, time, and kindness.
- **Detach from worldly distractions.** Focus on your purpose.

7. SEEK KNOWLEDGE AND LIFELONG GROWTH

A strong man is a student for life. The Prophet (PBUH) said, "Seeking knowledge is an obligation upon every Muslim."

- **Be a lifelong learner.** Read, reflect, and grow.
- **Teach others.** Knowledge is meant to be shared.
- **Regularly self-assess and improve.** The best investment is in your personal growth.

The Prophet Muhammad (PBUH) was the ultimate model of strength, wisdom, and compassion. To follow him is to strive every day for excellence in faith, character, relationships, work, and health. This journey is not about perfection, but about consistent effort. If you embody these principles, you will become the man you were meant to be: a man of faith, discipline, and purpose.

THE MAN YOU WERE MEANT TO BE

Throughout this journey, you have explored the philosophical, psychological, and physiological dimensions of self-transformation. You have dissected societal constructs, debunked misleading narratives of masculinity, and examined the foundational principles that define authentic strength. But none of that matters if you don't take action. Knowledge without action is wasted potential.

You are at a crossroads. One path leads to stagnation, complacency, and unfulfilled potential, while the other demands intellectual rigor, physical discipline, and an unwavering commitment to a higher purpose. The latter is arduous, but it is the only path that leads to greatness. Every hardship you have endured has been a refining fire, sharpening your resilience and molding your character. You were not designed for mediocrity. You were created to transcend it.

I know this because I have walked this path myself.

There was a time when I felt lost, where I questioned my direction and my worth. I remember nights staring at the ceiling, feeling an emptiness that no external success could fill. I had the accolades, the validation, and the physical strength, but something was missing. It wasn't until I committed myself to daily discipline, to something greater than my own desires, that everything changed. Strength training became my sanctuary, faith became my anchor, and surrounding myself with men of integrity became my North Star. Growth was no longer optional; it was necessary. And from that moment forward, everything shifted.

You have to make that choice for yourself. No one will do it for you.

Your legacy begins now. Not tomorrow. Not in some distant future. Your trajectory is defined by the choices you make today. True strength is not the product of comfort but of rigorous self-discipline, conscious decision-making, and beautiful wisdom. It is displayed in the courage to reject passivity, the intellectual fortitude to challenge established norms, and the conviction to prioritize long-term fulfillment over momentary gratification.

A man of substance does not seek external validation; his purpose is intrinsic, guided by ethical principles, disciplined habits, and a commitment to service. Success, physical prowess, and intellectual acumen are valuable, but they are hollow without integrity. A man of true depth does not merely exist. He constructs, leads, and elevates those around him.

But let's be clear: Transformation is not a one-time event. It is a lifelong commitment. Your attainment of self-mastery never ends. The great thinkers, scholars, and leaders of history never ceased their quest for knowledge and refinement. They understood that self-improvement is a perpetual endeavor requiring adaptability, introspection, and constant learning.

And you will stumble. You will face moments where motivation wanes, where discipline feels like a burden rather than a virtue. But mastery is not dictated by short-lived emotions, it is built in the moments you want to quit but refuse to do so. True growth emerges when, despite internal resistance, you persist. Every obstacle you overcome fortifies your mind. Every disciplined action strengthens your resolve. Every act of courage reaffirms your commitment to your highest potential.

1. **Commit to daily reflection.** Spend a few minutes each night reviewing your actions. Were they aligned with your highest principles? Where can you improve? Excellence isn't built overnight but forged through consistent, disciplined effort.
2. **Seek brotherhood.** Surround yourself with men who hold you accountable, challenge your thinking, and inspire growth. Find mentors; form or join groups focused on excellence, accountability, and spiritual growth. Brotherhood is essential; don't walk this path alone.
3. **Prioritize discipline and routine.** Whether through strength training, nutrition, spiritual practice, or sleep optimization, embrace the small daily habits that compound over time. Consistency creates mastery.
4. **Stay connected.** Join communities and forums, online or in your local area, where other like-minded individuals are on similar journeys. Exchange ideas, seek support, and continuously learn from one another.
5. **Consider mentorship.** Both as a mentee and eventually as a mentor yourself. Sharing your knowledge strengthens your growth and builds a legacy that lasts beyond your lifetime.
6. **Attend workshops, retreats, and seminars.** Places where you can deepen your knowledge, build relationships, and immerse yourself in environments that nurture excellence. Look for events and retreats that align with your values and goals, and commit to attending regularly.
7. **Continue your education.** Never stop learning. Subscribe to thought leaders, podcasts, and content that reinforce and expand upon the principles you've embraced here. Reflect on revisiting this book annually, as each new stage of life brings fresh insights and deeper understandings.

You now hold the roadmap, but it's up to you to walk the path. Live courageously. Love sincerely. Lead intentionally.

And when doubt creeps in, because it will, come back to this. Read these words again. Remind yourself why you started this journey. The world is filled with distractions and desires that pull you away from your mission. Resist their pull. Stay focused. Refine your vision. Advance with intent.

There will be moments of doubt, periods when the demands of this journey feel overwhelming. In those moments, recall your initial purpose. Recognize the progress you have made and reaffirm your dedication to continuous growth. Most importantly, understand that you are not alone in this endeavor. Draw strength from those who share your commitment to excellence, from the principles that guide you, and from the legacy of those who have walked this path before you.

Ask yourself, How will I put these lessons into practice today, tomorrow, and for the rest of my life?

You design your destiny. No one will hand you greatness or excellence, you must seize it. The world does not need more passive men, content to drift through life. It needs men of action, men of integrity, men who rise above mediocrity and embrace the responsibility of leadership and purpose. So rise. It is time. Go be the light.

"O God, place light in my heart, light on my tongue, light in my hearing, light in my sight, light before me, light behind me, light above me, and light below me."

In the name of God, the Most Gracious, the Most Merciful. By time, indeed, mankind is in loss, except for those who believe and do righteous deeds and advise each other to truth and advise each other to patience.

APPENDIX

THE MAN YOU'RE MEANT TO BE FIELD MANUAL: MASTER YOUR MIND, BODY, AND SOUL

DAILY ROUTINE OF A MAN ON MISSION

MORNING (FAJR–9:00 A.M.):

- Wake up before Fajr
- Wudu + Fajr prayer (ideally in congregation)
- Dhikr + Dua (ten minutes)
- Qur'an (one page minimum or audio during walk)
- Workout (cardio or walk for thirty minutes)
- High-protein, clean breakfast
- Review today's goals
- Avoid social media until after 9:00 a.m.

MIDDAY (9:00 A.M.–5:00 P.M.):

- Deep focus work blocks (ninety-minute intervals)
- Dhuhr + Asr on time

- Eat clean: protein, greens, hydration
- Midday walk or reflection
- Stay off distractions, gossip, mindless scrolling
- Workout (strength training for forty-five minutes to one hour)

EVENING (5:00 P.M.–10:00 P.M.):

- Maghrib + Isha
- Family, community, or focused downtime
- No phone after 9:00 p.m.
- Daily review: wins, slips, intentions
- Dua before sleep
- Sleep by 11:00 p.m. (seven to eight hours)

Dominate your day. Or the day will dominate you.

MORNING AFFIRMATIONS

Say these out loud daily:

1. I am a slave of God, not a slave to my desires.
2. Discipline is my freedom. I do hard things without complaint.
3. Today, I fight for my future. I choose action, not excuses.
4. My body is a trust. My mind is a weapon. My soul is eternal.
5. I protect my eyes, my tongue, my thoughts, and my private parts.
6. I don't chase women, followers, or approval. I chase Jannah.
7. My Lord sees me. My angels record me. My legacy is being written.
8. I lead myself before I try to lead others.
9. I am becoming the man my son will admire and my daughter will trust.
10. I live for God—not for this Dunya.

Repeat until you believe it. Live it until others feel it.

SINS TO AVOID/HABITS TO BUILD

SINS TO KILL IMMEDIATELY

- Porn/masturbation/Haram lust
- Riba (interest) and unethical money
- Gossip, backbiting, dirty jokes
- Missing prayers
- Arrogance, showing off
- Alcohol, drugs
- Disrespect to family
- Laziness with health and time

HABITS TO BUILD DAILY

- Salah on time
- Qur'an daily (recite, reflect, or listen)
- Train hard
- Lower your gaze
- Speak truth
- Eat clean, drink water
- Give in secret
- Wake before Fajr
- Reflect in a journal
- Dua daily with sincerity

Sin weakens the soul. Worship strengthens it.

DUAS FOR STRENGTH AND SINCERITY

DISCIPLINE AND PROTECTION:

- Allahumma a'inni 'ala dhikrika wa shukrika wa husni 'ibadatik
- Ya Muqallib al-qulub, thabbit qalbi 'ala deenik
- O Allah, protect me from the evil of my soul and deeds
- O Allah, shield me from laziness, cowardice, and burden of sins

FORGIVENESS AND RETURN:
- Allahumma innaka 'afuwwun tuhibbul 'afwa fa'fu 'anni
- O Allah, purify my intentions
- O Allah, let me die as a Muslim and resurrect me with the righteous

PURPOSE AND POWER:
- O Allah, make me sincere, strong, and pleasing to You
- O Allah, guide me, protect me, and use me for good

Speak to God like your life depends on it. It does.

RULES TO LIVE BY

1. Pray like you're already being watched.
2. Train like your survival depends on it.
3. Speak less. Do more.
4. Never miss Fajr. Never miss leg day.
5. Stay off the screen. Stay on your Deen.
6. If you're angry, stay silent. If tempted, remember Jannah.
7. Your eyes shape your heart. Guard them.
8. Fear Allah, and the right people will respect you.
9. Your family needs a leader, not a likeable boy.
10. You weren't built for average. Lock in. Submit. Win.

Print these. Live these. Become the man you were born to be.

www.ingramcontent.com/pod-product-compliance
Lightning Source LLC
Chambersburg PA
CBHW060511080526
44586CB00012B/455